Teachings from the
Heart

Teachings from the Heart

A CONTINUING JOURNEY

S. L. Waldie

To order additional copies of this book, contact:
Xlibris Corporation
1-888-795-4274
www.Xlibris.com
Orders@Xlibris.com
113047

Contents

I would like to say a very special thank you to all who contributed with their inspirations and Love and who has joined with me on this amazing journey of Spirit.,

Thank you to my husband, Bruce, for his hours of transcribing all the tapes and being patient while I adapted them for this book.

To my "sisters of the heart" Brenda and Jane, we have been through several "lifetimes" together, and I am so thankful we have met once again. Thank you for your love and encouragement and for being an integral part of my journey.

Acknowledgments

To all who remain dedicated to this journey we are on and to getting all the information out to those who will choose to read these words, I thank you for your time, efforts, and above all else, your love. It has been, and continues to be, an evolution in understanding who we truly are, and I know that it will be so for all who are on this journey with us.

Introduction

The previous Teachings from the Heart book was written in a slightly different format than this one is being written. I decided to have this be not only the questions, which as always resulted in a Teaching, but also to have it be an ongoing conversation between Bruce and the "Girls." I have also divided the book into chapters and dates. In each chapter, there will be approximately two months' worth of meetings.

While we were in Las Vegas, there was only Bruce and myself, so he is the one of course who is asking the questions. I did have him ask some for me as well, but mostly you will see my feelings in my commentaries.

I am so pleased that you have chosen to read this second book. The compiling of all the information from the tapes was a long process that Bruce took on, and he did an excellent job. I know that without his dedication in transcribing the tapes into written words, this would have been impossible.

The journey from the first book to this one has been life changing in so many ways. As I write this, we are currently living in Lake Havasu City, Arizona, but we know that we are about to be moved once again. This book will take you up to our return to Las Vegas in October 2008 and all that occurred since our last session of October 22, 2007, in the first book.

This book actually follows three others that have already been published. Two of those books written by my husband, Gordon (also called Bruce), are based on information from these original sessions of the "Girls." I felt it important to write this second *Teachings* book to show the progression of all we were given, as well as to introduce information not contained previously in the other published books.

It has taken me awhile to begin this project as I had been expending most of my energy providing an income, which allowed Bruce to write and publish the other books, as well as to meet our obligations. It certainly has not been what you would call "an easy road," but I am so very grateful that the opportunity to continue has been there, although it moves in our "time" at what seems to be a very slow pace.

Things once again are about to change, although as I write this, I am not sure where they will lead us. I do know that our desire to continue sharing this knowledge with others is as strong now as it was at the beginning over five years ago.

My energies are no longer divided between work and our "project," as I have officially retired. I know that this is the "time" to get this second book written. I also "know" that somehow we will be helped and guided just as we have always been.

At the conclusion of this book, I will share with you where all this is going as I will undoubtedly have more information.

Now, let us begin our journey once again.

Chapter One

October 26, 2007

On this date, we were back in Las Vegas, having arrived from Happy Camp the day before. We had been gone from our home for over six months. Today we were once again to begin sessions with the "Girls," Zelia and Astoria. It felt wonderful to be back. So now, we begin.

"We do greet thee. We understand that you have questions."

May we first discuss the Circles of Light? (This subject was first introduced toward the end of the first book.)

"Yes, we would be most pleased to answer your questions. What is it that you would like to know?"

Would you please expand upon the nature, composition, and purpose of the Circles of Light, as well as the role they play both individually and for humanity?

"The Circles of Light around the earth, moon, and sun are layers of energy that were placed there by the feminine aspect of the One. The purpose of this energy is determined by the user. The drawing of this energy is for those who have awakened and are in true understanding of who they are. One may draw this energy and utilize it during meditations, spiritual growth, physical healings, inspiration, and a myriad of other intended uses. This energy is also meant to begin balancing the masculine/feminine energies that reside now upon your earth. For long now has it been mostly masculine energy, the 'time' is Now for all to come into balance and unification to restore feminine energy to the earth. In this way is the direction to the One. Universal Life Force energy has the combination of both male/female energies while the Circles of Light are feminine energy. This energy is being, and will be, greatly utilized during the Awakening."

How do we draw upon the energy present within the Circles of Light?

"It is simply for you 'to be.' Be in the present, in the Now, and open your energy centers, what some call the chakras, and allow the energy to flow into you. That is very simple, but is also quite sufficient. So you would draw this energy to you simply by your intent and desire to do so."

How do we channel this energy for healing? Can this extra energy be drawn for when we conduct our healing sessions?

"Yes, you certainly may use the energy for any healing modality. The energy will simply be 'stored' until it is needed. It is stored in your body, generally in the abdominal region, in you solar plexus, and sacral energy centers. It is also stored in the heart energy center. It will simply be stored and available for your use as you desire it in your healing sessions. It is not as if you do not have the room to hold it, for you have received the openings. As you know, this allows for storage of energy."

What about using the Circles of Light for manifestation?

"Manifestation, Little Brother, is a trickier subject. We know the people on earth have the techniques, the ability, to manifest. It is difficult to explain to you exactly how this is done given your current stage in your evolutionary development. We are speaking, of course, of your desire to create not only that which you desire through thought/manifestation, but to also create through feeling/occurrence, or instantaneous creation as well. On our planet, of course, we do not have this concern because we simply 'feel' that which we desire and it manifests for us. This has always been our way. However, we do know that this is also your desire.

"We have been made known of late that because the human body and mind are very closely 'in sync' with each other, it is difficult for a person to stay focused on their desire to see it through to completion. Many are caught up in the 'time' it may take to manifest that which they desire. As you know, there is 'no time' in the Absolute, so many just give up if that which they desire does not materialize within the 'time' they expect it to. Some, as a result, decide that it does not work. If they remain true and concentrate upon that desire and 'see' it, they would be successful. We have asked the Council of the One if manifestation from nothing is possible. We are told that many miracles have occurred. Some we were informed did occur from nothing but it was by very learned masters who were able to accomplish this. So it is not that it will not happen, but it takes in your 'time' many days, months, or years to accomplish. We are not sure of the time of study it may take. One must be able to devote oneself to the study, and we understand that this is not practical in many instances. It is not that it cannot happen from nothing, but would be more likely to occur through action."

We have spoken of thought/action into thought/manifest into feeling/ occurrence. Is there anything that must happen within us in our preparation that would bring us closer to that, or is this just the process of remembering?

"It is not only the process of remembering, Little Brother, but it is also important that you—excuse us for a moment. Manifestation seems to be the question that all humans have. We understand they still have walls up that require these questions, so this is normal. To manifest with thought/ manifestation means to simply hold the desire within your energy, hold it in your heart, and 'know' that it will occur. Believe that it has already happened in the Spiritual but the physical manifestation is irrespective of 'time.' In order to move your created desires forward to the physical realm, at your current vibrational level, you will include inspired action along with your focus. We are not sure beyond that how this exactly occurs for this is not something we are privy to know."

Thank you. That is most helpful. There is a notation in my notes regarding the unveiling of mysteries. Is this kind of knowledge available to us at this time, or is it to come at some future Now?

"Little Brother, all mysteries are available to you, it is simply a matter of remembering that which you already know. We, of course, as we learn, will endeavor to show you. We are not told at this point whether the learning of these mysteries is even necessary. We are pleased that your desire to learn is strong. The mysteries, as you call them, are from the beginning of 'time' if there were a beginning of 'time.' They existed for the people of different eras. You have actually advanced much beyond that, so we will find out for you which ones, if any, will be necessary."

Thank you. Your guidance is so very much appreciated. It helps me to understand what is happening and this process more thoroughly.

"We had felt your worry. We had felt you're questioning. We would desire to do more than just send our love and energy, but that is all we are to do in this your 'time.' You may believe you go through this individually, but you must remember that you are all One."

Is the process that we have been going through part of our "blueprint"?

"You could say that, but part of what you are experiencing now is simply the residual of past choices and the effects of current choices that occurred before the time of your surgery. We know not the 'time' the residual of these choices shall remain in your surroundings. They work themselves out as they need be. As you change, and as you have changed the path you were upon, these residuals will fall by the wayside. We are informed that you will continue to go through what you Now experience, until you aren't."

This is something I came to the realization of early this morning. Thank you for all your help and energy to enable me to arrive at this place of acceptance of the process. However it manifests is okay, and for the greatest good. Now what remains is just our strong desire to move forward.

"Little Brother, we would strongly suggest that you would understand all of things to be done. We are referring to your writing. We have heard you say that it takes 'time,' and because we have no 'time,' this is a difficult concept. We do feel that it can be pursued and that it can be quickly realized. You simply have to, as you would say, put your nose to the grindstone. We know that you are being inspired not only through us, but through your guide, to write that which may bring to you the finances that are required. You are to write this book for the populace, something easy that they will understand, and it will be for all who are searching along many paths. They will pick it up and say, 'This seems to make sense.'"

Thank you very much for this information. I will begin to build upon the basic information that has been revealed, knowing the inspiration will come. May I now ask what will happen to the Circles of Light during earth changes?

"The energy of course will remain constant except for those times, which we have taught, when it will be stronger. It will not be depleted, for as you know, it is unlimited and eternal. As your people awaken, and are taught that this energy exists and how they may use it, it will simply be given to them by their intent."

We have spoken before of the animal kingdom and how they appear to respond in their behavior at the time of a full moon.

"That is because at those times they are receiving more energy. They do not of course understand the wall of humanity, the illusions of man. Therefore the energy is simply given to them."

With this in mind, does the full moon also cause behavioral actions in those who are not yet awake? The term "lunacy" comes to mind.

"We believe this to simply be an idea of your collective consciousness, for nothing actually occurs to someone at the time of a full moon. Only those who are receiving the energy by their intent will feel a 'change' within themselves."

So this is more a superstition that the collective consciousness believes to be true? Is it because of this commonly held belief that it becomes an actual experience for those who hold this belief as truth?

"Yes, the ones who are not awake would have no knowledge that the Circles of Light exist. Therefore, any effects others may attribute to the full moon have been created by the energy mankind has given to this idea. They have created their belief that the full moon is associated with various behaviors among your species. This belief is so strong that they actually create the very thing they experience."

What effect does the Circle of Light around the earth have as far as restoring the balance between earth, air, fire, and water?

"They would simply give energy to each one of those elements. This is why the earth, air, fire, and water also have their own energies."

You have previously taught us that the collective consciousness is an entity with a "mind" of its own. What about the four elements?

"They do of course have energy within themselves, and this energy can also be drawn upon. They do not have a consciousness as you understand that to be."

You have also taught us that the Circles of Light are not affected by the collective consciousness.

"This is because the collective consciousness is somewhat 'dense,' somewhat asleep if you will. They are not aware; therefore, they are not drawing the energy. Only those who awaken will 'know' of their existence, for they will no longer believe what the collective believes."

The ancient earth mother ceremonies were conducted according to the rhythms of the earth. Would you please comment on this?

"They understood and they were aware that they must respect and nurture that which they were given. The problem occurred, if you will, when they began to go beyond simple respect. They began to believe you had to sacrifice or perform certain rituals. It is simply a matter of thanking the earth, to take care of the earth, to make sure she is replenished when you have used her. This is sufficient."

Were certain geographical locations, such as Stonehenge, simply higher concentrations of energy?

"It was that area which received the energy of those who came, the entities who had come before and left their vibrations and essence."

Thank you for this information. We have talked about the return of Divine feminine energy to the earth. Has this energy been revealed at earlier times of our history? Was Isis one of her representatives?

"Yes, she was one of the representations of the feminine energy. The purpose for which she came was to help the people understand and respect the earth, and to give the feminine energy. The people of her era did not understand. They, as mankind always seems to do, wanted to lift her up and once again begin rituals. This is not what was intended. So Isis simply left long before they even knew she was gone, and they never understood why she had come.

"Little Brother, we have been listening to, and observing, your and Little One's thoughts about what you are now facing. We desire to offer you our feelings for your consideration. We would say to simply be aware of your choices, to see what the end result will be, and act accordingly. Know that there are times when you must take actions so that you are leading and not being led. As you know, we do not have these types of circumstances. But even though we have not experienced them, we certainly 'feel' for you. As we stated earlier, since the manifestation from nothing is a very difficult path, you must know that you cannot simply sit and wait. We would like you to be true to yourself. We certainly send you love and energy, and if it was different and we were here and allowed to simply create miracles, we would be overjoyed to do this. This is a difficult learning process for us as well to know that we must simply observe, but we do send energy and Love."

Your sentiments and the love that flows from you are more comforting than words could possibly express. Thank you very much. Little One was wondering, as you have mentioned your planet has collectively chosen to come and help us complete this project, is there a time when you would return? Would there be contact with you as we have now, or would it be an observing situation for you at that time?

"We would always be available, both at times of necessity and when you desire our presence. In the beginning, we believed we would be informed of the time when we would simply observe. Now we are in the 'knowing' that we shall never leave you, for it is our desire to show you and guide you in what is to come. It is our desire to come and lend ourselves to you as you walk this wondrous but difficult journey."

We are overjoyed to have "for this appointed time" the indescribable joy of your presence and guidance. We have a strong and deeply felt love for you, such that we have become family.

"We are most pleased to be here. As you know, there will come a time for us, as in all things, for we do have a planet to be a part of and we would return to that. We do not know when, just that we will. We would never just simply leave. The only reason that could arise that we would leave would be, of course, if we or our Teachings were no longer respected or if we were asked to leave. We have stated once before that should there be controversy or fighting amongst those in the council, we would come to you and speak about it. If it could not be corrected, then we may be asked to leave."

We have talked about this in great detail. We know you have heard not only from our discussions, but also from our promise to you, that it is of highest importance to us that there is absolute harmony. This is why we are counting on you, Dear Ones, for the selection of the people whom you have prepared for the council. We, under no circumstances, would

be happy or accepting of any person who could not coexist in complete harmony with all who choose to align themselves with either the council or any part of this important project.

"We believe that it will be as it should be. There are always those who bring their own energies, if you will."

We would deal with it in love, but swiftly. In regard to my writing, Dear Ones, may I call upon you for inspiration and guidance?

"We shall always be there."

You mentioned previously that I have not yet begun to see "the colors." Would you please expand upon this?

"The colors are the reflections of light, reflections of the Circles of Light, and the reflection of the light within your planet. If you look through a prism, you will see a myriad of colors. This is what the earth plane consists of and you will begin to see these colors. Some will see these as auras, but it is not just the human who has these auras. It is all living things. You will begin to be overwhelmed, if you will, as you see them and become more knowledgeable of them."

Thank you. The rest of the questions can be asked and answered in another session. We are so delighted and grateful for your presence this evening.

"We are most pleased, Little Brother. Now we would like you to go and do your full moon observance. We will lend you our energy, and then you may wish to call Sister of My Sister and relay to her all we have shared with you. So if there are no further questions, we do depart in Love and Blessings."

This was a wonderful teaching. Previously we had been introduced to the Circles of Light in sessions 13 and 14 in *Teachings of the Heart*. It was great to have our questions answered that came about from the teachings given to us in these sessions. We immediately began to gain experience with them. It was not long before all of us could not only "feel" this energy, but also be able to draw upon it just by our intent to do so. We have discovered this source of Divine feminine energy to be excellent for meditations, healings, balancing of energy, inspirations, and for our writings. The energy was strongly felt through our hands at first, but with time and experience, we could feel it at the crown and third eye energy centers. This energy does indeed vary in intensity through the different phases of the moon. What was an unexpected surprise was the intensity of the Circles of Light at the time of the Dark Moon that is the time each month when the moon is not visible. The first three days of the New Moon are also just as powerful as the Full Moon.

In *Teachings from the Heart*, an extraordinary event took place. We were blessed with the "appearance" of the Divine Mother. She is also referred to as the Divine feminine or the feminine energy when she is addressed by the "Girls" in a session. In session 13, we asked a series of questions to the Divine Mother; it was her answers that generated our first thoughts and impressions of not only Her, but of this project we had been asked to begin. We have since been given the acronym of ASTRID, which stand for All Spirits Together Rising in Divinity. Each time you see this name throughout this book, you will know that we are speaking of the Divine Mother, the feminine aspect of the One Spirit, the One Energy. Once we understood the true source behind the project and all that was being revealed to us, we began to see the magnitude of the scope of this awakening. We truly became aware of just how big this project is. This meeting was very humbling, not to mention a presence so intense that you felt as though your whole body was enveloped by an electric current. You felt as though your entire being was vibrating. You certainly do not forget an experience such as this.

As our energy has risen, and we have become more able to be in the presence of the Divine feminine energy, these encounters have become joyous experiences for us. They do not occur often, but when they do, the experience is so wonderful that we have no words to properly describe them. They can only be "felt" to "know" and comprehend them. Now you know the source of the Love, inspiration, guidance, and energy that empowers this appointed time of the awakening and the project we have begun. You will learn more about this as the Teaching sessions progress.

Our financial situation was steadily becoming quite intense, although we continued to do our best to meet our obligations. We were very hopeful of finding jobs and had voiced our desires concerning this. We were optimistic that a door would soon open for us. We received encouragement that the writing of these books could be a source of this income, and we began compiling the information that would be presented in Bruce's first book.

In discussing our financial situation with Zelia and Astoria, it became apparent that the scope of their involvement with us was for the purpose of bringing the Teachings. They would also prepare us for the coming of higher energy that would be directly associated with the awakening.

Even though they had the ability to do this instantly, they did not have permission as it would alter the process of experiences we were going through. We wondered about this at first, only to later understand the true meaning of our ability to have the freedom to create at will. We had to go through each experience and make our own decisions. We also had to endure the residual effects from each decision or choice, as they were designed to help us to awaken to remember who we truly are. To interfere with, or alter, this process in any way would be to deny us not only our freedom to create at will, but also to prevent us from learning the lessons these experiences were designed to teach. We will speak in depth on this subject as we continue on this journey, but this realization was a very important first step in understanding the importance of allowing each of us to create and experience the events or circumstances that help us to remember and understand who we are, and to grow as a result of them.

October 29, 2007

The morning after the first session, Bruce spent developing an outline for his first book. By the next afternoon, he already had chapter heading, topics, and a suggested title. Several questions had come to us the night before, so we requested a session for this evening.

"We do greet thee. We have come. Do you have questions for us?"

Greetings, Dear Ones. Yes, we do have some questions for you. When did separation begin to dominate the collective consciousness?

"We would have to say that it probably began from the start. Remember, you come into this incarnation forgetting what you knew in the Absolute. It would not have taken long for tribes to segregate themselves according to where they lived on your planet and what they were doing. Therefore, it began as we are assured, at the very beginning."

When we hear or read a truth that resonates within us, why do we soon forget about it? We do not make it a part of our experience. Is that because our minds and bodies are beginning to "see" but are still influenced by the walls of separation, limit, blindness, failure, necessity, anger/hatred, and suspicion/doubt?

"It would be two parts. Many times those who are beginning to awaken will read something that will resonate with them, but they are not quite ready for the truth of it. They will look at it but not put it into practice. If they are further along in their awakening when they read this, then they will certainly put it into practice. The second part, of course, would be the Walls that surround all. You may read a truth, feel a truth, but if you allow the Walls to close you in again, that truth can certainly be forgotten."

When we begin to meditate, it seems as if it is difficult to "drop out of mind." In other words, it is hard to quiet the mind and rid oneself of all incoming chatter.

"We would like to say to you that it is really not, to our understanding at least, that difficult to be 'out of mind.' It is simply to place yourself in a position of observation of all around you in your Now. You would do this without conscious thought or assessment of that which is around you, or any inner dialogue regarding your observations. When the chatter begins, simply refocus upon only observing and not judging. You become a part of all around you, and in doing this, you have fallen 'out of mind.' We believe anyone can learn to do this."

Thank you. I so enjoy the times we spend together and look forward to them.

"And we also. It has been our joy to be called this evening and shall await, of course, each calling. If there are no further questions, then we shall depart in Love and Blessings."

We began to consider the subject of separation. We experience so much of this in our daily lives. People, by and large, do not see themselves as connected to one another. Nor do they understand that we are all connected as one on a much-higher level. The conversations we had while in Happy Camp on the seven walls revealed that the wall of separation is our greatest challenge in order to transform the consciousness of humanity. This was a question we had been thinking of quite often. We had a strong desire to learn more about it, its origins, and to more fully understand its ability to influence every aspect of our lives—especially those who are still spiritually asleep.

The discussion concerning how many people read something, resonate with it, but do not make it a part of their lives, so they are actually living it, had interested us for many years. It now became clear that until one reaches the point where they are ready to awaken to a truth and live it, they are still searching and may continue to bounce from one "truth" to another. They may talk about a "truth," but not actually "feel" it. It does not become a living part of them. We so often talk about our "truth," but do not necessarily walk the talk. When we reach the point where we are walking the talk, we have made the "truth" our own.

We had been debating for months whether or not we would take a cruise that had previously been scheduled and paid for. We weren't sure if we should go based on our current situation. Once we found out that our payment would not be refunded, and when the "Girls" made reference to important experiences that we would have during the trip, we made the decision to go. We were now only several days from leaving. It was time to quickly pack our bags, call the cat sitter for Sarah, and make our arrangements to get to the airport. However, there was one more important session that would take place before we left.

November 1, 2007

"We do greet thee. We have been called and come to answer your questions."

We are curious about the capacity of someone who is not yet awake to store Universal Life Force Energy (ULFE). Because they are unaware of the Circles of Light, they would not be aware of the extra energy. Is this correct?

"Yes, that is correct. If you have not awakened yet, the energy is received unknowingly or unconsciously. It is just a continued movement. There is no storage. Once you awaken you can, on a cellular level, store some of that energy as it is being received and given. Those who have had the openings can actually store that energy. The capacity for storage is there but not necessarily used, as the person has not yet awakened to know that it is there. Nor have they received the energy centers openings that allow them to receive it."

Thank you. One of the things we are concerned about is our cat Sarah. Especially in light of us leaving on this cruise, do you have any information for us?

"She is an older cat; she is a remarkable little creature. All life-forms on your planet have a time for choosing. We do not sense that she has chosen yet as to her 'time.' We cannot be assured as to when that shall occur, just that it will."

We are concerned. As you know, we love her deeply and wonder if we should take her to a vet before we leave, or will she be fine until we return?

"We could simply say that if it is of concern to you at this moment, then the choice may well be to seek medical help for your creature. We do not sense that there will be any leaving, but as you know, it shall be her choice."

Yes, we really appreciate this answer as it gives us a sense of relief. Thank you. May I ask some questions pertaining to our present situation? These are asked so that your understanding may enlighten us. We are absolutely committed to the path we are one and to the monumental purpose for which we have incarnated. We do believe this is our life's purpose. Would you please comment?

"Yes, this is true. We encourage you to share your life story with those who will read your book. Talk about the things you have experienced on your journey. We know you will need a base for people to connect with you, the author. It would be important to tell them who you are and how you came to be where you are. We believe it is important for people to understand that this is coming from one of their own, and not a conglomerate of names. It is important that they connect. We know that you would prefer to remain, as you would say, in the background, but we know this is a good thing for you to do."

Thank you. Would you please comment on my surgery and the overwhelming feeling in the recovery room that enveloped me before and after the surgery?

"Your surgery was a series of events that resulted from your choices, through your actions. We have been told that had you not pushed yourself so hard, had you allowed yourself to 'let go' and allow your emotions to flow and not kept them bottled up, that the disease would have had another place to flow. This is not anything to be concerned about, for this is the way it went. The feeling that you experienced was the love of the Divine Parents."

Is all that happened part of an appointed time for us?

"Yes, it was a time of your choosing for is it not all your choice?"

Yes, what I was thinking on May 11 when we first saw the book *The Secret* and watched the movie was that life changed for both of us at that time.

"But you must remember, Little Brother, that it was your choice to listen; it was your choice to buy these things. You could simply walk on past them, but it was your 'time.' It was now upon you."

What I was thinking about was the series of events. For example, the surgery that came completely out of the blue became more significant after hearing you mention that you had been trying for a great length of time to get my attention, which it certainly did. Was this the vehicle that was chosen to get me to really wake up?

"It would not have been of our orchestrating, but it is possible that with your choosing and with that of the All, it could have indeed come to pass that way."

Was it ASTRID that came to me and carried me through surgery and enveloped me with the knowing that it was my "time" to begin this journey?

"It was, as you said, from the beginning the Parents carried you through. It simply is that you were 'feeling' more of the feminine essence."

I had the overwhelming feeling that it was time to stop working. If I had gone back and not heeded this guidance, perhaps a different outcome would have become my experience. Was this part of the "blueprint" and my purpose for this incarnation?

"As you know, a 'blueprint' is simply a drawing or schematic of things that can occur. Of course, it is your choices that make it occur. So to say that it was necessarily in an original 'blueprint,' we are not sure of that. We do know it was a series of choices, and events, which culminated in this."

The thought here is that it was not necessarily orchestrated by the One, but it was "time" for me to do this. It was the "time" in this incarnation to be consciously aware of being on the path.

"Yes, we have been able to observe but do not interfere. We have observed and see that removing yourself from that occupation was probably, as you would say, a good thing, although there is no 'good' or 'bad.' Possibly you could have made some other choices that would have allowed you to have an interim 'time.'"

I had wondered if all the events and circumstances had been a direct output from my "blueprint." Whatever decisions that were made, and the series of things that just came to be, were a part of what was to be learned from this experience.

"These choices you must realize go back to many, many of your years, even prior to your meeting Little One. It is simply a culmination of all these choices that have brought you to your path you are now on."

It is clear that we have to go through this financial ordeal. Apparently, in some way, it is a part of that plan. It was something I must have chosen at some point before this incarnation. If I had gone back to work, I would still have had to face, at some point, the exact same thing that is happening now. Is this something that was also in Little One's "blueprint?"

"If it occurs it would at some point have to have been your choice. It is possible you would still have had to face this, but we do not know this for sure. You would 'know' this within you. As to Little One, this may not necessarily have been in her 'blueprint,' but it was her choice to either continue in your experience or to remove herself. It is always your choice to either stay or leave another's experience."

There is the feeling inside and the sense that no matter what had happened this would still have to be faced. This repetitive situation of no matter how hard I tried or what I did would end up, from time to time, in progressively more severe financial situations. Now it is reaching its final and most severe version in what is happening now. There has to be a progressive learning experience here. All of this has to be a preparation to be able to do what I came here to do. Is this an accurate assessment?

"We would say that this is fairly accurate, yes. We, of course, know not what your plan, your 'blueprint,' is completely. We need not be privy to that. The forming of the 'blueprint' is only between you and the ONE, the Divine Parents. But because these are your circumstances, we must believe that this is the path you have set yourself upon."

Yes, from your teachings, it is clear that we make choices. Deep inside is the feeling that this is now, as you would say, the "appointed time" for all these events to happen. The series of repetitive events throughout my life have led to this point of culmination.

"Then, Little Brother, if this is what you feel, then it must be so."

Thank you, this is so very helpful. Can it then be said that everything that has transpired to this date had been a careful unveiling of all that has been planned long, long ago?

"It would be what you had requested."

So this is what Spirit knew I had to go through in order to prepare myself for my life's mission and purpose?

"Yes, Little Brother, and usually once you have been told, once you come to that totally awakening of those facts, then at that point, there is no more attachment, if you will, to things that are not an expression of what your purpose or mission for your incarnation is. Things in your life can then change to come into alignment with what you know your purpose to be. As you know, there is perfection in this process of unveiling, or unfolding, of the events that will appear in your experience."

Then, everything that has, and is going to, unfold is inseparably linked with all these series of events?

"Yes, we see that you now understand this."

Was this also part of Little One's "blueprint"? Or did she become linked with my experiences through her choice of being with me? We now are on the same path toward the completion of this "Awakening" project.

"As you know, Little One has not spent much 'time' in the physical realm. Due to the fact that she has spent her 'time' in the Absolute or the spiritual realm so much, she has been, as we have said, a renegade angel. She is basically gone wherever she has desired, and her path in the incarnation led her to you. It was known to her that it would be important for her to stay by you. She chose to do this. There were other choices, other paths. This was the one, due to who she is, that she chose. She has remained out of love and understanding, even though we sense that Now is a difficult 'time' for her. We understand that she is suffering, if you will, from the pangs of physical mortality and being in a physical environment that would not have been of her choosing. She will go through this as she has linked her path with yours. We know that she will remain true to completion."

This causes me to be a little sad, because her pain becomes my pain.

"Is this not how it should be when you love someone? There is no other response given what has been learned."

The thought just came about how the desire to go gold prospecting was a "hook" that brought us to Happy Camp, which in turn led to our meeting Sister of My Sister. So many unexpected things unfolded, particularly in learning Reiki. It was like a door opening to a whole new experience that had previously been only a desire.

"When one door closes, we have heard that another door opens. As we have mentioned to you before, your meeting of Sister of My Sister was no accident. As you know, there are no coincidences. This meeting had been long planned. It was a series of events and circumstances that led each of you to this 'time' of meeting."

There was a substantial amount of gold envisioned to be found while mining in Happy Camp. This, as you know, did not occur. However, I had the feeling that it did not manifest in order for us to experience the things we are experiencing at this time. As this was a "blueprint" event, nothing would have changed that.

"We are not so sure of that, Little Brother. We do know there are substantial amounts of gold in that area, for there are those who are finding it. It does not mean that in your 'time' you did not find it. It only means that it still awaits you."

In regards to financing the project, we know that everything will come together in the appointed "time," so it is not something to be dwelled upon.

"You may need action, not necessarily by yourself, of course, but no man, as you know, is an island. If you think you are, then you are still within the wall of separation. Do not be afraid to ask others for help and guidance. Do not be prideful or embarrassed if you must reach out to those with the resources to help you fund the project. We believe that sometimes the things that you desire, not that they are wrong of course, may not be practical. When you say you wish to finance everything, unless you are writing a library, this would not be possible at this 'time' on your earth. For those who give financial aid will feel vested and, therefore, are able to give more of themselves to the project. Many people will contribute to this project, and you will let them do so, for it is a blessing to them."

I do desire to participate to the extent it is possible for the unfolding of this project.

"You must know that you, Little One, and Sister of My Sister are the founders. You are the beginning. If it were not for you, nothing would have been able to unfold, but there is no control. Just let it flow and you will be guided."

Thank you. This is excellent advice. We have spoken in the past regarding our awareness of evolution. Is it possible here on the earth plane, over time, to have mastery over feeling/occurrence?

"Yes, we believe that this could occur but we do not know in your 'time' when it would occur. As we have said to you before, we do know that this shall occur within your current lifetime. You know that your physical vehicle has certain limitations, not that these can't be overcome. You must, as you would say, stay serviced. Exercise, eat properly, be of a good weight, keep your mind sharp, keep your body strong, for these things will aid your physical vehicle to continue."

It is certainly our heart's desire to see this project through to completion. We are dedicated to that goal and appreciate your advice and guidance.

We have been talking about my guide. There is one very important thing I would like to share with you. I have been attempting to understand who the guide is since you first revealed his presence. Is he the masculine aspect of the One who is All?

"Yes, and we thought that by now you would have gotten the name."

A request for the name has been presented, but nothing has come through as of yet.

"We would suggest you study the name we were given to give to you, for you will find much information that will be helpful for you. We have led Little One to a source that will give you insight into the questions you have asked and will provide the answers you seek."

Good, we will take this information with us on the trip. Now, as you know, Little One is somewhat hesitant concerning the information you have given her as to one of her previous incarnations. Will her current studies help her to remember who she was?

"We believe that she is aware. It is something that her mind, if you will, needs to wrap itself around. She has always felt second best in this life, and this incarnation for her has not always been pleasant. She has been made to feel, in many cases, invalidated. It is because of this invalidation that she finds it hard to accept and believe what has been revealed to her. We know that she will come to this understanding and realization of what this means."

We know we are to relax on the cruise, but there is a strong feeling that something extremely important is going to take place on board.

"You must at all times be aware. Listen to people as they speak to you, and do not isolate yourselves on this trip. Take your time to do your book, your study, but be among others for you know not what can occur. It will be a time of enlightenment, a time of understanding. So, yes, we believe it is a 'good' thing to take this trip although it will appear to others, because of your situation, not to be so. There will be Teachings and much to show you during your cruise. Remember, Little Brother, it is through your questions that you learn."

We have already been informed about the veils that are part of the forgetfulness that accompanies us into this physical realm, and it would be our desire to have the veil or veils that might inhibit us from receiving clear and unmistakable communication from our guides lifted away. You know my past and the considerable resistance on my part that has colored my thoughts concerning the truth of things I thought I was hearing. It is clear now that a lot of what was heard, which led me to past responses, was me not understanding the nature of how this communication took place, and I know that Little One has experienced much of the same. We

placed a time frame upon receiving information that was not meant to be understood in the context of time. However, many things that were revealed did eventually come to pass. We simply did not understand that you cannot place a passage of time upon information or inspiration that will be given. It was difficult for us because of the responses that we received from others when we shared with them some of these communications.

"Yes, Little Brother, a spirit, if you will, of the All would not give you a 'time' frame for those things are the direct results of your choices, of your free will. Also, if what you hear or 'feel' does not resonate as a truth, or if you think you are hearing an amount of money being revealed, this is your own mind and not a true communication from either your guide, us, or others who are sent to help, guide, and give inspirations to you. If it is 'pie in the sky,' if that is how it is said, then you will know. When it is us or others who speak to you, and when you exercise this gift that has been given to you, the more you will 'feel' the truth of our words and guidance. You will 'know' when it is ego or self-speaking or when the communication comes from outside of yourself."

We desire at this time to have any and all impediment removed in order to receive absolutely accurate communication. The request is for all filters to be removed as we desire only the truth be placed into the books. Would you kindly help us to reach this level of awareness and clarity?

"Yes, of course, we will do all we are able."

Thank you. We choose not to run from this any longer. We desire to face this directly and no longer close ourselves off from any communications received simply because we might have been afraid that it was coming from ourselves and not true communication from you or others sent to guide us.

"This is good. Always stay aware to all things, inspirations, and ideas that may require action and to all that you may hear."

We accept the situation that we are in, either way it goes. Whether our desires will be answered at this time or whether they are not, be it bankruptcy or miraculous recovery, we choose to advance as rapidly as allowed on our path. We believe that the wondrous work, which ASTRID called our path, is the purpose for which Little One and I incarnated and

that our appointed "time" has come. Would you please comment upon this?

"We believe that what you have stated is accurate. You know that to achieve anything you must make conscious choices. When you are in complete awareness of all you choose along your journey, and you stay consciously aware during those times, you can accomplish all that you desire. Little Brother, we have been most pleased to have been of assistance. If you would excuse us for one moment."

"My beloved, I have taken this opportunity to come into your presence, for I 'feel' and 'know' what you are going through. Paths can be quite arduous and we understand this. We would like to help you, of course, to lower the veils as you have requested. Place your hands over Little One's hands, and through her physical body, I wish to send to you the lowering of the veils. This will be helpful and necessary on your journey along your chosen path. You know that it is not our choice the path you follow, as it is always your choice. I trust that you will look at this path, not necessarily to the future of it, but to the choices you Now make upon it. I come through now to give you my Blessings of Love and that you will know I am lowering these veils. I shall now depart."

Thank you so much, ASTRID.

"Little Brother, we were requested to leave and we know that this was helpful for you. Now, because of this, we will depart so that Little One may rest."

Yes, I have transcribed all the material for the seven walls and will be putting questions together. I had planned to present some to you during this session, but felt it important to share with you what was on my heart.

"This was most appropriate. We know there will be much said regarding the walls while you are upon your voyage. There will be many learning's upon this voyage, but we also wish for you to relax. We wish for you a peaceful time, as we know this will be an excellent thing for you. Much will be necessary once you return from this voyage. We are quite looking forward to this trip, although we have already traveled far. This will be our opportunity to interact with others, if you will. When a ship is at sea, it is of itself, and those upon it are of their own consciousness. It will be interesting to see people who are enjoying their traveling and to experience along with you what the consciousness is onboard. It is a

work in and of itself. This will be most interesting. If there is nothing
further, we shall now depart in Love and Blessings."

The impact this session had upon us has not diminished with time.
So many important lessons were taught in such a brief span. The one
lesson that really stands out is that we alone choose our path and create
our journey. All the events and circumstances we face in this life, and
the lessons we learn from them, are our creations, and they all begin
with a choice. The "Girls" do not tell us what to do, nor would they ever
interfere with the choices we make. For them to do so would be to take
away our "freedom to create at will." They do help us to understand that
it is our choices that bring about our life experiences. What we learn
from them (our choices) are not only purposeful but enable us to, step
by step, travel our intended path and create our journey. Through our
understanding and the guidance from the "Girls," we are able to face a
situation or phase we are going through. They give just the right amount
of input, allowing us to arrive at our own answers. This process builds a
strong connection for us as we continue in our remembrance of who we
truly are and why we experience things the way we do.

Nothing happens in our lives by coincidence. Everything we
experience is by design. When we need encouragement, or help,
in connecting the dots, just the right words are spoken to spark an
understanding. We have come to realize how invaluable this type of
inspiration and guidance can be. Especially as you begin to awaken and
travel your path to Oneness. We are truly blessed to have been given the
Teachings, and their love, energy, patience, and encouragement always
moves us forward as the project continues to expand.

We found special comfort in knowing that our cat Sarah had no
intention of departing the physical world at this time. In fact, she became
more active, alert, and engaging upon our return. She was with us for
another year and every moment was a joy. This information given to us
certainly allowed us to be free from worry on our trip and it helped to
create a phenomenal experience.

One subject that had a great impact on us was the discussion
concerning the events, beginning with Bruce's surgery that changed the
course of our lives. At the time, the "Girls" were quite guarded about the
details that surrounded the circumstances that came together so fast.
These had a profound influence and completely shifted the course of
Bruce's life to a purely spiritual path. It was later revealed that indeed all
these events had been carefully orchestrated and left for his choosing. As
time went on, and with each new experience, the big picture came into
focus. This understanding really had to be experienced. It definitely could
not have been explained before the actual happenings. So many other

events became a part of the main experience and created an expanded experience. These experiences would have been too "far out" to have been understood simply by an explanation. It is not always for the best to know how an event will unfold. You must make your decisions along the way, and your freedom to create at will must be upheld, otherwise you learn nothing from the experience. This was a pivotal lesson learned. Through the experiences themselves, and the knowledge and awareness that were gained, we were creating the very thing that enabled us to advance along our path. We certainly would not be where we are today had things not manifested as they did.

The appearance of the Divine Mother was only the second time she had revealed Herself. The first time was in Happy Camp, and I have spoken of that moment in the first book. I know that this concept will be difficult for many to understand. Believe me when I say I was even reluctant to speak of it at all. It is so important that the Teachings and inspirations we are given be shared with everyone. There was that moment of fear when I felt that sharing this amazing information would put the whole thing in the "gone off the deep end" category. I know now that I couldn't have been true to myself or you without sharing this with you. Her Love is eternal and brings nothing but joy. I desire you to know this. Of course, when I say Her, I do not mean to indicate that there are two individuals, for there is only the One, and the One contains within the feminine and masculine aspects of the One Energy. I will try as we go to give you a clearer understanding, but if you open your heart, you will begin to "know."

Looking back, I can see how this session proved to be another important event in our spiritual journeys. It was at that moment, during the session, when we "knew" to put everything else aside to travel this path. Now was the "time" to put into practical application all that we had learned so far.

So after this session, we packed our bags for our flight the next day. We made sure to pack all the materials and information we had so far accumulated, along with questions to be asked once we were onboard. I cleaned the house as I hate coming back from a trip to a dirty house! Sarah was all set for her cat sitter, everyone was notified of our itinerary, and we headed off to try and get some sleep.

Early the next morning, our ride arrived, so we said goodbye to Sarah, locked up the house, and excitedly headed to the airport. We certainly didn't know then what a truly amazing trip this would be.

November 6, 2007

We arrived in Florida the next afternoon after a very smooth flight across the country. The afternoon was sunny, warm, and a perfect time to do a little exploring. We walked down to a gazebo overlooking Tampa Bay and watched the sun set over the Gulf of Mexico. It was our first time in Florida and it was truly a beautiful sight. After a really good night's sleep, we boarded a bus and were dropped off at the cruise terminal in Tampa. The process of checking in went smoothly, and before long, we found ourselves standing at the rail on the Promenade Deck gazing at the skyline that quickly disappeared as we made our way toward open water.

At dinner that night, we were treated to another beautiful sunset. After eating and getting somewhat settled in, we decided to explore the ship. We walked around for several hours before returning to our room, and we were pooped. The bed proved to be as comfortable as it looked, and we had a restful night of sleep. We were several days away from our first port of call, so our time was our own. Each morning we headed down to the library and checked out a Scrabble game. Of course, I always won, but we enjoyed the relaxed atmosphere on board. As the "Girls" had suggested to us, we began to take notice and become more aware of others and the happenings taking place around us. By the afternoon of November 6, questions for the seven walls had been completed, and later that same afternoon, we settled in for our first and, surprisingly, only session while on board.

"We do greet thee. We have come for your questions."

Yes, the questions concerning the seven walls of humanity are finished. In the previous teachings, you brought to us regarding the walls, you asked if we knew how difficult the task would be to break down each one of them. Would you please tell us more about this?

"It will be quite a monumental endeavor. As you know, there are not many who are upon this path to tearing down the walls, as they still do not know, nor believe, that these walls exist. We do not want to discourage you from breaking down these walls, for it is certainly possible to tear them down. As in all things, it must start with one. This tearing down will be first for your own journey, but the effect will be for the entire collective consciousness as more and more understand these walls and dismantle them. It will be according to your perception of them that will aid you in the dismantling of them."

What specifically is our task to be?

"In regard to tearing down these walls, you simply share what you are learning with those you meet, with those who come to you. Explain to them exactly what the walls are. Show them and point out to those who will choose to listen, how they are there, and how they continue to exist. It is by this recognition of all who would see that they shall fall."

Will all necessary resources be provided along the way?

"You will require action, as we have stated, to accomplish this. We know that the resources exist, but if you are intending them to fall into your lap, this is not the way of creation. We do believe that the resources will come due to your actions. If you do not scribe the books, how will others learn of these teachings?"

How much time will we need to set aside in order to walk this path? Should we suspend our other desired activities, as your planet has done, in order to devote all of our time and energy toward this project?

"Little Brother, our planet chose this time to help, but you must remember that we are quite advanced from where you are. Our joy, our leisure, if you will, is in a different way than you have here. We would not ask you to give up your life. We ask that you devote some of your time, your energy, but certainly we do not expect you to take time away from your own leisure. These experiences are the reason you are here and to create in only one direction would be to remove yourself from all else you would desire to know."

Thank you. Will we be given information beforehand if a significant event is to happen so that we will be prepared for it?

"That would, of course, be giving you your future. You realize that what occurs in your future is based upon your choices now. In the 'Now' you must just continue. Therefore, when something does occur, you will know it."

Was it the desire of the One to experience the concept of separation in all its forms, degrees, and expressions? Is this one of the principal reasons for all spirits to enter the physical realm in forgetfulness?

"We do not believe it was the desire of the All to experience separation, for you cannot experience separation of yourself, and as you know, separation is that which occurs when the perception of the observer is to see things outside of themselves as separate from themselves. Forgetfulness upon entering your physical realm, and taking a physical form, happens so that each may remember who they truly are and their connection to the All. As you know, there are those who chose to come in with less forgetfulness than others. They were here to be teachers, just as we have come to teach."

We know that we come in to this experience having forgotten what we knew in the Absolute in order to experience awareness, feelings, thoughts, and the actions that arise as a result of them. This is in order to remember who we are as we proceed on our path toward Oneness. Is that correct?

"Yes, you came in forgetting so that you would not only have the experience with your physical body, mind, and spirit, but also to experience the All and who you really are in the Absolute and in physical form, for they are the same. The One has no need, or desire, to experience separation. The One simply experiences all that you do through you."

So is it more accurate to say that this forgetfulness is to allow us to have the contrast within this earth plane, between the understanding of who we truly are, and who we are not? Having come in forgetfulness, we are then able to have the experiences of closing the gap of separation so that we may "know" the reunion with the One?

"Of course, otherwise you would have chosen another planet, another universe, to have a different type of incarnation. Not all that come into their incarnation come in with the wall of separation. We, on our planet, did not do that. We have always known Oneness. When one comes to your planet, they desire a different experience and they may then choose to know this separation."

Is this process of taking down the wall of separation not only to bring us into Oneness, but also to teach us the whole process of unifying spirit and matter? Is this part of the process of renewing the earth?

"This is well said. The more who remember, the more the wall must fall. Of course, it shall not only help each other, it shall help the earth as you cannot help, but remember what the earth is and what it was originally intended for."

Thank you. Is this awareness then a vehicle to reach a higher consciousness in order to realize and understand separation from the One and to serve as a catalyst for reunion with the All?

"Awareness is, of course, just what it is. It is being aware of yourself and, therefore, your separation. If you are seeing something as separate, then you are creating that separation. As you remember, you come to that place where you understand this, and you know that there is only the One and you are eternally connected to it. This remembering enables you to have that experience."

In Oneness we will remember the All. So then does each one of our life experiences have the explicit purpose of awakening us? As we consciously awake, and we recognize separation, would it be fair to say that there would be levels of awareness that would lead to Oneness?

"If those have been your choices, then yes. Many do not know that their choices or experiences can be used to awaken. They simply just go on as they always have because their choice has not been to remember. All of this remembering, if that was your choice, does not happen all at once. It is like the building of anything, it starts with the foundation, and as your awareness increases, your memories increase as well. At the completion of the building, you will be with the One and 'know' who you are and your purpose."

I have written down a series of five levels to this process. I'm not sure if they are accurate though. It seems that level one is when we first come into our physical body in forgetfulness. We would, in essence, be asleep to the understanding that we are spiritually asleep. The second level would be our first recognition that separation exists. Beyond that, would knowledge of the existence of a higher SOURCE be the next logical step?

"First, yes, you would not be aware that you are spiritually asleep. This first recognition would be of self as an individual, of being on your own, so to speak. It would be your first recognition of being isolated. It sometimes takes several steps to get to the level of awareness to understand the existence of a higher Source. Many do not know this, and some just take a longer period of 'time' to reach the point of understanding. It is not the same for each one, but for the collective as a whole, this first step of recognition would be seeing yourself beyond your belief of separation and recognizing the existence of a connected Source."

So then we could say that the next step would be the individual recognizing the unity of the oneness of body, mind, and spirit?

"Yes, and of all humanity as well."

Would the final step be the unity or reunification with the One who is All?

"Yes, that could be looked at as the final step, but as you know, all things are eternal, and in this is the continuation of union with the One."

We have talked about the levels of consciousness and that there are many levels in this process of awakening. Does each one have a separate consciousness, or is all a part of a total consciousness?

"The levels of awakening, if you will, would certainly be part of your consciousness of which there is only ONE. It would be different levels within your consciousness. So as you take the first step of awakening, your consciousness is also beginning to awaken. As you proceed along these levels, you will become more and more aware."

Does each level of consciousness correspond to a different level of vibration?

"Yes."

Are we to understand from the law of attraction that one of the reasons certain groups will form, and unite, is through like vibration?

"Yes, there is more than just one level of consciousness. On one level, the vibration for a particular thing, such as your meditations, will draw together those of like mind. This is why the more you give to something, that is energy through feeling or emotion, the more it raises the intensity of the vibration, especially when the heart is filled with love."

What is the part miracles will play in the awakening of humanity?

"It will be, if you will, a catalyst. There will be miracles that will cause people to stop and look. They will see that there is more to life, the universe, and the power of All that is. This will open their eyes and help them to awaken."

The discussion that followed in this session addressed each of the seven walls of humanity, one wall at a time. The questions and answers, and the Teachings that were added to the discussion, are combined to form the content of the chapter "The Seven Walls of Humanity" in Bruce's book *Living Your Life in Joy*. There were a number of questions asked during the course of this Teaching that were not included in Bruce's book, so we will include them here.

Is there a common approach to the process of dismantling the wall of separation?

"As you speak with someone, start with the basics. You do not want this to seem complicated, for it is really quite simple. Start by speaking to them that there is, in truth, no such thing as separation. Ask them about their thoughts, or belief, that they are separate. Obtain the idea of how they think and believe, and go on from there."

Would it be an accurate statement to say that there are degrees of separation in regard to the intensity of this belief in different areas of the world?

"Yes, that is well put. Upon your ship, have you noticed the consciousness as far as the wall of separation is concerned?"

Yes, we have noticed a certain feeling of resignation on the part of many people and that they believe they are going through the last steps of their lives without anything beyond that.

"Pay particular attention to those you observe without a partner. They are not even enjoying this voyage. They believe themselves to be alone and separate. They are simply putting on a face, if you will, for someone else, but generally not for themselves. It is these people who believe they are in their last days or years who will benefit by awakening to the fact that they are not alone. Give them the ability to choose their passing by having the knowledge that their passing is their choice and that the illusion of being alone is a misunderstanding. There will be many to meet them when they choose to depart, for they as well are eternal."

Little One mentioned today that she noticed a woman by herself who was in a wheelchair. This was at the formal dinner last night. She was very nicely dressed, but all by herself and appeared to be deep in thought

at the time. Little One went up to her and told her how beautiful she looked. The woman instantly brightened up, smiled, and thanked Little One for her kind comment.

"This is something everyone can do for each other. 'You look lovely today,' 'How are you doing today?' 'How are you feeling today?' A kind word or sincere offer to be helpful, you understand, can brighten a person's day in ways you may not have thought of before."

Yes, just a smile seems to make all the difference.

"An unspoken Blessing is good, but a spoken Blessing goes much, much further."

Are we going to be able during the process of our transformation, or renewal, be able to sense a total planetary collective consciousness? Currently we are limited to understanding the consciousness of the geographical area we live, or travel, in.

"We believe there will come a time when you will 'feel' the collective consciousness from larger areas. We would impress upon you in this Now to simply get the 'feel' of where you are and with the people around you."

Thank you. Does the earth's evolution in awareness depend upon the sum total of the planetary collective consciousness?

"Yes, it will."

We feel that to accomplish this task it will involve you, Dear Ones, to train and help us. Even the ones looking on have such an important part in this as we feel their love and support. We feel that this wondrous work is actually the work of many.

"There are millions upon your earth who have already begun this pursuit. We have simply chosen to work with you, whereas others are working with those of their choice upon your planet. They may not all be aware of this of course. Little Brother, we have worked with you for many of your years without your knowledge. To our joy, your awakening has brought you to this place of remembrance. Know that others will reach this place of understanding as they too begin to awaken."

So this is a very highly coordinated project?

"Yes, it is."

We feel your direct involvement in all facets of our lives. We know that you are of the highest of evolved beings. The direct involvement of both the masculine and feminine aspects of the One indicates the importance and magnitude of this project.

"Yes, Little Brother, you have been chosen to work with the highest. Know that there are others who have been chosen as well. Their view shall be given in a different light, but when all these viewpoints unite, things will certainly pick up and change rapidly."

We are aware that there are vast numbers of our highly evolved brothers and sisters looking on and lending their Love and Energy for this monumental endeavor. We are very thankful and most respectful of their desire and choice to join with you on this project.

"Thank you, it is our joy, and you are most welcome."

Would you please elaborate on the relationship between the wall of separation and the other walls?

"It is the wall, if you will, that holds all the other walls up. If it was not there, the other walls would soon crumble and be toppled. They would not be able to stand independent. They will come down much quicker once the wall of separation is down, for it is the most important of the seven walls."

What have we not asked, that is necessary at this point, for us to understand the wall of separation?

"We believe from your questions, which were very good indeed, that you have gotten a grasp of this wall. It is just simply to remember this is the one we wish to see fall. For with its falling the others shall be more easily dismantled. It is also the hardest one to fall. People must be aware and in complete understanding that they are not separate. You can do this through your example and then through your conversation with them. This is how you will begin and 'know' you have begun. We believe you have enough now to write upon this subject as well and shall include this in your book."

Thank you. We have been talking today with others about this, including a gentleman who felt he didn't have much longer to be alive. We shared with him that he was the author of his own life. He responded positively to this.

"Yes, this is a good way to speak with people. You and Little One, and all who are on this path, will instinctively know that each individual may require a different approach depending upon where they are on their path. But this is good."

In terms of healing, wouldn't the actual experience of receiving a healing have more impact than just learning about it? If they actually experience it instead of just being told about, they will truly understand it. As I look at the whole process of miracles and healing, it seems as though a miracle happens not for the miracle's sake, nor the healing for the healing's sake alone, but perhaps more as a point for awakening.

"Yes, if you offer for a person to receive a healing modality, they will absorb it into their being rather than just their mind. The healing goes to the intent of the one receiving it and becomes more than just the healing—it becomes a step to their awakening."

Can these people who are caught in a downward vibrational cycle expend their life's energy to the point where they cannot sustain the human condition?

"Yes, without them even knowing this. You must keep Love, keep happiness, and keep joy, always as who you are. This will raise your vibration and keep you on your path. This will extend your life."

We know that you said the wall of separation is the hardest one to fall, but would the wall of anger/hatred come right behind it in terms of difficulty?

"Yes. You will know these people. People who have this wall erected exude an energy you can 'feel.' We suggest that you start with the wall of separation at this 'time,' for it is not the 'time' for you to deal with the wall of anger/hatred. We would rather that you just observe them, bless them, and let them go by."

What about those countries that are known for their collective hatred of others who do not believe as they do?

"As more and more awaken, and the New Collective becomes stronger, these others will begin to isolate, or separate, themselves from those who are awakening."

Is there any additional information vital to our understanding the wall of anger/hatred that we have not yet addressed?

"We would simply state for now to be aware of it and to not mingle with it. You are not ready to deal with it yet. By dealing with the other walls around them, you will be able to begin to lower that particular wall."

Is this appointed time the earth's last opportunity to collectively raise the level of its consciousness? Would awakening now save us from having to face global consequences later, especially because of the previous rejection of the masters who came to teach?

"This is the beginning of another opportunity. There have been several others. This is the beginning of what we believe to be the fourth opportunity. As yet, man has not 'gotten it,' as you would say. There will be more earth changes because you will not be recognizing what you are doing to the earth. You will continue to see it as separate from yourself. You have not husbanded the earth. You have not had enough Love, so yes, it could be the cause of many catastrophic changes."

How late in the game is it?

"There will be other opportunities, but we know not when of course, nor to what extent will your population still be here. This we cannot say."

It seems that we as a collective body are destroying the very mother who nurtures us. Many, if not all, are unaware that this is an appointed time for the earth and all of her inhabitants. It is not that there is no return, but we sense that even if there is acceptance, or nonacceptance, earth changes will still occur.

"There will be earth changes, but as you know, there is no such thing as no return. It is simply a continuum of the Eternal. If you do not learn now, and if the earth must be gone, it will simply be brought back."

For all those sent by the One who bring the message of truth to the earth, it seems that they have not only been met with suspicion and doubt, but anger and hatred have led to their persecution and murder.

"The opposing groups, if you will, were suspicious of the ones sent, of their words and their works. They became afraid, and with that fear, they began to hate them. For there was a belief that they were harming their life. This emotion ties in with every other wall. It was because of that first suspicion that doubt, that the wall of anger and hatred was created and built. If there are no further questions, we shall now depart in much Love and Blessings."

This session was a profound one for us. The information the "Girls" presented, which expanded their earlier teachings on the seven walls, really brought this subject into focus. Especially when they tied everything together with the current collective consciousness and the Awakening that is now under way. It was a new way to look at the project in terms of how it would unfold rather than when. This was not an easy thing to do at first. Normally when we plan something, there is always a timetable that governs all the activities, objectives, and outcomes. I mean if there wasn't a time schedule, how were we to know what should come next, when it should come, and if we were on schedule? We soon learned the lesson well that there is "no time" at the level of evolvement the "Girls" have attained. We had to shift our thinking to look at the projects unfolding in terms of sequences of events, not the time it took for these events to manifest. We were somewhat confused and it took some time before we finally made the transformation. Zelia and Astoria were always so patient with us and kept guiding our transformation until it became our own. We now understood how to undertake a project of this magnitude regardless of the concept of how long it may take to unfold.

One of the most important things we have learned is that, as Eternal Spirit, we cannot be less than who we are in the Absolute, even when incarnated on earth. Who we truly are does not change. We can only decide to voluntarily forget who we truly are in order to remember who we are and have always been. We remember through our experiences as we journey the path to Oneness. Our lifetime, as such, can be a joyful and glorious journey of remembering, if we only choose to walk this path. Those who choose to maximize their experience on earth will choose the path of Awakening. Not all do. We have the freedom to create at will, to awaken, and remember who we truly are during our lifetime on earth.

Our experiences on board the ship, and visiting the islands, were far greater than we could have ever imagined. Especially when it came to observing the collective consciousness present from island to island and the walls that were observed at various occasions during our trip.

It did not take us long to realize how huge this project is. At first it was very overwhelming, but with time and the Teachings, we felt more comfortable. It was fascinating to learn that this "Awakening" had been attempted before, and not once but three times. As time and experiences grew, we were given a larger and more complete picture of the evolution of this process on earth.

After a wonderful, relaxing, and very eye-opening voyage, it was time to return home and address all the challenges that would face us over the coming months. So fresh with new inspirations, impressions, and great memories, we arrived home.

November 20, 2007

Once we returned, it did not take long before the pressure of our financial situation began to weigh heavy on us. We had put out so many resumes that I lost count, but still had not heard anything from a potential employer. We did begin receiving calls from creditors demanding payment. Some were considerate of our situation, but for the most part, the calls were anything but understanding. Some were outright rude and threatening. We allowed the situation to so affect us that we began to become very discouraged. You could say that we created circumstances in our minds that, for an intense period of time, clouded our vision and we lost some of our focus. What we were facing at the time proved to be nothing compared with what was to come. We learned by experience how easy it is to lose your perspective and momentum when facing one of life's big challenges. We needed a perception check to bring us back into balance. We looked to the "Girls" for help and asked for the first session since returning home.

"We do greet thee. We feel much sorrow. We would desire to help. We know not what we can do though. We, as you would say, have our hands tied. It is not our mission to interfere, but to give Love and support. We do wish to help by answering any questions."

Well, you have heard the conversations regarding our finances, and you know our circumstances.

"Yes, we understand the emotions that you are feeling. We wish for you to stay strong, know that this path for you, and for us, continues."

It is our desire also. We are reaching out to receive the help we need to continue.

"We understand this. We do 'feel' this. We have asked the question as to why this is occurring, but we are only told that it is the choice and the result of choices. We do not perform, as you would say, miracles. If that would be our right to do so, we certainly would have done so. We simply must observe. Please know that we 'feel' for both of you. We also are concerned that it may become difficult for us to come through if Little One's energy is low. We are strong and are giving both of you our energy."

We would like you to know that even in the light of how we are feeling right now that we choose to continue. We have made a promise to you, and we are going to fulfill the commitment we have made. We do not know how, where, or when, but we will fulfill our promise.

"We would desire that circumstances were somewhat different that would enable us to do for you what we can do on our own planet, but we realize this is not your evolution."

How we wish it were for we would know exactly what to do.

"Of this we are quite aware. At this point, to go faster in your evolution would simply destroy your physical vehicle. You must realize that there is a restraint upon the physical that you inhabit. You are quite strong, probably stronger than you are aware. You have been told, and this is a truth, that your writing, your books, shall be the answer to much for you. We do not know in what 'Now' this shall be completed, for these Teachings must be discovered by those who will resonate with them, and then they shall share them with others."

What I am trying to understand is whether or not every communication is for the immediate "time," or is for a "time" to come at some point in a future Now?

"There is so much that we all have to learn when we hear a truth that may not be for this time continuum. This is confusing for us as well. When you hear not to leave your home, would it be referring to this home, or to possibly a different home? It does not mean that what you have heard is not the truth, it simply means that this truth may be in a different continuum, if you will."

The reason for asking about this is the fact that even though we are in the center of this hurricane, it is so important to be clearly and accurately hearing the inspirations as they come. Only the truth can be written into all the books that we are writing and will write.

"We understand your concern. We can assure you that you are receiving inspirations as they are being given to you."

We know that we are not supposed to know the future. However, we desire to have our "glass full" so that the decisions that are to be made are based upon not what we think, but what is known.

"You understand, of course, that your future has not happened. It cannot occur until decisions, as you call them, or choices that you have made have started. Everything that you do is based upon the 'Now,' for it is the choice you make now that creates your next 'Now.'"

One of the main areas that cause frustration knows that the ability is present in the Absolute to instantly manifest what is desired, but that it doesn't seem we are able to do this in the physical realm at this time.

"It is simply because physical body is at a much slower and reduced vibration. It is the physical vibration that keeps you back from creating miracles and manifesting. You must learn to be without. In the spiritual realm, all your desires have been created and exist, it shall be for you to stay focused upon that which you know you already have, and through your choices, actions, and raised vibration, you will begin to 'know' and see it as complete in the physical world as well."

Thank you. I would now like to address some questions on healing. It seems to be most helpful, before beginning a healing, to go into that place of silence and stillness that existed before time and the creation of the physical universes. This seems to be the place where you can draw the greatest amount of energy where it is the most powerful and is the most abundant.

"Yes, for in the Absolute there is 'no time,' therefore, there is abundant energy. This energy has not been sullied, if you will, by the time constraints you have upon the earth. This energy is simply constant, simply flowing."

It has also been noticed that while conducting each healing, it is almost like going into an altered state. Especially when the energy is being applied to the recipient in the area of their spine.

"This is a very powerful energy position, which is why, in healings, you balance that energy. It is bringing the energy from the crown through the back, and through the entire body. It is a very powerful place to be."

Thank you so much for coming. We feel much better now with the explanations and understandings you have presented to us in this session. It is clear now that to swim against the river does not serve us. It is time to turn and just flow with the direction in which the project, and all aspects of it, are flowing.

"Yes, because the things that are not needed will simply flow behind and the things that are needed will stay with you. The realization of this will occur when all of this has gone by."

Will we be guided regarding the things that are critical for the days that are coming?

"You must keep those things for which you have a strong emotional attachment and those things that will enable you to carry on the work. Of those things that you let go, simply keep the memory. In much Love and Blessings we do depart."

We all face difficult times in our lives. Times that challenge what we believe, how we feel, and whether we can find the desire, balance, and energy to keep going through them no matter what we may be experiencing. Our financial pressure, and the way we dealt with it, was an event in our lives that gave us the opportunity to prove to ourselves that our commitment and belief in all we knew was strong. We were going to continue walking toward the desires of our heart and the purpose we had chosen for our lives. Of course, at the time, we didn't understand this, and we were overwhelmed by what we saw in front of us. We did not truly understand its purpose and intended outcome. Little did we comprehend that this traumatic event manifested for our ultimate good. We were very new to all of this, but with the help, Love, and energy we received from everyone, we forged ahead. We went through cycles where we had little energy or interest in going on, but somehow the considerable support to continue on this path came to us. This was to be a very long journey. You have been introduced to only the beginning of it.

Throughout this ordeal, all the books Bruce was asked to write have been written. Four have been published. It has not been an easy journey. The many difficulties and countless obstacles, and what seemed at the time to be insurmountable circumstances, have brought us to the understanding and awareness that we could not have arrived at this place of growth by any other means. The references we make to this ordeal have been such a powerful force in refining an understanding of who we truly are and our potential as an eternal spiritual being in human form.

The help from the "Girls" has been so strengthening that their energy and Love completely transforms our thoughts the moment their energy wraps around us. This enables us to be clear-headed, as they would say, while still allowing us the freedom to create at will our experiences, and to exercise our choices at each step along the path we are traveling on. They are so willing to lend of themselves to our discussion, both during and between sessions, and to help us through this and many other ordeals we have faced and will face.

We did not understand, at first, why they could not intervene on our behalf. They are more than capable of accomplishing any feat we could ask of them. It was not until we found out exactly how things really "work" in our universe that we finally understood that we came here to experience life and all that this entails. If they intervened, what would we learn? We would be deprived of the very experiences that help us to remember who we are and why we came to earth. Actually it took some time for this to sink in.

We also did not really understand that we create the events and circumstances we experience in life and that our choices, whether we are consciously aware of them or not, create each and everything that we experience. These choices also produce residual effects that can continue to be a part of our experiences long after the choices are made. These residuals have to play out. This is another truth about "how things really work" in our universe that we had to learn. Of course, we learned it the hard way, but in doing so, the lessons were permanently imprinted upon us. This understanding of choices and residuals had the power to transform the way we think, feel, what we say, and what we do. The financial challenges facing us were the result of past choices magnified by an unexpected event, that being Bruce's surgery. He wrote of his experience in his book *Living Your Life in Joy*. That event, while opening him up to the world of spirit, also carried with it a monumental challenge as well. It is often very difficult at the time you are going through such a challenge to realize its potential for growth in your understanding of who you really are.

In my first book, *Teachings from the Heart*, I discussed the subject of guides. This was not a new concept for me as I had always been very intimately connected to the spiritual realm. Although Bruce had been receiving communications from an early age, he knew far less about this wonderful gift each of us has been given. Each one of us comes into this incarnation with a guide, even if we have no knowledge of it, or do not believe that it even exists. For Bruce, it has always been more of a question as to whether it is truly from the spiritual realm or something that he desired to hear and came from that desire. This is something many people wrestle with. Gradually things for us began to come clearer. As mentioned earlier, the concern and stumbling block was in thinking that a particular message has to be for that exact moment in which it was given. We didn't realize that there is "no time" in the Absolute where these messages originate. These messages are given regardless of our knowledge of "time" as we know it on earth, for "time" is a creation only experienced in the physical realm. A message given to comfort or to announce some very important information may not happen for weeks, months, years, or in several instances, decades. These messages are absolutely true, but our insistence for them to manifest in a particular timeframe caused considerable confusion and lots of frustration. Thankfully the "Girls" cleared up this entire issue. It was then that a whole new perspective opened up for Bruce. Now it was much easier for him to become receptive to communications from the spiritual realm and be able to clearly and audibly hear the messages that came forth. This is an ability every one of us has; we only have to awaken to it. It is part of who we truly are and the connection we always have with the Infinite and all life no matter where that life may be found.

The Reiki sessions Bruce and I conducted while on board the ship were extremely memorable. In fact, a considerable portion of our time became devoted to these sessions. Once it was known that we were Reiki master teachers, a number of inquisitive people came forth. This was one of the high points of the voyage. I also conducted a great deal of "readings" for those who requested them. I don't do as many "readings" now, especially since I spend much of my time with the Divine Mother and being her "voice." Reiki was a stepping-stone for us in understanding healing energy, and we have been very blessed to have been given our own modality by the "Girls." Being Reiki masters, we knew our desire was for a modality that brought it down to simply the deliverance of healing energy and the opening of all energy centers, without all the other mind/concentration aspects of Reiki. All healing modalities use the One Energy; it is the application that differs from one to the other.

Bruce's first book will be referenced as we go along in this book and in our discussions. Its completion was a wondrous accomplishment in light of all that was transpiring around us. All the support, love, guidance, and inspirations he received from the "Girls" and his guides brought his book from conception to completion. He told me that his writing and his "inputting" sessions were an oasis of calm, balance, and peace that he experienced during this stage of our journey. I also discovered the same oasis when I began the first book in this Teachings from the Heart series in early 2008. We would join together every day in the library to write. These are wonderful memories. After Bruce transcribed the sessions from the tapes, we would spend the morning working on my first book. He would read the transcribed sessions to me as I sat at the computer. I would receive inspirations at that time to further explain what had occurred in the sessions. These were the sessions from the beginning of this journey October 2, 2007 through October 22, 2007. In the afternoon, I would read, or do some jewelry design, while Bruce continued working on *Living Your Life in Joy*. These moments lifted us over the turmoil we were facing, but it took us some time to come to this understanding. As we now look back at those times, we can see that the "Girls" had already given us the combination to open a lock to find peace, joy, happiness, and balance within the storm of our physical lives. This indeed was a precious gift of their Love for us.

November 30, 2007

We now go to the next session. Much had happened since the previous session ten days before. We had been given much to think about, and the time spent working on our books seemed to make the days pass quickly. Since we had questions for Zelia and Astoria, as we always did, we requested our next session. It was so helpful to receive their feedback on how we were doing.

"We do greet thee. It has been long in your 'time' since we have spoken. We are pleased to be here and answer the questions you have for us."

Yes, we are delighted that you are here. Little One has a question to start with, and then, if you wouldn't mind, Dear Ones, we would like you to address all the things that you know are on our hearts. If you would comment on them, we would be most appreciative. We would like this

to be your session. Little One would like to know, is the Divine Mother going to work in a different way with her than just channeling?

"Yes, it has been decided that it would be much more appropriate if the Divine Mother did indeed work with Little One in a varied amount of ways. One would be simply encompassing her, if you will. She will know when this begins to occur for she will have knowledge that she previously did not. This will also enable the council and the alliance, if you will, to get direct communication without having to channel."

Little One mentioned the day before that she felt it was going to be more than just channeling, as if the Divine Mother's inspirations would reside within her.

"This is indeed what we are hoping for. This is what is being worked toward. We, of course, understand that at this time there is much going on emotionally. Until that emotion begins to level out, this will take some of your 'time.'

"We also understand your frustration. We desire that we could simply take this away, but as you know, that is not the way it was meant to be. We would like to speak to you about your question regarding why the help is not there. We would say to you that when you look through the eyes of fog, you cannot see what is ahead of you. When you allow frustration, emotion, to cloud your spiritual eyes, you cannot always see what is there and what is there is not always clear. This would be advice that we would give to you."

Thank you. This is very sound advice and is deeply appreciated. I am trying to get myself into a place of balance and to be centered in the energy.

"You are working well toward that. We know that in being a human, you have certain mental and intellectual restrictions. When these are compromised, the emotion takes over, but this is fine. That is as it is to be here, but we also know you have been chosen because of your ability to overcome."

Sometimes there is a tendency for us to overreact. At times, especially right now, we seem to have stretched too far too soon.

"We do not know that we would call it overachieving, for to overachieve means to have achieved. We believe you are still struggling with that achievement. It is necessary for you to find balance, for you to find continuity. You must begin a planned walk. We wish you both to continue your writing. We understand that you are having somewhat of a blockage, and this is fine. There are many who have written who have this from time to time as well."

Should writing be my occupation? Should I be devoting all of my attention to this?

"Should writing become your occupation, then yes, we know that this would certainly be good for you to focus upon it. At this time where you currently are, you will need to split your focus between writing and, as you would say, bringing in the money. It is necessary for your survival. We are not saying that you should be working for long periods of time, but there must be an income, an energy. We know that this has been, and continues to be, a difficult time for you. We have spoken with the Council of the One, and we see that this is all for your benefit even though you are not aware of this. Just hold in your heart that it is all for the good."

This is for our greatest good?

"Yes, you may fight against it, but it would be as if you were fighting against the tide of the ocean coming in. You cannot stop it. It must continue its course. If you had looked, had noticed, you would see that things are looking up. The tide has changed somewhat in your favor."

Yes, all of a sudden we have received counsel in very important areas where decisions were to be made.

"Follow this counsel, for counsel will be sent to you. The assistance that you shall be receiving shall be of your own energy. At this time you, and Little One, must extend your energy to bring in that which you require. Know that this is right; it is for the good, for we are still here. We shall not go. We are yours, if you will, and this path is continuing. There are works being done. There are things happening even though you are not aware. We know that you are involved emotionally and mentally right now in this situation you find yourselves in, but we are still continuing the work and you are still a pivotal part of that."

We are so grateful for your kindness. Your presence is the primary reason for us being able to get through this. We desire to acknowledge respectfully, and in Love, how grateful we both are that you are here and for all that you are doing to help us. This feeling is so hard to express in words.

"We are most pleased as this is our purpose. This is why we are here. As you know, we have 'no time,' so it seems very fleeting these things that are occurring. Do not worry, it is perfect."

Several evenings ago, we experienced a strange phenomenon. In the middle of the night, our television set came on and the computer went haywire. There was all this energy present in the house. Would you please explain what happened?

"What happened on that night is that the energy that was left upon the earth was turned up. It was necessary to take these areas of energy and accelerate them. This is why, at this moment in 'time' for you, there are many earth changes occurring. This is simply the acceleration, if you will, of the energy that had been previously placed upon your earth. There were pockets of lower-frequency energy upon the earth plane, and this simply eradicated them. The energy was turned up to move them aside."

We feel more energy here in our home than we do in other places in Las Vegas. Was this once a meeting place for ancient native tribes that may have gathered here?

"We are not sure of that, but we do know that this desert, any desert, is filled with energy. We believe the feeling that you both have in this place would be more emotional than actual.

"We would again say to you that we believe at this 'time' that things are changing for you. We wish for you not to be clouded too much by emotion, although we do understand that it is there."

It is better now knowing that the tide has turned somewhat in our favor. We will do our best to set aside our concerns and be about our business of writing the books.

"We have heard you speak of your writing machine, a computer as you call it. We understand they grow obsolete quickly. Mankind has not quite understood that to make something last 'forever,' if you will, is more efficient than to create something that goes obsolete so quickly. This is the way your things are packaged. As the knowledge advances, so do the machines. When you are in a position to do so, look at more advanced machines as these will give you more capability for that which you shall do. We understand that what you have, in the Now, is sufficient."

Earlier you were speaking about the fact that everything is continuing to happen even without us being aware, does this refer to even subtle things? I know that when we first began there were a lot of things we would describe as surges of energy; that we all felt. It seems like now it's a finer-tuning or more subtle energy. Is this accurate?

"It is. The best example we could tell you is to take your pool for instance. It is full of water. It does not need to be continually filled. It is only occasionally necessary to get back that which has been used."

This would then be more of a fine-tuning that we are sensing?

"Yes, the energy you are feeling now is helping to replenish energy you use; you can never be depleted of energy for it is a constant flow. It is just that when you use a large amount, an equal amount will fill you."

Do you have any guidance for us now that would really be helpful to get us going more assertively on our path?

"Simply to, as you would say, keep the faith. Understand that where you are is perfect and is where you need to be at this point in your 'time.' Simply go forth, always forward. Do not go backward. Do what is needed to be done. If that is to expend energy to receive energy in the form of finances, then this is what you should do. Stay on your path, continue your writing. You will find the 'time' to do this, it will be given to you. Do not concern yourself with this. Know where you are, is where you should be. We are with you. Many are with you and we shall continue to be so. Just know that at the end, it shall all be the way it should be for your highest purpose."

We are so happy to know of your collaborative effort. This helps to explain the appearance, during deep meditation, of what seems like a very large gathering or audience of people who are watching.

"Yes, we are all aware and watching. We do not go where you would desire us not to be. We do respect your privacy. We know that this does not 'freak you out,' Little Brother. There are much of your colloquialisms that are quite interesting, but it appears at times that there are many within your own planet that do not seem to understand each other."

A number of the people of this planet have their own language within a language. Of course, for those in separation, they do not even begin to understand who they are, let alone what they are saying to each other.

"Yes, indeed this is true. Your people separate themselves in many, many ways, language being one way."

I am so appreciative of Little One's grasp of this and so many other areas. Sometimes I will go to her with an insight only to have her say that she already has an awareness of it.

"Yes, she has this ability. You will be able to see in her, although she may not be aware of it, a change. It will not occur until she has reached more of a place of peace. We are working with her, but she is quite stubborn at times. This is why we have always called her the Renegade Angel, for she is very hardheaded when she desires to be."

This is quite true, although I see the beauty, the spiritual beauty, within her.

"She is not yet fully aware of this. She feels that to admit this would be to put herself above others, which she would never do. Sister of My Sister saw who she is from the first moment of meeting. She saw both of you from the beginning. We would encourage you again to sit down and send her a message.

"We shall begin to speak, in your 'time,' once a week. Put your questions upon paper. For now, we shall depart in Love and Blessings."

We had come a long way emotionally in the ten days since our last session. We were also able to sell a number of items that we had forgotten we had. All together we generated enough resources to keep us going. This really raised our spirits. The session was more lighthearted and relaxed, as though we had turned the corner and that things would now improve for us.

We were beginning to learn from our meltdown before the last session, how important it was to remain balanced no matter what circumstance we found ourselves to be in. Zelia and Astoria's constant encouragement to remain balanced took on a much more universal meaning for us. We began to understand that when we are balanced, we maintain not only our energy levels, but gain access to the abundant energy that was there for us for the asking. Communication between the "Girls" and our guides definitely began to flow quicker and the inspirations rose considerably. It was a painful lesson, but the message came in loud and clear about how easy it is to allow the emotions to run rampant. We learned this the hard way.

We both appreciated the encouragement to stay focused upon the writing of the books. This was especially helpful for me as I steadily gained the strength to work on my first book in this series. Both Bruce and I understood that to devote our energies to combat our circumstances only fueled the intensity of them. We needed to allow this challenge to unfold and run its course.

It was really interesting to hear about the lower pockets of energy that were on the earth and how they had neutralized them in order to bring about a balance in energy level worldwide. There had been a number of weird occurrences that were centered around energy since we had come back home. It was nice to know and understand what was going on.

Somehow, with everything that was happening, we had really dropped the ball with our meditations. It was a blessing that the "Girls" gently reminded us of this. We once again began our practice of meditation in the early morning and right at sunset. We certainly felt more centered and balanced as a result, as well as being more aware and connected with the energy. Meditation also brought us to a deeper connection with the "Girls" and the Divine Mother. We wondered how we ever got so sidetracked especially since this had been a daily routine for quite some time. I know that when your mind joins with your ego, you "forget" a lot of things that are for your growth, that is exactly what the ego intends. Definitely allowing ourselves to fall into despair and doubt brought the ego its jollies. This was another lesson learned and I am thankful we listened.

We have already discussed how we began to realize exactly how large an undertaking this project truly is. I mean the Awakening of all mankind—really? It took me awhile to wrap my head around this, and I am sure many reading this book feel the same. I just had to stop and realize it wasn't all going to happen at once and that there would be sufficient "time." It all starts with a drop of understanding and begins to flow like a river of truth. This book and all the books are there for you to further understand who you are, why you are here, and what the heck does it all mean. So we continue on understanding, learning, "feeling," and beginning to understand this truth.

This is the last session that was conducted in what I am calling chapter 1. We now continue on with chapter 2.

Chapter Two

December 19, 2007

Encouraged by the information received at the last session, it became easier to focus on writing our books. Our "time" was devoted to writing and relaxing in our home. In the afternoon (after typing for several hours), I would either do some jewelry design or read. In the evenings, we would watch a movie or go for a sunset swim in the pool. I really wanted to enjoy my home as much as possible since I didn't know how long we would have it. These were also times to think about what we had been taught so far and to apply these teachings to our everyday lives. We did try our best to stay calm, centered, and joyful no matter what each day brought our way.

It was also around this time that I began communicating with the "Girls" in a different way; this was my direct link. I began to be able to receive and relay their messages at times when specific questions were of immediate concern or to receive explanations for previous Teachings that required clarification while writing the book. This type of guidance became an almost daily form of communication and interaction. Bruce would ask a question and the "Girls" would relay the answer to me. This was very helpful. We felt so close to them, almost like a family. Since I had done "readings" for many years, it didn't seem to strange to receive messages this way. Some questions did arise concerning the steps to awakening, and it was better to receive the answers during a normal session, so we requested to meet with them.

"We do greet thee. How is everyone on this day?"

Greetings, Dear Ones, we are well, thank you. It seems it has been awhile since we met, and we apologize.

"Since we have no 'time,' this is not a bother. We have observed you both typing away on your machines. We are most pleased with what you have written. You have given the truth, and it is in a way that people will understand. We would simply caution about being possibly too wordy,

Little Brother, for the more words there are in a phrase, the harder it may be for others to grasp."

Yes, thank you for that. I will tighten it up. There is a question I have for you. I would like to rate each of the walls of humanity from one to seven in order of their importance. This would relate to the way they affect the collective consciousness. Would you please address that and let me know the number that each wall would be assigned?

"Yes. Separation is 1, anger/hatred 2, suspicion/doubt 3, limit 4, necessity 5, blindness 6, and failure is 7."

Thank you so very much. These will be assigned to their respective walls. As you know, the chapter on the awakening of humanity has just been started. I thought to begin with the first step that is, at present, being called life on automatic pilot. Would this be an appropriate title and place to start? Also, in relation to that, we would then go into the steps of the awakening process. Is that the next logical step, or should there be something else in between?

"Yes, before they understand what they need to awaken, they must understand where they have been. Speak to your readers about what 'automatic' means and that they understand what 'to awaken' means. Then you should include the steps for them to achieve this."

Thank you. We have talked about the steps in the awakening process, and step one would be people who are spiritually asleep to the knowledge of separation and to the understanding that they are spiritually asleep. If you would be so kind, what are the remaining steps in the awakening process as you desire them to be revealed?

"You have already explained to your readers what separation is, so at this point, they have that understanding. Now you begin to list for them the steps to awaken. First would be them recognizing that they are or have been asleep. This is most important for those who have yet to begin to awaken. They will begin to look at separation in their life and all that is around them without seeing anything as separate from themselves. They will then begin to see this connection in the lives of others around them and in the lives of the world as well. Once they can identify and recognize separation, then they can begin, in their selves, to dismantle it.

"The next progression of awakening after the recognition of separation is searching within yourself for any of the other walls. If a wall is found, then it must consciously be dealt with. You can only deal with your own walls and the dismantling of them before you can be of assistance to anyone else. So it is important to identify separation and be aware that, within yourself, other walls do exist. You begin one by one in recognizing and breaking down these walls. Once you have done that, you begin to put into practice that which you have discovered. There are many steps within that process. We believe, Little Brother, that as you are writing you will be inspired to what those steps are."

Thank you. What would the step following be?

"You must point out to them that as their eyes are opened and their 'veils' of misunderstanding removed, how easily they can be reconstructed by the egos of others around them. They must be aware of this. As we have said, be consciously aware of this so as not to allow those 'veils' to be implanted again. These steps are not necessarily short; they will take 'time.' Once they have arrived at the point of recognizing, understanding within themselves these walls, they understand this need to be aware that others can throw these walls up. At this point, we would suggest, in the act of awakening, beginning meditation. There would be care of the body, care of the mind, and care of spirit, for they must become united and whole. They will understand they are part of the whole and begin to 'be' such."

What other steps do you suggest be included for the Awakening process?

"That each must find joy and happiness in all that they do and all that they are. They must understand who they are, for you cannot be truly awake if you do not understand this. So part of the Awakening process would be to understand who you truly are. Ask this question, Little Brother. 'If your eyes were beginning to awaken to this mystery that you had not previously known, what do you believe the steps would be that you would take?' The answer to this question from all who hear it will give you insight. Listen to what they say and use what you hear to reach others."

Thank you, that is a wonderful suggestion. Is there anything else I can tell those individuals who are beginning to awaken? Anything else I should write about in this first book?

"You may talk about energy to a degree. Talk about receiving energy from plants, those you love, and Love in general. That would be a first step for people who feel they are isolated, who have felt themselves alone, that will be important for their understanding. Reach out to that which is already within them. They are just not yet aware that it dwells within.

"Your creature is feeling our energy. We hear her sounds. She is happy and we are pleased that she decided to stay with you. She will make a decision when it is 'time.'"

We are very happy about her decision to stay. We did not know for a while what was going to happen. We are delighted to have her and very pleased that you are so delighted with her. Let me ask a little about the upcoming earth changes.

"Simply put, earth changes are, and will continue to be, happening. These changes shall bring about the balancing of masculine and feminine energy upon the earth, and this shall in turn aid in the Awakening of those who chose to understand and hear what we bring. We do not create these occurrences; they are created by the earth's energy itself. It is to protect and cleanse itself of all that has happened to it since its creation by the Divine One. There will be many storms that shall appear in times when they are normally silent, much drought, floods, winds, and climates that appear outside of their normalcy. These changes are not punishments or something to be feared, they are simply the reinstatement of conditions as they are intended to be."

We know that our awakening affects the collective conscious geographically and on a planetary level. As the vibrational levels of our physical bodies begin to rise, this will, of course, help bring about the unification of body, mind, and Spirit.

"Yes, of course, it is okay for people to understand that their bodies do have a frequency that they do indeed vibrate."

That brings to mind a question. My understanding is that the mind is the playground for the both ego and Spirit to express themselves. Is this accurate? I have read others who have a different interpretation, or understanding, of this.

"There have been many misconceptions and there will continue to be many. Each person will go toward that which is comfortable for them. If you understand that the mind arrives with Spirit into the physical and is not attached to the physical. Once Spirit encompasses the physical and mind is introduced to ego, it then shall choose, in each moment, where it shall reside. As you Awaken to the remembrance of your true self, mind will remain with Spirit, but if you remain asleep to that remembrance mind will associate with ego. You can see where one is on their journey by viewing if mind is in Spirit, or mind is in ego. By this we mean what are the choices of a particular person. Are they making, and creating, their journey with Love and compassion, or are they leading with want, need, and the misunderstanding that they are, what they have been identified by the collective to be? There is much to learn regarding ego, and we shall teach on this as we go along on the journey."

We look forward to more understanding on this subject. Is there anything Little One and I need to know right now?

"You keep your peace, keep your happiness. We are not sure how long in your 'time' you will remain in this home. We do know that it is intended for the council to be together now and, amidst what is occurring, find unity. It is important to look at what you are doing as your purpose, your quest. This is to enlighten those that are asleep to their true essence and created journey. We desire to begin to gather in numbers and grow in the knowledge of Love upon your earth. It is with the expansion of those who are now asleep that we begin to gain insight, and we begin to affect the collective consciousness. This is your quest, if you will."

The other night I experienced a feeling of having scabs, or a crust, being torn off from the inside. This was very new to me. Was this an important happening to remove deep-seated scars from past experiences?

"Yes, and many times the removal of a scab, or debris from a wound, is quite painful because the wound is still so raw. That pain will dissolve with the healing. Once the healing begins to occur, the memory of that pain leaves. These were layers, or crusts, that your ego had deposited.

You remove these by remembering, and feeling, how they began. Once they are remembered, felt, and understood, you will see them through your Awakening spiritual eyes. You then choose to let them go because they no longer serve who you know yourself to be. Each ego placed scab that is removed allows you to advance upon your path."

I feel so much better now that this understanding from you has become clear. This explains the purpose and intent of it. As always these things, while painful, are for our greatest good and continued growth.

"You understand that if we or any other of your guides told you of these things ahead of 'time,' would you have grasped them?"

No. Had all this been known beforehand, there would not have been the growth that came from this experience. A very important lesson was learned. Thank you.

"You can tell a child that the stove is hot, but until they experience that heat, they know not of what you speak. We, of course, would not have a child harmed to learn this; it would be enough to simply let them experience the heat from a distance so as not to harm."

Very true, and so what transpired was actually a blessing. This was not known at the time, but it certainly is now. We are attempting to eat the way you earlier suggested. How are we doing?

"You are doing quite well. We understand that you are somewhat on a budget due to your circumstances, but we believe you are doing all you can to follow the guidelines for the health of your physical bodies."

Thank you, Dear Ones, this is all we have for today. We will endeavor to get together more often.

"We are here whenever you are ready. As you know, we have 'no time.' When we are called upon, we shall come through. Know that we are always there to lend our Love, our energy, and through Little One, our inspirations. For now, in Love and Blessings, we do depart."

This session addressed some of the scope of material that Bruce was to present in his first book, *Living Your Life in Joy*. As a result of this session, his work on the book accelerated. By the twenty-third, he only had two chapters left to write. It was a wonderful feeling to see him approaching the final stages of finishing his manuscript.

The joy we were allowing and choosing to have in our lives helped greatly to offset our concern over the financial challenges we were still facing. We continued to sell items to pay our obligations as best we could. We had unfortunately fallen behind on several of our accounts and received daily calls from their collection departments. Some understood while others harassed, threatened, and did their best to make our lives as difficult as possible. Even though they were often rude, debasing, and devoid of any concern for our welfare, they could no longer take our joy from us. This was a lesson in choices that we, again, had to learn the hard way. They did indeed have a lasting impression on us.

The experience Bruce spoke to the "Girls" about, of having scabs pulled from the inside of his body, was one of the strangest things he ever experienced. He told me that he awoke to the feeling of a tearing sensation inside of his body and that he felt it throughout his chest cavity. It was as if adhesive strips, or scabs, were being torn off one after another. This continued for about thirty seconds and he said it was a very uncomfortable feeling. His response to this was, shall we say, less than complimentary. He felt somewhat picked on and made sure that the Divine Parents were aware of this and how he felt about the whole situation. Patiently they explained to him the purpose behind the experience. The "wounds" that required healing were residual scars from past feelings of persecution and resentment he held toward the Divine Parents. These feelings were caused by a number of very painful events in his past. The whole incident was an intervention to remove those old scars and the energy they represented that would have continued to hold him back from further advancement on the Path. He felt better after this explanation, but it was also a lesson in how ego could still lead our reactions when we didn't stay aware of it.

Once removed, the old scars, or rather the feelings they represented to him, were healed. He really felt lighter, more joyful, peaceful, and thankful for the experience. The old feelings were gone, "torn" out of him. All the years of his harbored resentment and the emotions that accompanied them vanished with each painful "tear." Then the pain subsided and also vanished. Even though this was a painful experience, it was Infinite Love at work for the greatest good.

It is so hard when you are in the middle of an emotional storm to stop and examine what is really happening. Are you pushing those feelings deeper? Are you creating the "wounds" that will need healing? If you aren't aware of your true nature, the most natural thing is to blame what is happening on someone or something else. You don't see where your choices have created the residual you will have to deal with later on (or maybe not if you don't awaken). You simply push all those emotions down to the point where you no longer have to think about them, or most importantly, "feel" them. In many instances, you even forget they exist. At other times, you think you have dealt with them, only to discover later that you allowed yourself to believe they were gone. If we but allow ourselves to be open, in a moment of inspiration and guidance, to pull up the "old garbage," truly recognize it for what it is, "feel" it, and then let it go, we can and will create our own healing. The storm and suppression of the emotion is created by ego, maintained by ego, and held in place by ego. Recognize who you really are, live that knowledge, and allow the removal of those "scabs" that no longer serve you. You will find your peace and joy in that moment of action and recognition.

As I look back on this period of time, I realize that through the events that so strongly challenged us, we continuously remained joyful and continue to be so to this day. It is how we choose to conduct ourselves as we go through them that teaches us our most important and significant lessons. We are presented with the opportunities to make giant strides in becoming, and remembering, who we truly are.

December 21, 2007

We had a short session on the eve of the winter solstice to ask a few questions and to share the solstice with Zelia and Astoria. Even though the session was relatively short, it put into focus several important aspects of how we can conduct ourselves on a daily basis. It gave us a larger perspective on the greatest gift we receive, and give, which is unconditional Love.

"We do greet thee on your winter solstice. Do you have any questions for us, for as always, we would be pleased to answer them."

We do have several questions. They skip around a bit, but the answers to them will help to fill in some areas in regards to all of the Teachings you have given us to date. Is it basically our fears that form our greatest obstacle to believing that our desires will manifest for us?

"Yes, fear is the 'glue,' if you will, to all the walls and can indeed prevent you from being able to raise the vibration of your physical body. Because of where we come from, we are able to reach a vibration that enables us to simply 'feel' that which we desire. We do not know this emotion of fear, nor do we have your strong emotions that weigh down your body and keep you from Awakening. Please understand that it has taken millennia for us to attain this ability. Upon earth you are now beginning to travel the path toward this ability, although you are in the infancy at this 'Now.' We know that it is your desire to attain this, but we do not know the 'time' it will take to achieve the raising of your vibration to enable this to be your experience.

"This is a difficult subject for you to understand as you awaken. It is one you have personally had difficulty with. We have seen how frustrating it is for you to understand what your potential is, yet not see it manifest in your experiences. This is a form of fear that can create a blockage on your path. Many on your earth are so strongly influenced by fears of many kinds. Some bury their fears or try to cover them up with false, or ego, courage. It is difficult for us to 'get through' these emotions and the wall they create. To face your fears, to realize that they are of your own creation, will help you go far in lowering the walls and speeding up your awakening.

"Many people do not even know they have fears buried deep within. They do not understand that what is buried deep inside, that what is feared the most, will create your experiences as they are brought to the surface. Many tend to fight against or resist bringing up these fears. If they are not faced when they are first recognized, it is often more difficult to face and resolve them when they all surface at once. Each one should be 'felt,' understood, and 'let go' as they arise within.

"You are advancing in your understanding and we see that. Even though you have your moments, you are letting go of what you have feared when you were asleep. As you master this 'letting go,' you will experience an acceleration of bringing into the physical that which you have created in the spiritual. When you are calm, when you are in balance with body, mind, and Spirit, you are not so strongly under the influence of these fears. This is why we have often brought you guidance to help you to understand this, for when you put away fear, you are no longer in ego-mind. To be 'out of mind' is to be Spirit where all things are possible for you. Every day put into practice that which you know and live this understanding."

Thank you so much, this is most helpful. You have, in this Teaching, revealed a "key" that has unlocked the door to knowledge and understanding fear. This will help us greatly as this journey on the Path continues. Also I know that your words will be a blessing to all who receive them.

Recently you were commenting on how our cat Sarah was feeling your presence. Would you please expand upon this?

"She 'feels' our presence. We felt her vibration and her joy at our presence. Your animal kingdom is much more attuned to Oneness than many would understand or accept. They 'feel' the presence of all energy around them. You have noticed how animals will just go up to some people whereas they back away from others, or they 'talk' [by this we figured they meant to meow or bark] to those whose vibration they choose not to be in the presence of. They are very perceptive and aware of what is happening around them, much more so than many of your people. Some on your earth do not even acknowledge, for the most part, that animals are also an expression of Divine Love. They may not have 'intelligence' as your people describe and understand it, but they do have an awareness and consciousness that most do not understand. They are also Spirit and will choose the one they wish to attach themselves to. You have had animals in your life that have been before with you. You recognized them without knowing this, but we see that you are beginning to understand. This is as it should be. We will explain more at another 'time' that will be more appropriate to this subject."

This connection you spoke about was felt very strongly with Abigail, my Siamese cat. The "feeling" inside right now, even though she no longer inhabits what was her physical body, is that there is so much more to this than is currently believed, let alone accepted by the collective consciousness.

"We will let you in on a little knowledge. She will come again in a 'Now' of her choosing, a 'time' when you are more settled and have traveled to where your heart is leading you. You will know her for she will approach you as she has done before."

Thank you, that is indeed fabulous news. You mentioned in our last session in Happy Camp about the Sanctuary that we would begin. Did the planning of this Sanctuary begin a long time ago?

"As we mentioned to you before, planning for the Sanctuary occurred at the beginning. It is difficult for us to say how long this has been since we do not share your concept of 'time.' We will say it has been since the combined memory of both of us. We work as one, so you can imagine our memory is quite long. The planning began when you created your 'blueprints,' before the expansion for, and creation of, your physical universe. We are joyed to be speaking of it and to see it beginning its formation."

You see things clearly from start to finish. It is our distinct advantage to not see it so clearly as to enable and allow us to participate in its unfolding.

"Yes, that was the purpose for you coming into this incarnation, to experience. We could not take that joy from you by predicting, or revealing, the future for you."

There are many times when it seems like knowing what lies ahead would be comforting, but you are quite right that if we knew the future, it would significantly take away from all that we learn and remember from the choices we make. In regard to beginning the Sanctuary, will all three of you be there to give information as you now do for us?

"Mainly Astoria and I will be there for you. You will find that the Divine Mother will also be present for continued guidance and counsel. For the council as a whole, we may, from time to time, pop in. Primarily it will be the Divine Mother in the lead for all twelve on the council. Know that you will receive continued Love, energy, and guidance from all as you request it."

We would not be at this place of awareness where we are now if it was not for your inspiration and guidance. These are all the questions that we have prepared for this session.

"We would encourage you and Little One to go outside and 'be' in nature on this night of your winter solstice. Feel the energy and be with the One. We shall now depart in Love and Blessings."

Again, there was so much that we learned, and we were able to make significant progress on the books we were writing. Even though the circumstances around us seemed like a roller-coaster ride, we managed to find our "place of stillness" within that storm, to continue our advancement upon our chosen path.

It was very helpful to understand how fear, any kind of fear, can really influence all we think, say, and do. Once we understood that fear was the "glue" and underlying theme behind each of the seven walls, that knowledge allowed us to recognize it within ourselves and let it go. As we now understood its ability to prevent us from manifesting our desires, we would no longer allow it to be present in any aspect of our lives. Believe me this is not easy to do. There is a lot of "garbage" down there hiding in the depths, but when it does raise its ugly head, grab it and hold on. Look at it for what it truly is, a convenience created and stored by your ego, to use in order to block you from being and becoming who you really are. Don't misunderstand me, there will be tears, hurt, and sometimes anger, but once you have taken back your power from what your ego created, you will feel liberated. The rest of the garbage that rises to the surface becomes easier and easier to be rid of, until you are free to continue your path in complete awareness of who you are, free from fear. It is the subtle forms that prove to be the most difficult to identify, let alone address, so always be aware of your "gut" feeling when issues surface. You will still be dealing with ego, but you won't allow fear to be created and used against you again.

It was fascinating to learn about the sensitivity of animals to the energy around them. Years ago Bruce had a Siamese cat, Abigail, who was so "tuned in" that she seemed able to read him like a book. He had such a strong connection with her, and they shared some of the most difficult times in his life. They communicated on a level of consciousness that went beyond any "language" barrier. For all who have had a beloved pet, I know that this resonates with you. They seem to sense our moods and unspoken words. What could be more comforting than your pet curled up in your lap, or beside you, at times when you are feeling low? There is no better feeling that I know of. From my own experience, I have felt so blessed to have shared a part of their journeys with them.

We had already discussed several times about the planning of the Sanctuary, but the reality of the "time" span involved had not really hit home until this session. It seems that all this had been planned and in our "blueprints" from the very beginning. It became clear that the purpose of every lifetime, or incarnation, had been to prepare for this monumental event of the Awakening. Every experience, every event, and all that had been learned by everyone involved manifested in this lifetime exactly for this purpose. I began to really understand what they mean by "no time." These experiences and events had occurred over a huge stretch of our "time," and we couldn't know how much more "time" would be involved. All we did and do know is that we are here in this Now to do all we can to share what we have learned with all who would hear. It is our greatest desire to be a part of something that can change the lives of both individuals and the collective as a whole. No matter the "time" involved, we will continue on our chosen path.

One of the "hopes" we had at the beginning of meeting the "Girls" was to have events revealed to us prior to them happening. We quickly learned that Zelia and Astoria, and all those who have come to help us, are not allowed to reveal our future Now's. They will aid us in understanding how events could unfold, based on our choices, but the outcome of the events themselves will not be revealed. Our choices create our experiences, and until they have run their course, we often don't understand what may have been hinted at. To come out and tell us what will happen takes away not only our Freedom to Create at Will, but also robs us of the experience created from those choices. Sometimes I so wish they would just tell us, but then I must remember that that is why I came here in the first place, to experience all that I create, and remember who I truly am. There are hints given, and with time, experience, and constant communication, we have become more skilled at staying aware, at all times, of where our choices may lead us and to choose accordingly.

The "Girls" had requested that we go out into "our nature" and experience the winter solstice, which we did. It was truly a magical evening. There was a great energy that surrounded us and brought about a comforting sense of peace. There are these times within our earth that the energy is so strong, all we have to do is have the intent to receive it, and we do. Next solstice or any of the moon cycles, go outside and breathe in that energy that is ours for the taking.

Even as I write this, I remember how excited we were about all the upcoming sessions and the things we would learn and be taught. We knew there would be great "Spirit opening" insights as there had been since the beginning of this journey. So let's continue.

December 27, 2007

We started at this time to plan for our return to Happy Camp for the reunion with Annie. Even though it would not be until spring, we were already anticipating the time.

Our next session with the "Girls" took place on December 27 and it was quite comprehensive.

"We do greet thee. How are you, Little Brother?"

I am very good, thank you. Would you please speak more on the subject of energy?

"Yes, of course. It is important for all to understand that energy is always there and always present. It is what everything consists of and what is given and received by all. Energy is used for many purposes, such as meditating, healing, psychic abilities, manifesting, and much more. It is the continuance of all things. We believe the knowledge of this should not be complicated because it is not complicated. It is very simple, if you will, but people believe that to reach the highest, it must be complicated. For if it is not hard, then how can it be real? Using energy is simply drawing upon your intent to use it and letting it flow from its Source to and through you. You are not really 'using' energy as much as you are allowing yourself to be open and letting it seek and find its purpose. Energy is something that indeed can be felt and 'known' by the one seeking to employ it as well as the one who is receiving it. It is by your 'knowing' that this comes to you."

Can we address exactly what "knowing" means?

"Yes, exactly what is 'knowing'? How would you know that you 'know'? How would this 'knowing' make you feel? How will this 'knowing' affect you and others? It seems like a very simple word, of course, but it entails much. We wish to always stay with simplicity. It does not have to be hard to be correct. You do not have to undergo an inquisition, if you will, to find out the truth. It is there for all who reach for it. Are you created with it? Yes, it is a part of who you truly are. Is it cellular, of the mind, or of Spirit? Since it encompasses all parts that create the whole—both the physical vehicle and your true self, Spirit—it comes in with you and joins with the physical to be 'felt' in physical ways. That 'gut feeling' we have spoken of, for instance. It is important for those who are awake or awakening to understand this. What it means, this understanding, this 'knowing,' is that they can now be who they truly are and no longer walk those paths that no longer serve them. They use both the physical feelings of their vehicle combined with the true understanding of self to make their choices. They can look at the light at the end of the tunnel knowing that the length of the tunnel is dependent upon their choices. Their 'knowing,' and the trust in it, will take them along to their desired conclusion. Their tunnel can be short and they come into the light, or it can be long with much residual along the way before they emerge. It depends upon your perceptions, choices, and the using of that gift you contain within of 'knowing.' Do you have any comments?"

This explanation is wonderful. When you were talking about "knowing," the impression that immediately came through was how was this "knowing" known? It is not something intellectual. It is by "feeling" that we "know," and that is how I now "know" something to be true. This "knowing" was felt. There was no thought involved, just the physical feeling that accompanied the "knowing." This may sound somewhat confusing, but it truly works. This knowledge and paying attention to your own signals

will guide you as you go along. This information created a totally new experience for me.

"Let us speak about this word 'feeling.' When you say, 'I felt good,' 'I feel bad,' 'I felt sick,' 'I felt well,' what does that mean? Is it the same as 'feeling' that you know something? How do you know that these 'feelings' are correct? By what measure do you understand that these 'feelings' work? As with 'knowing,' 'feeling' is a part of all, and it is that combination of body, mind, and Spirit that will direct and guide you. Do not go on intellect alone for it will trip you up. It will make you stumble. It is not where you should be, be with 'feeling.' It is, simply put, a process of becoming aware of any physical changes that are happening at the moment of these 'feelings.' A stomach flutter, or as it is called 'a gut feeling,' is a strong indicator to pay attention."

You are absolutely right. Having spent so many years trying to intellectualize everything, this is truly a light of understanding. Another thing I understand completely is how each and every one of us is connected to the other. I have realized that each and every experience and the understanding that came from them have brought us to this place in this "Now."

"Do not forget the experiences that are also occurring in this 'Now.' In each breath will be a choice resulting in an experience. So each 'Now' as it passes leaves residual from its having been, and this residual will be a passing experience in your 'Now.' Of course not all choices will contain what one in the physical would consider 'bad' residual for there will also be that which is considered 'good.' When making a 'Now' choice, always take into your consciousness that residual which is still occurring from a passing choice and incorporate that into what you choose."

Sometimes when events happen, people think they are being punished. Maybe things are going well and they took their eyes off their Path for a while. They may then find themselves on the gravel and off the road. Isn't this true?

"Yes, this is quite true for this is what can happen once a desire is met. You look upon the desire rather than why it was given to you for your continuance on your Path. If you simply indulge in the desire itself, money, fame, fortunes, then you will lose sight of where you are going. You will find yourself then looking upon other things you were given as a way of identifying who you are. If you believe you deserve accolades, if you believe you deserve this or that, then you have certainly lost sight of your Path in that 'Now.'

"For the majority, fame or fortune will take them in a direction that does not follow their intended Path. Depression also serves to pull one off as it almost becomes cellular. This detour away from your intended direction is the creation of ego, and it puts a blanket on who you are for you do not see beyond the fame, fortune, or your perceived misery. While you are in that state, you are not walking upon your Path. You may simply be standing still or you may have gone by the side. We are not saying that all who experience fame and fortune will be detoured, for many in this situation are awake and reach out to others, they understand their connection with all. The fame or fortune simply allows them the 'time' and opportunity to be who they are and, with that understanding, create experiences that benefit many."

We have seen how easy it is if we are not diligent, alert, and conscious about where we are on our path to become sidetracked.

"It is quite easy. Walking one's Path is not a difficult thing to do if you remain constant in your desired and intended direction. There is much that can pull you off, and it is generally based upon the ego. Whether the ego needs to be stroked, needs to be satisfied, or just desires the lead, it is that part of you that you should be aware of and keep in check. You understand that ego serves no one and no thing, its desire is to be the lead."

This has been a constant underlying current of thought, suggestion, and guidance in my first book.

"This is well for people should understand this. Do not be preachy for that will turn people away and that is not your intention."

My desire and intent was to draw the reader into the narrative so that they may see a correspondence within their own lives.

"Yes, they should be able to see themselves within your writing. This will be a most meaningful way for them to understand what they have previously experienced along their journey. It is much like your movies. There are several we have viewed where a child opens a book and becomes a part of the story within the pages of that book. This is important as you and Little One write your books to take your reader into that story. Describe to them what the Path looks like when it is traveled with the true understanding of who one is, and when all choices are made with awareness so as to create the desired experience. Everyone will see their Path somewhat differently of course, but it is the visual image—the imagination—that is also a part of Spirit."

Thank you, this is excellent advice. There is a strong knowing inside that what we are doing is what we are supposed to do. We know people are being prepared to receive the message. Our most important consideration is to make sure that the message we relay is exactly as we have received it from you. Our primary focus is to ensure that the books are totally representative of the inspirations that are being received.

"You are being true to this. We see that Little One has severed the emotional ties that have bound her to this place, this home. It is always to look forward and not back. Should you lose or not lose this home, you need not be tied to it for it has served its purpose, which was to provide an energy-filled environment for you both to write. When a 'Now' passes, you sometimes do things within that 'Now.' Let them pass in joy and peace, knowing that in the next 'Now,' things will be as they are intended."

That is something we shall remember. People who are spiritually asleep, what is the best way to reach them?

"When speaking with those who are asleep, whose spiritual eyes are firmly closed, simply talk to them. Do this in a way to help them understand who they truly are and what it means to have the freedom to create at will. What can you say to them to draw them in, to help them change a belief or beliefs they have held all their lifetime. Some of these beliefs may have even been created from a perceived pain or illusion. Show them the meaning of separation and that they are not separate but a part of All. Think of all who desire wealth. They may attain this, yet still not believe it. No matter what their wealth was, they would not see it, for they are separated from the truth of who they are and dwell only upon the physical. The physical rules as far as they are concerned at the moment. In order to help them awaken first show them that they are not separate, not alone. Tell them who they truly are. You may share all this but also know that it will ultimately be their choice to hear or not. If they choose to not hear and reject what you have come to share, simply let them be on their way with all your love and blessings. Not all who you shall meet have chosen to awaken and that is fine. They will pass through this lifetime and, upon their return to the Absolute, shall 'know' the truth. It is then once again their choice to come again or not and to awaken or not. We know that the joy and peace experienced with the remembering, and all that you create while in the physical is well worth the journey. You shall simply give them the opportunity to know that joy and understand how to create their experience. You shall give them the choice to accept or pass, then you shall continue on your own journey and Path to remembering.

"If there are no further questions, then we shall depart in Love and Blessings."

This particular session contained so much information on what the meaning of "knowing," or "feeling," something meant. I thought I had understood what they had taught, but it wasn't until now that I really "got it." We have all had that "gut feeling" they talked about, but I wonder how many of us really paid any attention to it? I know that I certainly became much more aware of what my physical body was trying to tell me whenever I was trying to make a choice about something. You know, I did find that nine times out of ten, those "feelings" were right on. Wish I could say that I always followed them, but no, I had to learn just like everyone else. It was those experiences of learning that have really given me a truer understanding of myself, my choices, and my Path.

I also finally understood about residuals. When we make a choice, it will always have a residual, and that residual will have to pass through our life. Sometimes these residuals are things that are wonderful and sometimes not so much. So if every choice we make is made in awareness of that fact, it helps us to make the choice. I do think that it can be difficult to figure out what the potential residual of that choice may be, but again this is where that "feeling" comes into play. The saying "If it feels good, do it" has more meaning than one would think. We all have gotten that yucky feeling when we are about to decide something, but how much do we pay attention to it? Believe me, I now follow those hints I am being given.

The "Girls" also spoke again about the ego. I don't think this subject is one you can talk about too much. That ego can definitely take us in the direction away from where we intend to go. That seems to be its purpose, to be "in charge." I mean, after all, we have allowed it to have its way for a long time, we allowed ourselves to be identified by it, led by it, blindsided by it, and because we didn't understand its creation, we believed it. Now that it is understood how it is created and how it keeps its "control," I am always on the lookout for it. I know who I am and that I am not what others may identify me as. The joy I have discovered in completely understanding this fact is beyond anything I could have imagined. I completely know that I and I alone create my experiences.

No one can do anything to me that I don't allow, and I can choose to be a part of anyone else's created experience. Wow! It makes this journey so much more than I ever imagined it to be.

They also shared with us how we can help others to awaken. Of course that is one of our greatest desires, and because of that, we felt we had to share with everyone everything at once. Overload completely. Now we know to just start with baby steps, the same way it was given to us at the beginning. All we can do is share what we know and then leave it to them to choose and hear more. It's okay if they don't because that is their journey. That's a hard one to digest because I really desire everyone to "know" and "feel" and remember, but that is up to each and every one to decide for themselves. I will just do all I can to get the information out there to those who it will resonate with and love those who it may not reach (at least in this Now).

I am so grateful to be on this Path and will do all I can to make the choices that continue to keep me toward my ultimate conclusion—the Sanctuary. I don't know in this Now how or when this shall happen, I will just continue in my trust that it will. To be a part of this unfolding that can change the world is amazing. By being with me on this journey, you are also making a choice. Listen, learn, and choose. I love you no matter what.

January 11, 2008

We spent our time between the last session and this one working on our projects. Bruce had finished his first book by this time. It had been completed, proofread, and was ready to submit to the publisher. Looking back on the months since we had returned home, it seemed amazing that the book had been written so quickly with the entire financial storm we were in. I was in the process of just beginning to really put the first Teachings from the Heart book together. All these months also gave us the time to reflect on all that had transpired, all we had learned and were learning, and the motivation to continue.

Bruce had questions to ask the "Girls" regarding the book I was writing.

"We do greet thee. How is everyone on this your day?"

We are well, thank you. I desire to help Little One get her book finished. May we please have your thoughts and feelings about the book?

"It is going well. The transcription you have made from the tapes is as it occurred. The messages we are adding now, to what had been said, and are now being received by Little One."

I can see by the transcribed material that this is going to be a fascinating book. This book lays the foundation for others that are to come. It is our strongest desire that it be accepted by those who choose to read it.

"It is difficult to say, Little Brother, how it will be accepted. We know that there are a myriad of different opinions and feelings among your people. We also know that now is the 'time' for its writing. There are many who have awakened quite sufficiently to understand this and to grasp the meanings. We wish we could tell you how it will sell, but it is again the old collective consciousness. There has been so much given as truth that has confused many. All things written will have some truth; it just depends on how much the ego is an influence on the author. This can be said for much in your world, how much is the influence of ego? The New Collective that is forming shall be the ones who, of course, will reach for this book. We know these words will resonate with many for there is an inherent energy within the pages that will be 'felt.' Continue to share what we have come to teach, and as we have said before, it shall be their choice."

Thank you for that. That is all I have to ask at the moment on Little One's book. I would ask you about our cat Sarah. We are concerned and wondering if she is feeling well.

"We believe her to be in what you call stress, for it seems that her body is not cooperating with Spirit. There are things that are occurring that are causing her discomfort. This is why she is very disrupted and restless. There are things going on within her body that are not comforting her."

Is there something we can do for her? She is meowing often and pacing around the house quite often. Right now, we are trying to hang on financially, and that doesn't leave money available for the veterinarian, but we will take some of what very little we have left and get an opinion medically. It is like being between the rock and the hard place, desiring to do this knowing it is really going to take a miracle for us to hang on.

"The animal doctor will give you some enlightenment on what is happening with her. She will eventually decide when it is time to leave. Keep in mind that she is an older animal, and animals do not have the same abilities as humans are afforded of prolonging their life. These spirits are free. Once their animal body no longer serves them, they simply leave. Right now, we do not believe her spirit is ready, but her physical body is becoming weaker."

We will do something. This is going to affect each of us emotionally. We are very much attached to her and do not want her to suffer. We honor her desires, but do not want her to suffer in any way.

"We understand this attachment for she has been with your family for a great long 'time,' but do not allow attachments to affect you adversely. When you truly understand and believe that there is more beyond what you physically know, then you know that whether it is human or animal, Spirit shall always simply continue. Attachment keeps you and them on a level that is not of Spirit. Know that all are eternal and it is only the physical vehicle that is finite."

Thank you for all of this information. I would like to ask you a question regarding our physical bodies and the care we are taking of them. What more would you suggest then what we are currently doing in the way of exercise and the foods we eat? I know that it is important for me to get out in the afternoons and exercise.

"It is not just the walking outside. We strongly urge you to be in fresh air as this is very important. We have noticed that with the walking machine Little One is using, she is actually working her body more than the walks you are taking. So we would suggest that you do both things. We have looked into what you are consuming and believe there are those foods that you eat that are not of any real aid to the physical body. By this we refer to carbohydrates, especially those that are white in color, such as white rice, white bread, or pasta that is made from white flour. Potatoes should be limited. When eating bread, have whole grains and limit this to one slice a day. Eat more fresh fruits and vegetables. Limit your red meat to once a week and then make choices that are lean. Fish is wonderful in all its forms, just beware of overeating those that may contain mercury. Beans are a good source of protein, and cheese in moderation is fine. Limit sugar. Eat smaller meals more often, and if possible, eat your main meal before four in the afternoon of your time."

This is very good advice, thank you. It is also something that we can easily do to improve our eating habits. That is all the questions I have for now. We will continue to work on Little One's book.

"As always, we shall await your questions, for as you know, the Teachings will come from them. We will be with you again once you are ready with your questions. So now, in Love and Blessings, we do depart."

It seemed like even when a topic had already been discussed, the next time it came up, more information was given. They never seem to give more than you are able to grasp and let you think about it and have the Teaching settle in before they continue. This was especially true when we learned that whether or not the books would sell rested so much with the collective consciousness. Believe me, this was not something we wanted to hear, it was a bit unnerving. However, we had been assured that this was the "time" to write the books and for them to be released. Sooner or later, the books would sell, even though no "time" frames were given. There were still experiences left to go through in order for the proper sequence of events to unfold. Thankfully all of this was not revealed at the time as the "Girls" knew it would have been hard for us to hear. We did learn an important lesson from this, and it was, just because we had been informed of the success of something didn't mean that it would immediately manifest. Any thoughts or expectations as to when things may occur had to be taken out of our thinking. We learned to be able to receive information about events, or occurrences, in the context of "no time" and not limit to our "time" for manifestation. We were to remain in the "Now," the moment, completely outside the concept of physical time. We were to devote our energies to what was unfolding in the moment with the comfort of knowing that at some future "Now" that which we were assured would manifest. We did, and are, doing exactly that. I would like to tell you that after this particular length of "time," things have manifested in the way we would desire them to. That's not entirely the case. Yes, there have been moments of rapid forward movement only to be met with times of standing still (or so it seems). In this "Now," there is still much to unfold, to manifest. You may ask then why are we still writing books, maintaining a website, teaching others about what we have learned, training healing practitioners, etc. I believe that it is because no matter what, I know with every fiber of my being that these messages, and this healing modality, will indeed change people's lives. The desire to share all we have learned is so strong within all of us who are now involved in The Light Alliance that the "Teachings" and the modality have become an integral part of who we are. This is our path, our walk in this incarnation. I continue to believe that those who do receive these Teachings will be forever changed, and as they share with others, who share with others, we can build the New Collective Consciousness one step at a time. When everything will manifest as we desire, I don't know. What I do know is that we will continue to be who we know we are, teach what we have been given, find our peace and joy in all things, and live our lives in each moment, each "Now," as it unfolds.

Sarah, our beautiful furry companion, had rallied once we got back home from our voyage in November, however, for the past several weeks had been going downhill. She did a lot of meowing for no apparent reason and we were very concerned. She was not just a pet to us. She had lived in five states, traveled in ten, logged over fifty thousand miles in the truck, and was a very seasoned traveler. Like all devoted animal lovers, we had learned all her sounds and behaviors. We knew that once again she was distressed, uncomfortable, and calling out to us to help her. Prior to our last session with the "Girls," we had decided to spend as much as we had left to help her. We took her into her veterinarian and learned that she had a growth, or tumor, that was restricting her ability to breathe. We immediately scheduled her for surgery. They were able to remove most, but not all, of the tumor. Once removed, she began to feel much better, although her urine output increased and she was now showing all signs of being in early kidney disease. The vet advised us to put her on a new diet to slow down the disease's progress, which of course we did. Being a finicky eater, she wasn't fond of the new cuisine but soon adjusted and her appetite returned. Little did we know that events were also occurring on a completely different level. More on this as we go on.

During this financial implosion that we found ourselves in the middle of, Bruce and I, for some reason, couldn't seem to get either the energy or discipline to continue daily with our meditations. I was doing better than Bruce, but we both went through moments of exhaustion, low energy, and emotional drain. Some days it seemed a major effort just to get out of bed. We lost sight, at times, of any good thing that may be happening. We were surviving somehow, but the appreciation of this really wasn't even noticed, especially when going through such a traumatic life experience.

We still had so much to learn, so much to remember, and so much to experience. As always the "Girls" had their way of shifting our focus onto things that would benefit us. A good example was getting some form of daily exercise. Bruce had been finding it easier to just sit in his chair all day and write. He gradually fell out of a routine where he would get out and walk a couple of miles around our neighborhood. I was still doing the treadmill but not as often as I had been. The very afternoon of the last session, we went out for a walk. We noticed an immediate improvement in our outlook and how much better it felt to be outside in the fresh air. We tried looking at our cup as half full rather than half empty, and it is amazing how our perspective on something really does influence how we feel about everything that is happening in our lives.

At the same time we were gently reminded about getting some exercise, we were reminded about healthy eating. We knew what our physical bodies required in the way of proper nutrition, but had descended somewhat into the so-called comfort foods. We had been taught that eating healthy would greatly benefit our ability to travel to the end of this journey we were on. Remembering these lessons was a good reality check for both of us. It really was, and is, our desire to take care of our physical vehicle and keep it as healthy as possible. Without this vehicle, we could not experience those things we desired and could not continue this journey. With the "Girls'" help, we began again toward our goal of being in good shape physically knowing that this would also benefit us mentally and emotionally.

January 17, 2008

On this somewhat cool day in January, we asked the "Girls" to join with us. We were excited as always to hear them and learn what they came to share. Bruce of course had questions, as always.

"We do greet thee. How are you this evening?"

We are well, thank you. We are so pleased you are here with us. I would like to ask some questions.

"We would be joyed to answer them for you."

How does a person know they are spiritually awake?

"They would begin to experience a different 'feeling,' a clearness of vision. There would be a deeper understanding of people and things around them. Most of all, there will be a 'feeling' of peace and joy. It is a 'knowing' that no matter what occurs in your life, it is right and good. We would have to say that this knowledge will come from 'feeling' all that they experience."

What will this "feeling" feel like?

"This is very difficult to answer. Each individual expression of the One upon this earth will 'feel' it differently. It will depend upon their makeup. It will depend upon who they have been as they traveled upon the Path. One 'feeling' would be that of peace within. This is warmth, a peace where they truly 'know' that all is as it should be. There is no longer need for controversy. There is no longer any strife in their life for everything that is occurring is occurring the way that it should, especially when they are going forward in awareness of each choice in each 'Now.' They go forward in the knowledge they are indeed creating but hold no recrimination if it does not occur as they may desire. They 'know' that something which serves that creation will occur.

"As we stated, each will 'feel' this being awake in different way. Some will experience a giddy joy, others simply a deep sense of peace and 'knowing.' Still for others may be the desire to go out and reach others to extend beyond themselves that which they are 'feeling.'"

Why would they feel so differently now?

"This would be because their spiritual eyes are now open. The veils that kept back the remembering are falling or gone. There may still be walls around your complete understanding for it is going to take the shifting of the collective consciousness to completely dismantle them. Eventually, for each who is awakening, they will use their 'knowing' and 'feeling' to also dismantle any wall that still exists for them."

It is then important for all to be content right where they are at the present time.

"Certainly, and know that where you are, is where you should be. There should be no worry in your life anymore. Just know that each moment will unfold in your life at its proper 'time,' for your highest purpose. Each moment will bring with it the experience of your creation, your choices. Be content in this understanding."

A lot of people are going to ask themselves what are they to do now that they are awake.

"Their lives will continue, of course, as they have been. If they have a job, a family, these will, of course, continue. The difference will lie within their understanding of this new 'feeling.' The 'knowing' that they are connected to their coworkers, their neighbors, their family, and all others who share this earth with them. They will realize that all humanity is their family and that they are truly a part of, and connected to, all. The only changes that may occur are those that they will create as they journey awake. They will create without fear and go forward in their lives."

They may also ask, once they have this understanding, where they are going and what is out there ahead of them.

"Ahead is whatever they desire. They go forward, knowing they are no longer an individual, alone, not connected to others on their planet. They go forward with this knowledge of who they truly are. They begin to take an active role in those things which they know can, and will, be changed."

It seems that as you continue in the "awakening" process, you can no longer identify with the current collective consciousness, but you begin to identify with a "knowing" and understanding much greater than that.

"Yes, this is what all who are awakening, or have awakened, are feeling. They will now see the current collective thought differently. For instance, you may see a homeless person who is in that state due to drug abuse. You can truly see that they are there due to their choices. Choices will send you in the direction of that which you create. You will also understand that you can choose to take part in an experience someone else has created. As with drug abuse, you will observe and understand but choose not to participate. Your choice may be in helping them to understand what you now 'know' and allowing them to understand about choices. You will have a deeper level of 'knowing' about the walls and your interaction with them. You can now choose to no longer participate in the experience of their creation and continuation. They will begin to fall around you as you awaken and dismantle them. The New Collective will be built upon the ruins of the old."

People are going to want to know how others are going to perceive them. This may be a very difficult thing. It is a very tender topic for others. Some will have a tendency to fall back into old thought because of this perception of others.

"It will, of course, depend upon where the person who is observing stands along their own path. Unfortunately many will be observed as being cuckoo because it threatens those who are still outside of Awakening. They do not understand how someone could be so happy. What is wrong with them? What are they trying to do? Who do they think they are? They will pin many names upon those who are awake. It will be for those who have awakened to observe these name-callers, understand where they are, what their understanding of themselves may be, and not be pulled back into their blindness by their words. It is your choice to simply not be a part of their consciousness and continue on your own journey with your 'knowing.'"

Are we then encouraging the awakened person, at this point, to only respond with Love and understanding?

"It is okay to say to the person who is mocking you that you understand they do not know where you are now coming from. This is fine. They do not need to know because you know within yourself where you are coming from and who you are. Tell them that you Love them. That is all that is necessary. You may also say that this is your journey and you are not asking them to follow you. Many times this will promote the opportunity for them to ask questions and for you to share."

The awakened person knows that they were once in the exact, or similar, place before when they were still spiritually asleep.

"Have compassion for these other people. Your greatest desire is that they feel the Love and joy that you now feel. Have compassion for them because they have yet to reach that moment of 'awakening' in their own lives."

What about those people who are closest and dearest to us, such as partners, friends, and family? Is it different than dealing with someone we are not close to?

"The best thing to share with someone who is in your emotional circle is that you Love them and are dedicated to your relationship with them. Your awakening does not change that, it simply intensifies your commitment. The promises are so much deeper. Even if they do not understand, from their current place on their Path, where you are on yours, assure them that you are with them and not going anywhere. Spirit will hear you even if they are unable. This new you is not leaving them, you are joining with them more in your understanding of who you are and of who they can awaken to be."

Even with these assurances, the partner, friend, or family member may not want to stay. This will be one of the hardest things for most to overcome. I know it was for me. I hung on when I should have just let go, although at the time, I thought it was the right thing to do. My

eyes weren't open enough yet to understand that I was actually doing the opposite of what I should have done.

"Let us explain that Love is, and was always, intended to be shared by all. Love was not originally intended to be paired. It was not intended for two to go off alone. Love is for everyone, to be shared communally. It is the giving, sharing, taking, and caring of Love that creates such strong energy. On our planet, for example, we are not bound to one another solely. We desire to share and know Love from all. It is that sharing, it is that emotion of connection that all want to feel. Is it fair that there are those on your planet who do not know Love? How is it that because of their physical looks, size, or for a myriad of reasons, that they go without Love. They do not share in that most important thing that life consists of. It was never meant, this custom that you have on your planet called marriage. This was never the intent for two to isolate and go off together, to live within their own confines. Love is meant to go to all.

"Children are the complete essence of Love, and this Love is given to them, in most cases, by those who physically created them. But what about the children who have been born and abandoned? What about the children sitting throughout your planet in orphanages? Even though they are being taken care of, being given food, shelter, and clothing, do they truly know or receive Love? Love is the essence that you grow with, it is the essence that you are.

"We do not understand this concept of what you have termed 'gay.' We see that you believe it is 'wrong' for a male to be with a male, or a female to be with a female. Why is this so? Is it not all Love? There is simply the love for each other, the sharing of their lives. Is this not what you do when you understand that who you are is Love? You are the expanded creation of the Divine Parents whose pure essence is Love. Do you believe that the Divine Parents would love only a selected few? No, that Love encompasses all things that exist.

"We believe you took the word *Love* and associated it only with the sexual expression, and you made it into something that it was never intended to be. Many have, and do, believe that it is only for the procreation of your species. It has been looked upon as forbidden, dirty, reckless, sinful, and much more. This belief has been so strong that it has taken away from its other purposes. The intent, and the reason male and female were created physically as they are, was for the ultimate expression of the body, mind, Spirit, together as One. Would the Divine Parents have created such a strong feeling within you, that feeling that occurs during this act, if this was not a joining of all these parts of who you are? No, there would simply have been no feeling, only an act that resulted in procreation.

"Love and sex do not necessarily go hand in hand. You are to Love all with the complete understanding and recognition of each as Spirit. In some circumstances, this Love results in sexual expression, but sometimes this expression is shared only for the experience. As in all things, there come choices in the sharing of this expression. We understand that because of past and current beliefs there have been created illnesses out of this act. You should be aware of these illnesses and make your choice according to your knowledge of them. This act should always be done with the complete choosing of your partner as well, for anything less than total agreement would be violating another's Freedom to Create at Will. In Love, you would protect those unable to make this choice for themselves.

"Love in its true nature is to be known, shared, and felt by all. It is with Love that all things flourish and energy is at its highest. The absence of Love creates a withering and energy turned down for all who do not experience it."

The separated consciousness, the hallmark of the collective consciousness currently upon the earth, would not accept this. Love or what they have confused as pure love, as it is experienced here, denotes possessiveness and is ego-based and ego-gratifying. It is often self-centered, self-gratifying, and a mode of control over another. I understand now how it was intended to be, but as long as there is separated consciousness, things will stay the same way.

"Yes, this is so. You are in better understanding of the spiritual connection of Love as well as the physical expression."

What advice would be appropriate to give the person who has just awakened to enable them to proceed along the Path to Oneness?

"They would continue their meditations and begin to outreach. They will begin to fully understand what this Love, this peace that they are now 'feeling' and experiencing truly is. Share what you are learning with others. There are so many ways this new experience and 'feeling' can be expressed."

What tools will be available to those that are awakening, such as support groups as an example?

"We believe your Light Alliance will be a support group. There are many such groups. Each will find the group that resonates the most with them. One thing that they could do would be to become involved with people and things. Maybe, if you are not comfortable enough yet to show this new understanding of Love to other people, show it to animals and plants. Start a recycling program upon the roads, or pick up garbage and debris to help clean up the earth. There is so much you can become involved in."

Many who are awakening do not know of their personal guides. What can we say to them about that?

"Once you are awake and understand that spiritual guides do exist, you will want to become connected with your own personal guide(s). They will be able to help you to a more clear understanding of your path and reach you with inspiration. At first it may take an intermediary, someone like Little One, who has the capacity to see guides and introduce you to them. They can let you know that you have now made a contact, or that a guide desires to contact you. Once this introduction has taken place, they will begin to work upon their chosen method to seek and receive inspiration and guidance."

Is the identity of your guide known and decided on before your incarnation?

"Yes, you know your spiritual guide as this had been agreed upon before you incarnated. They came with you, in Spirit, into the physical world and have chosen to stand by you. This is why you are never alone. Often you will see infants cooing, grunting, and talking away. They 'see' what you cannot. Their eyes have not yet been closed by ego and they still remain connected to the spiritual guide that came in with them. As you awaken and begin clearing ego, you also will begin to connect with your guide."

Is it common to have more than one guide?

"Yes, some have chosen to travel into the physical with several. Some are gained during the physical experience. If Spirit leaves its physical body through the body's passing, then it can choose to remain within the earth's vibration or what is called 'earthbound.' Sometimes it may not be the choosing of Spirit to leave but the physical body's. Spirit may then choose to stay in order to help, guide, or continue to share in the experience of one whom it loves. Spirits that are 'earthbound' will never interfere unless you request it. Many can see these spirits around those who are still in their physical body. If it is your desire, you can also be made aware of them and continue to 'feel' their Love and receive their guidance."

Once people understand Oneness, they are going to try to integrate all their experiences and knowledge into a cohesive whole in order to see how everything fits into a Grand Design. How do we understand this Grand Design?

"It simply is that which you desire. There is no preset design. When you are in the Absolute, you choose to come in to this physical incarnation and experience whatever it is you choose in that life. It is through those choices that you create your experience. There is not preset destiny, if you will. Your destiny is what you create it to be. Each will do this for themselves."

We desire to have people understand that before they were incarnated, they did have a basic plan or "blueprint" of what they will accomplish, or what their purpose is to be for this lifetime.

"Yes, you are here to experience life in a physical vehicle and to be Love. That is it. It is that simple. It is humorous to us that this has been made so complicated. While you were in the Absolute, you created a sketch, a 'blueprint.' Sketches change, they are redrawn, lines are erased, and new ones entered. Things grow upon other things. This is how your life unfolds as you experience each new thing that you have created. One experience creates another sketch. Each occurrence in your life creates, or erases, a line. It is that simple."

People make complex the simplest of things.

"That is why your world is in the condition it now finds itself, because they don't see that it is just that simple. It does not have to be the complex thing they have made it out to be, but now that they have made it that way it will be up to them to create it differently. It will take those who are awakening to begin these changes and to remember that they now must live through the residual effects of those prior choices."

Is the "blueprint," guideline, or sketch, one we make ourselves, or is it made in concert with the One?

"When you are in the Absolute, you are not an individual. If you were to take a drop of water and put it under a magnifying glass, you will see that what appeared as only a single drop contains within it a multitude of movement. When you are in the Absolute, this is what you are, an inseparable part of that multitude of movement that is the One. It is a forging of Spirit, a 'knowing' that creates these sketches. It is together that this 'blueprint' is created."

Is there anything else people need to know about inner guidance?

"Inner guidance is from your true self, Spirit. Ego can be a guide, but not the guide you would necessarily choose to walk with. Inner guidance is just that, leading with Spirit. Other 'guidance' may only be that which your mind has chosen, ego. Your mind will be the reflection of that which it allows itself to be led by, either Spirit or ego.

"Little Brother, we would like to broach upon a subject Little One brought up yesterday. This concept to which she has awakened is very important. This is the concept of the Divine Mother and Divine Father. This concept is not one which many upon your planet are ready to understand or accept. Each will chose, and that choice will be where they are and where they are supposed to be. For those who will listen and are ready to hear, we would share this. It is very important to understand that the Divine Mother and Father are ONE. They are the pure essence of Love together, for Love is in All and of All. Each essence of the One has its own purpose, if you will, and different attributes. We say you are made in the image and likeness of the One. This is why there is a male and a female of your species. It is the representation of both the masculine and feminine aspects and attributes of the One. In your physical incarnations, when two join, they bring with them their own likes, dislikes, creations, and desires. In this joining and in this Love, there is the capability of coming together as one voice on one journey. It is similar to the combined essences of the One with the exception that they have always been One, and you, in your incarnated state, remain individual even while joined."

We have had a feeling of this by your past wordage, but it really didn't sink in until now.

"Yes, the Divine Mother and Father are One. The imbalance of this energy on your planet began when the male of your species, because they are physically stronger, started to assert control. This is why they have called themselves warriors. The concept that they also had more intelligence was created by their own egos and completely in error. It became the belief that the woman, the feminine, was less and less and actually became the property of a male. Traditionally the female gender on your planet has had to fight for rights that man assumed were his alone. It has slowly been changing, but now the Divine Mother is saying 'enough.' All are the same and each must treat, believe, and understand each as the same. This imbalance is destroying your world. It is now time to bring back the balance as it was intended to be."

This session has been very enlightening. Little One will love your answers. What brought about the understanding that the Divine Parents are One but have their own attributes were a couple of things. Even though you were discussing a particular individual attribute of the Divine, you always addressed them as One. You got us to thinking that each of the attributes of the Divine Parents is to be addressed for specific concerns. The Divine Father for information concerning universal knowledge, and the Divine Mother for guidance, teaching, healing, and the understanding of how to restore the balance of Divine masculine/feminine energy upon the earth. I understand that each of the Divine Parents have a division of labor within the ONE. They are absolutely One but with different attributes and are doing different things that are totally united within the completely comingled union of the One.

"Yes, it is the comingling, if you will, of the two attributes that is the Creation. Consider, for example, the glue you have on your planet that you call two-part epoxy. Each in and of itself has its own attributes. It does its own thing, but if you put a drop of each one together, it creates another essence. It creates a bond. Even though the Divine Mother and Divine Father have their own attributes, they are still that One Essence. This bond is because they are Love in its truest form. When these two attributes, within the One essence, comingle, then Creation occurs.

"We of course shall join with you again, but for now, we do depart in Love and Blessings."

Many of the Teachings in this session came about through the questions that Bruce asked concerning the first chapter of his book *Now That You Are Awake*. They covered the subject of how we know when we are awake, what that means, and how that knowledge moves us forward on our walk. We also received unexpected Teachings, not from our questions but by design. These Teachings were to introduce, and explain, important topics that as always were intended for our, and the people we share them with, enlightenment.

The first unexpected topic was on Love and how it was intended to be expressed on our planet. They indicated that Love, as it is commonly viewed on our planet, is not Love at all. It has become an ego state of separated consciousness and is used as a means to control another, or for self-centered or self-gratifying reasons. True Love was to be unconditional in nature and extend to every living thing. Too much emphasis seems to have been placed upon the interchangeable meaning of Love with the term *sex*. Love is reaching out to everything equally and unconditionally. Sex is that act which is shared by two and is the ultimate "energy" connection between body, mind, and Spirit. When this act is expressed with two who are also showing unconditional Love toward each other, it is "out of this world"! They also explained that, in this Now, we have created diseases based upon how we have viewed the sexual act in the past and that you must be guarded when choosing a partner.

Love, as they see it, on our planet is often hallmarked by a sense of ownership in which we become possessive, jealous, angry, hurt, resentful, vindictive, and seek retribution from those who have "broken our hearts" or bruised our ego in some way. This is not love, actually it is just the opposite. Love is energy turned up to its highest level and what it has become, in some cases, is Love turned down and in some cases turned off. Unconditional Love does not keep score, is not possessive, conditional, or used as a means to control others in order to get what we want, or for the many other reasons we employ this emotion to satisfy our own self-seeking wants or needs. We may call this Love, but it surely is not. Love, in its purest form, is spiritual in nature, understands and embraces Oneness, is unconditional and meant to be expressed to all living things in acts of kindness, compassion, acceptance, and allowance. This Love raises the physical to the level of Spirit. All are worthy of being Loved and of being shown the respect, appreciation, and equality that unconditional Love was always intended to be.

The second unexpected area of information concerned our spiritual guides. We gained additional insight on how they are chosen, what relationships we have with them, and what their purpose is. We also learned that we may pick up more guides as we continue on our journeys. One of the most interesting comments concerned the ability of a spirit to choose, after departing its physical body, to stay earthbound in order to help, guide, or assist the one they chose to help along on their journey. This can occur for specific reasons: such as to share the knowledge they gained during their incarnation. There are many reasons for their decision not to immediately return to the Absolute. Please note that I said their purpose, their true intention, is to "help," or "assist" the person, not to haunt them or cause them harm. I know that within the current collective consciousness are the beliefs in demons, evil, malevolent spirits, and the devil. We asked the "Girls" about this and their response was quite eye-opening. These beliefs are from separated consciousness. This separation actually creates and manifests such phenomena in the experiences of those who devote their energy toward these so-called "truths." Mankind, as a whole, does not understand who they truly are, let alone the fact that we are eternal creative spiritual beings who have come to earth to experience life in a physical form. We, as such, can create any experience in our lives. This is given to us by our Divine Parents as the freedom to create at will. This means that our fears, superstitions, and flights of fantasy, which are the manifestation of our separated consciousness or ego, may also become manifest as our experiences. In the misunderstanding of our true nature, we can, and do, create our own experiences that will reflect what we believe to be true. This once again is the creative act of the ego-influenced mind separated from its Source, which is Pure Spirit. Haven't you ever been walking down a dark street or through a darkened house and just knew there was something behind you or just around the corner? You proceeded to scare the — out of yourself by this belief; some even will see things through this perception although nothing is actually there. As long as we do not understand, or accept, that unconditional Love is the Spirit we truly are and that all life was created in unconditional Love, we will continue to experience all the things that are the expression of a consciousness that believes itself separated from the true Source of all life energy.

The subject concerning the attributes of the Divine Mother and Divine Father answered so many questions in understanding the true nature of the Divine. I know there are so many who have wondered about, and asked, these questions. This knowledge may go against what has, and is, being taught in some religious circles. For those asking, and seeking answers, I believe this will resonate with them and touch within to that place of "knowing." Their true self, Spirit, will recognize the truth that lies within themselves.

Bruce had noticed that during this session, and for a couple of earlier ones, there was a "presence" during the talks that was different from how he had come to recognize the presence of the "Girls." The energy, he stated, seemed much higher and more intense, and it was something that was "felt" by all who were present. Sometimes it seemed to him as if the room was filled with electricity and the air became dense, almost as if you could cut it. The tape recorder had some static at first, but did not last long as the "Girls" adjusted the energy so the recorder could function properly. Bruce asked what it was that was happening. They explained that many times they were being joined by the Divine Mother, which resulted in the feeling of more energy. This combined energy also produced Teachings that were much deeper in understanding and contained many layers of that understanding. The more that was understood on a subject created the revealing of another layer. Meanings that were not completely grasped became, as we grew in our awareness, crystal clear. Now that we had been made aware of the Divine Mother's joining with the "Girls" for some of the Teachings, we also noticed how each time we listened to the recorded tapes something new would jump up at us. Now, we can always tell when She is coming through. Not only does the energy rise, but the "Girls" speak to us much slower than they normally do. Their normal combined voices are pretty fast, so the slowing of their speech is a signal that they have been joined.

As always, we left this session with so much to discuss, review, understand, and share. This is my gift to you, this continuing journey.

January 27, 2008

In this session, questions were presented to the "Girls" that addressed a subject that has sparked many debates throughout the course of human history. This subject resulted in countless conflicts and incalculable human suffering as well. We had been given some information on this subject in our last session, but were looking for more ways to explain this to the reader.

"We do greet thee. It is our joy to once again be in your presence. You come with questions for us?"

Greetings, Dear Ones. Yes, I would like to address what it means to be created in the image and likeness of God. This is an area that is confusing for much of humanity. It seems as though very few people really do comprehend this. The objective of asking this question, if acceptable, is to present a basic understanding that anyone can understand.

"Yes, Little Brother. We believe that far too much has been made of this wording in your religious texts regarding the image and likeness of God. This is simply man's interpretations. The image and likeness of God, the One, the All, is simply referring to those attributes of Love, of trust, peace, and joy. This would be the image and likeness. If you are in the image of something, then you are surely in the likeness of that same something. We were never sure why both words were used to mean the same thing. Image, of course, means that you do not look like the One, you do not look like the All. You understand that the word image is implied to mean 'looks like.' The One is spirit, and Spirit has no physical form or matter. So whoever wrote this in the beginning had, of course, their own image in mind. Likeness means the attributes of the One. That you were made in the likeness of the One simply states that you were made with Love, you were made pure Spirit. Your 'conception,' if you will, or the expansion of your creation, was done in peace and joy. You knew of nothing else for there was nothing else in the One. For the One is all there is.

"Being created in the image and likeness of the Divine Mother and Divine Father is to share in that Love, that joy, that peace. Physical image is dependent upon the physical form you chose to incarnate into. Each physical form or image will be different. Not all eyes, noses, mouth, and bodies are going to be alike. This is the image you portray upon the earth in your incarnation. The image of the One is Spirit, not physical. So you would say that the 'image' is your true self which also is Spirit."

Many people have interpreted that this actually means that the One has a physical body. There are religions that teach this.

"This is because they do not see beyond that which is physical. Being a visual people, how would your concept of image be something which you cannot see? If you believe you were created in the image and likeness of something, then therefore that something must be also physical as you are. They do not understand the concept that when you decided to incarnate into the physical you were coming from a spiritual realm, not a physical one. You, as eternal Spirit, chose to incarnate into a physical realm and into a physical body."

What higher level of understanding can we bring to people?

"To understand how much your belief in something will truly affect who you are. You are what you believe, what you think, and what you create. Nothing more and nothing less. If you do not believe it, if you do not think it, it cannot be so. It is important for each person to understand this, that they are what they think they are. If they have feelings of inferiority, abandonment, that is what they will experience. You choose what you feel and think, and what you will, or will not, allow to be a part of your experience. In order for you to be who you truly desire to be, free from fear, full of Love, peace, and joy, then you must believe that is who you are. It begins with the understanding of your true nature, Spirit, and knowing the true meaning of being created in the 'image and likeness of.'"

At this point, is there a way that would best enable those who are awake, or awakening, to comprehend this truth?

"They should search within. Look deep with no game playing. If you look only with honesty, you can discover these truths within. Look inside your heart. What are you feeling? What do you know? What resonates with you? Is there a voice in your head that is still saying, 'Oh, this may not be true'? Once you awaken to your truth, there will be a glow, warmth that will encompass you entirely. Not just your physical body, but your mind and Spirit as well. You will 'feel' it; you will 'know' it. If you have not yet realized these truths, if there are still doubts, you simply haven't reached that point yet. Each will make these discoveries for themselves in the proper 'time.' They may choose to stay where they are and that is all as it should be. You simply bless them and bid them joyous travels on their chosen path. We bring this to you and those who are in a place to hear, to resonate with what is being given. When one has heard what we bring and they 'know' and 'feel' our words as truth, then they will travel along that path, and then we say you are truly awakening."

Thank you for that Teaching. A number of people reading this book at this point may still have some foggy notions of where they came from. What can we do to help them, at their current understanding, to reach that place of knowledge and consciousness?

"We would say to start with the basics. It goes far beyond the fact that your physical body comes from an egg that was fertilized by a sperm cell. Your scientists have shown that when this process is taken back and broken down, all evaporates into nothingness. It all started from something most do not comprehend and think to be impossible. You 'came,' if you will, from something that scientifically can't be categorized. It can't be neatly filed away with complete awareness of where it truly began. We have told you that you came from that which you have always been. This can't be seen through a microscope or tested in a laboratory. You know that being Spirit is far more than just physical. If you were only the physical, you would be a robot with no 'life' within. It is the joining, the comingling of Spirit with physical that creates what you are and what you become while in this incarnation. We can only tell you these things, but it is for you to choose to understand, 'feel,' and 'know' them."

We have talked before about the Grand Design and the "blueprint" within. There is much talk in some circle about a Universal Grand Design, or the principal of predestination or predetermination. Would you please comment?

"The only design that exists is that which you create. Each person upon your planet is creating their own design. To say that there exists a universal design, or a predetermination, would not be correct. If that were so, then how would your freedom to create at will be honored? Each individual design, if you will, is a brushstroke upon the canvas of life. Each design from each individual creates the general design upon the canvas, and it is these myriad of patterns and directions that compose what you have previously misinterpreted as a predestined Grand Design. Life upon your planet is meant to unfold through your series of choices.

"As we stated earlier, you came from the Absolute, from the Divine Parents. You are here not only for the growth and remembering by Spirit, but for the enlightenment and the experiencing of the One from which you came. This is not something we can repeat too many times. It takes several times for someone to understand the meaning of what we come to say. When it is understood where you have come from, and who you were created by [as Spirit], then you will also begin to 'know' that it is the desire of the Divine Parents to experience with you that which you create.

"Your purpose, and that of all who are awakening, is to be Love, to bring joy and compassion to every living thing. You will create experiences through choices made with conscious awareness so that you can grow as you travel on your journey back to the Absolute."

There is a lot of discussion about how the "image" and "likeness" of the One is revealed in the created world beyond what we have already discussed.

"This is revealed every day with any birth, with every person that walks upon the face of this earth. It is revealed in all living things, as well as in a sunrise or sunset, a rainstorm, a crystal clear lake, in everything around you. How much more revealing could anyone desire? When you have awakened to the words we bring, and the Love behind all, you will truly understand that you see the reflection of the Spirit of the One in all things."

There also seems to be a misconception that the spiritual realm is "out there somewhere" and not reachable while we are in physical form. They

don't know that it is all a part of the One, a universal web of life that connects everyone, everything, and everywhere with the One. This may be a tough one for all people to understand, let alone accept.

"It is a hard concept for people to understand that they are a part and parcel of the homeless, part of the web that includes mass murderers and child molesters. It is not their consciousness that creates these conditions, but nonetheless they are connected by virtue that all are connected."

It is because they believe in the separated consciousness that has produced the duality of good and evil.

"They are separated in their thought only, in their perspective of separation. If they truly knew 'who they are,' and acted within this knowledge, there would be no prisons. There would be no mass murderers. That type of anger and hatred would not exist if there was not that type of perceived separation. Many people view this type of behavior and creation as either good or evil, not as points of individual expression along a continuum of expression. When these expressions and creations result in the use of energy being completely turned down, then those who have chosen to act in this way will have the residual of those creations to experience. Those residuals may be prison, death, or any number of consequences. If they had truly understood 'who they are,' they would not have created any experience that was the opposite of the energy at its highest. All human behavior is a reflection of the myriad of choices one can make."

The next question is one that has been a topic of much debate and discussion among Christian faiths. They looked at the word "we" and "us" in the creation narrative and assumed that the Godhead was composed of a multiple of individual persons that were involved in the creation of the physical universe.

"Little Brother, the context in which the words 'we' or 'us' were used were correct, but it was the interpretation by man that was in error. These words referred to the two aspects or attributes of the One, the Divine Mother and the Divine Father. It was let 'us' as One Spirit create. Because the truth of God, or Divine Parents as they are called by us, is not understood, it has led to many misconceptions and misinterpretations. On the subject of creation, we would say to understand that it is, and was, only the Divine Mother and Father who are the One Spirit. It is that

One Spirit that created all life everywhere. As we teach, you will begin to grasp and understand this."

My studies have revealed that the masculine-based faith systems followed the feminine-based ones. Is this not the case?

"Yes, the masculine-based beliefs came long after the time of the feminine-led beliefs. It became the 'strength' of the masculine that condemned those who followed the ways of the feminine, or Mother, religions. It became no longer safe to worship and thank the feminine for fertility, prosperity, and continued abundance. These beliefs were hidden for a great many years. There were still believers who worshipped in the 'old ways,' but as in all things, they eventually became silent out of fear. Their future generations, for the most part, integrated into the new masculine-based faiths."

During my research, I discovered that often in religious texts, the worship of the Queen of Heaven is condemned as well as other feminine rites and rituals. The fact that so much is now extremely masculine-based has always bothered me. There does not appear to be a balance of the masculine and feminine aspects of the One within any of the contemporary "religions" or "beliefs."

"In the beginning, there was a balance of both these aspects. Even though it was the Feminine that was thanked for Her nurturing essence, fertility, Love, and guidance, it was still the Masculine aspect that was the 'strength,' if you will. The balance was equal as many men, as well as women, thanked the Feminine for her attributes and the Masculine for his. But when man decided they wanted to be the forerunner, the only one recognized, the shift from the Feminine/Masculine to only the Masculine began. The thinking today is shifting back to the old truths, but it is a long journey with many involved in bringing back that balance.

"The original intention for your experience on this earth was not for man to attempt control over the female. It was never said that man was to 'own' or 'rule' over the woman. At one point in your history, women were actually chattel and ruled by their husbands. They had no rights, property, or seemingly any mind of their own. This of course is no longer true due to women standing up for their beliefs and understanding of balance, with that they began creating a change out of their choices. There is still though a strong feeling of masculine dominance, superior intelligence, and the need to be the leader in all things. We see this reflected in much of your current collective consciousness."

We know that with the blessed return of the Divine Mother that the balance between the masculine/feminine energies on earth will be restored. What can we say and reveal at this time concerning this process?

"At this point, one must understand that the restoration of this balance is simply going to make the earth plane more cohesive. Not only will there not be as much anger, but this restoration will begin to dismantle many of the walls which are held, and kept, in place by the beliefs of the collective consciousness. Veils of mistruths, misunderstandings, and misconceptions shall be lowered. It will not be something that will occur overnight, as you would say. Many must dismantle their own walls within their own understanding first. The restoration and rebalancing of masculine/feminine energies upon your earth will bring about the ending of anger, strife, fear, and create the understanding of one to the other. There will be no 'need' to see war as the only option, a 'need' to conquer. There will be the feminine understanding of what it means to sit and talk it out, to 'feel' the solutions and in Love actively pursue them. It will once again be the way it was intended to have been, the way it was begun."

Would it be correct to say that these understandings are a part of the awakening process?

"Yes, for it certainly is."

Also this is all a part of the renewal of the earth?

"Yes. The awakening processes for each one on the earth, as well as the earth changes that are occurring, are together, hand in hand, creating the restoration of the balance between the masculine/feminine energy of the One."

The concept of the One has always been shrouded in mysteries. From all that you have revealed, it would appear that it is man who has created them.

"Yes, man wants it to be a mystery. If you have a mystery, then you have those who supposedly hold the key to that mystery. These 'key holders' set themselves up as authorities to everyone's truth, and there is created the premise that one must go through these 'key holders' to learn the 'truth.' It gives them an assumed amount of control over their 'flock.' If the mystery is taken away and the truth is freely given to all who would hear and resonate with it, then the control would no longer exist. This 'control' was created by an abundance of masculine energies."

Can we say, at this point, that this is the time in the evolution of humanity where the keys are being removed and the doors are being opened to every single human being on the face of the earth?

"This is a time for all to look through the eyes of Spirit at what is being taught and not at what you have been led to believe. The ultimate choice of course lies with each who hears."

So then many of the mysteries have been created, or invented, by individuals seeking to gain control and mastery over other individuals? Are there many mysteries that are real?

"Yes, there are many of the ancient mysteries that are truth. Many mysteries were put into motion by the One at the beginning of creation and have not yet been touched upon by man. They have barely glimpsed the enormity of them for it was more to their purpose to have 'mysteries' that only they could reveal. Once you are evolving, awakening to your true essence and purpose, you will begin noticing more of these unexplainable things occurring. These mysteries become truly revealed the more you tap into them with the complete awareness of yourself and everything around you."

May we return to the concept we were discussing about the creation? I understand that this occurred with the comingling of the essences and attributes of the Divine Masculine/Feminine as One. Is this sharing of each of the Divine Parents attributes to form a blended expression of the One Spirit? Does this then express the intent of the "two" within the One Spirit?

"Yes, that is exactly what it is. It is much as if you were creating a recipe. You would need certain ingredients. If you were baking a cake, you would need all the necessary ingredients to make that cake, to create it. It takes several ingredients to make one cake. You wouldn't have two cakes because you used two ingredients. The result of using the two ingredients is only the one cake. So you could say it is two in one. It is the same with the Divine Mother and Father. It is the One Spirit that has attributes of both feminine and masculine. It is the giving and taking of these attributes, each to the other, that creates and contains the Spirit of the One."

I think that all you have given us on this subject will be understood by most people. It resonates to have this seemingly complex concept reduced to such a simple explanation. This is what we have attempted to do not only in this book but in all the books that have been written. Take the most complex concepts and reduce them to the simplest explanation and form.

"Yes, for this is the way most will learn. They are not only visual learners, but also learn by having it layered out before them. This is a good way to teach as it helps lend to the understanding of those being taught. If you attempted something too complex at the beginning of their awakening, it would simply go over their head and be lost. This simplicity gets the point across and it is that which causes them to begin to 'know' and 'feel' the truth. Sometimes the simplest explanations are the most precise."

Thank you. It is also a good thing for people to understand they are living that which they are creating, and that becomes their experience.

"To simplify it again, as we were saying, if you had a parent who was not an honest person and that parent taught their child dishonesty, and raised that child in anger, then that child will, in turn, become a reflection of that parent. For example, take a family that has an alcoholic parent or parents. Many times the children within that family become alcoholics themselves. That child becomes a myriad of reflections of the ones who raised them. There are many who choose to change this because they have the spark of 'knowing' within them that it does not have to be that way. They begin to understand that they do not have to identify themselves, or be identified by others, as that which their parents told them were truths. They do not have to have the experiences that their parents are creating, they can choose for themselves and create their own experiences. This is why we have brought these Teachings forth. To give to all who would hear these words, the opportunity to explore and learn of their true self and purpose. To reflect the true Spirit of the Divine Mother and Father to the world, one would be out amongst the people giving unconditional Love to all, being kind and compassionate, listening, Teaching, and most of all being who you are [Spirit]. Not everyone will be that 100 percent of the time, so just do what you can when making your choices to reflect this. Do not reflect those things which you are not."

Thank you. This is wonderful guidance. Over the last week, I've come to change my whole perspective on the collective consciousness. I understand now to wrap the entire collective in Love while only joining with the expanding consciousness of those who are awakening to form the new one.

"The current collective has been created through the thoughts and beliefs of the many. The strength of the collective is based upon how 'close-minded' people remain to anything that takes them outside of the comfort zone that they have created for themselves. It actually contains an energy that is the result of these many created beliefs. The New Collective will be created by those who no longer hold to the old beliefs as truths for their own created experiences. These Teachings are for the New Collective, for those who have and are awakening to the understanding of themselves and their connection to all life around them. It is not for the collective consciousness of anger or any of the other seven created walls. It is for, and of, those who are changing. There will come a 'time' of equal strength between the old and the new. Then it will be quite interesting. The New Collective is indeed growing rapidly. You cannot appeal to the mind of the existing old collective, only to the New that is being created. At this moment in your 'time' exists both collectives. The old will begin to fragment as the new is constructed. This growing New Collective is of unity, Love, joy, and the true understanding of Spirit. Even though it still seems in its infant stage, we are so pleased to witness its growth. It is within the New that the balance between the Divine Masculine/Feminine energies is restored. Changes upon your earth are to realign you to properly reflect the aspects of the Masculine/Feminine to create again the balance that was always intended for your earth."

Thank you, you have more than answered my questions in this session.

"You are most welcome, Little Brother. As always, it is our joy to hear your questions and to give you answers. Now, if there are no further questions, we shall depart in Love and Blessings."

This was a wonderful session as the "Girls" took what could easily have been a delicate or complex subject, made in the image and likeness, and reduced it to such a simple message that anyone who is receptive to the teaching would understand. To reduce such a widely debated topic to two words, *unconditional Love,* spoke volumes. If we could understand that Love is all there is we would truly transform the current collective consciousness of humanity. Since so much in our world reflects just the opposite of Love, it is quite plain to see that, on the whole, mankind does not yet know who they are. If they did have this understanding, we would see what is our true nature reflected in all aspects of our lives, in our interactions with all life around us, and in regards to how we treat the planet that supports our physical existence.

Humanity's extreme concentration on the purely physical aspect of our being, and the results this has produced, is another example that as a whole, humanity does not know who they are. It also makes it easy to understand the perspectives and biases that are reflected in our beliefs, philosophies, and worldviews. The current collective beliefs pertaining to the death of the physical body has become somewhat of an obsession and is a prime example of fear. The physical body is not who we are. It is simply the vehicle for our journey, for our experiences, while we are incarnated on earth. It certainly does not define or represent our true nature. From the "Girls'" Teachings, it is more than readily apparent that our beliefs, truths, and understanding of who we think we are is based upon a physical understanding of the world we live in. In order for us to arrive at the truth, it requires nothing less than a transformation from being led by the ego, or physical mind, to that of the Spirit, or Spirit-led mind.

All of our misconceptions will never be solved through the physical mind of the ego. We can't solve these issues and misconceptions on the same level from which they occurred. Think about it, it is, and was, this separated consciousness that created all of these problems in the first place. It is the transformation from ego-led mind to Spirit-led mind that will open the door to new teachings and advancements in the consciousness of mankind. Every living thing everywhere will benefit with this transformation.

There are many subjects discussed in this session that Bruce addresses in greater depth in his second book. When it was being written, new inspirations came forth to expand and clarify what was being discussed. Rather than try to present them in this book, out of context of the other Teachings, it would be more to your benefit to read them in the context of how they are presented in his book. The title of that book is *Now That You Are Awake.*

One subject that was fascinating was about earth changes. These changes will be one of the most visible occurrences of the Awakening as they unfold in our experiences. In addition to allowing earth energy to come back into balance, these changes also serve to balance the Divine masculine and feminine energy as experienced by all life on earth. The imbalances that are currently present in our world are being corrected by the rise of feminine energy. This will reestablish the balance that was always intended. Because the Divine Parents honor our freedom to create at will, and the fact that we came into our physical body in forgetfulness of all we 'knew' in the spiritual realm, this balance was lost or rather forgotten. In our unawake state, we created a world full of disharmony, misery, suffering, and every other conceivable expression of separation. Mankind knowingly, or unknowingly, created this through thought, word, and deed. All of this energy is contained within the current collective consciousness. It has the ability and energy to influence the thoughts, feelings, and behaviors of every living thing, particularly of those who remain spiritually asleep. Without being aware, we give our life force energy to its establishment and, in turn, are influenced in every aspect of our lives because of it. This is the created experience for countless numbers who have no understanding or knowledge of the existence of this collective. You can't physically see it, but you can physically see the results it produces each and every day of your life. You can change this by being a part of the construction of the New Collective. All it takes is remembering who you are, your purpose, and why you are here. These Teachings are intended to guide you in that remembering.

The New Collective is currently growing alongside the old one and is being built upon Love. Its expressions are joy, peace, harmony, happiness, compassion, unity, knowledge of, and the ability to live in oneness with all life everywhere. It will be this consciousness that will transform humanity and renew the earth. Earth changes go hand in hand with the New Collective as they are designed to awaken us to a much-higher level of consciousness. When you see things happening around you, think beyond what you may see or hear, or what your physical brain can comprehend, and "know" that they are universal in nature and purpose.

January 30, 2008

This session followed quickly on the heels of the previous one. We felt we were "in a groove" as far as extended Teachings were concerned.

"We do greet thee. We are so pleased that our teachings are bringing forth many questions. As we have stated, we know by your questions where you are in your understanding of what we bring. Little Brother, please ask your questions."

Yes, thank you. How do we unify all into Oneness with what seems to be huge diversity in the world?

"This diversity is, of course, the collective consciousness of mankind. Each one comes in as an individual expression of the whole and therefore would, in and of itself, be diverse. It is these likes, these dislikes, if you will, which create the whole. To join all these diversities into one understanding of the One may not be possible. It is important that each remain an individual expression with the ability, and the freedom to create at will, to make a choice regarding the understanding of the One. As Spirit, each individual expression can unite within the spiritual level. As the collective awakens (those who have chosen or choose this path), and they become aware of their connection to the One and to all living things, then you will recognize those who have united in their purpose. You understand that everyone and everything is already connected on the spiritual level, even if they are not aware."

So that is how we unite all things?

"Yes, to know it is so, on a spiritual level."

For the person who is awake and approaching the subject of One Energy / One Voice / One Purpose, what does that mean for them?

"It should simply mean 'knowing' that there is only the One Energy that is All. It is in and of everything that has or ever will exist. One Voice is for all those voices who are speaking in Love, who are speaking in truth, they are speaking in harmony as One. One Purpose would be the speaking of these truths about Oneness to all who have chosen to hear."

How do we begin to truly understand this Oneness?

"It is not an understanding, if you will, of the intellect. It is a 'feeling' of Spirit. It is a 'knowing' of Spirit. The intellect can never quite grasp this concept for it knows only what it is taught, what it reads, and what it physically experiences. The connection with the One goes beyond the physical intellects ability and lies with Spirit and the understanding that that is who you truly are. This understanding joins you in Oneness."

What about people who are awake but are being approached by those who are either not awake or just awakening? How do we help them best explain Oneness to others?

"Besides what we have already shared, Little Brother, the best explanation of Oneness would be by example. If someone approaches who is either not awake or just awakening and asks you a question such as this, then know that they must be 'in tune' enough with their inner vibrations, and those around them, to ask. You can, of course, explain to them with just your words but they will not touch them as deeply as the example you set. You will of course use words, but be sure they come from Spirit and not your ego-led intellect. Once your words and your example are seen, heard, and 'felt,' their comprehension will widen."

Feeling does reinforce the concept. We really do see now what you meant when you said that we would come to know things when we began to "feel" them. You were absolutely right. In fact it is happening for us on both an intellectual and a "feeling" level.

"Yes, this will happen. We have stressed 'feeling' from the very beginning. It is important to teach others to begin to follow their 'feelings' and let ego simply go to the wayside. There will be times, of course, when people will say that is what they did, follow their feelings, and it got them into trouble. This occurs because the feelings they are following are not from Spirit, but from ego. You will know the difference when you are truly in tune with your true nature. Feelings from ego will be made in haste, for self-gratification, and without any, or much, awareness of the residuals. A 'feeling' from Spirit will be made with the conscious awareness of the residuals. You will begin to know the difference between the two as you awaken."

At this point, it should be apparent to anyone reading this, or hearing about Oneness, what it means.

"If they have not grasped the meaning, they are simply not ready. They have not reached the place in 'time' along their journey where they can understand this. They may simply need more 'time,' they may have stalled on their path, or they may be going backward. One's journey is not always a forward motion as it is dependent upon choices, experiences, perceptions, and residuals. It may be that one needs to stop occasionally and assimilate all that they have learned. Also understand that not all have chosen to have the experience of awakening. Everyone is where they should be at any given time."

We have noticed that some of the newly awakened we have met are sometimes a bit arrogant and pushy with their newfound understanding. I know that they are new and therefore may not yet be in complete "control" of their ego.

"There is an important lesson to be learned. One must be careful not to become a 'bible thumper' as you would say, for this drives away others who are questioning. There are those who believe that they know what others should know and do not allow others their 'freedom to create at will' and make their own choices. When teaching, always do it with Love, and always remember, it is the choice of others to hear or not. Do not push, be an example, a listener, not a 'preacher.'"

The young people who are coming from various religions seem to be searching for something more. They don't seem to be getting fed.

"Yes, and they don't want to have something shoved down their throat. They want to make their own choices as to whether or not something resonates with them. They want to be told, 'Here it is, if you wish to know more, you certainly may.' More young desire change and are searching beyond what they have been previously taught. They will find that which speaks to them of their truth. When they come to you for answers, share what you have learned, but remember it is their choice to hear."

I feel we have covered the Oneness of the Divine Masculine / Divine Feminine. Is there anything else that we can or should do to explain the oneness within the Oneness?

"It is the unexplainable. It is that which you believe and must be taken on trust. It is that which is known by Spirit. You must simply 'feel' it. Feel the truth in it. Resonate with what has been said, that there is no reason why two can't be One in all ways. It is not like the joining of two physical bodies, for they physically cannot become one. But if you have the joining of two raindrops, they do indeed become one, retaining and containing the individual expressions of their own identity. It is the same way with the One who is All. The Divine Mother and Father are, if you will, the two drops of water. Each of them having within their own attributes, their own strengths, and their own purpose. They join and become One Energy, One Purpose, One Love. It is the true state of being in Oneness.

"Understand that Oneness is a state of being. It is the state of being One with everything, not just the understanding of the One but the truth that you are an integral part of All there is."

Your explanation should help people come away with a very good understanding. We have heard people talk about what they refer to as the Divine dichotomy. What can be said about that?

"If the One was to be made knowable by the churches, made understandable without the necessary 'inspired' interpretations of the clergy, then what hold would they continue to have over their congregations? They would no longer be elevated above anyone else's understanding. When they don't have the answers, they tell others they would not be able to understand the true meaning on their own, or that they alone are the ones who are capable of understanding them. It has long been the desire of religions to cloud the One in mystery. This has been done for control, for power, and for general purposes of ego. To give a simple explanation would feel to them anticlimactic and would be a release of all they have held on to."

Our experiences have been that there are many who do not know the true answers, especially when they are matters of Spirit.

"Many do and many do not. It is because their faiths have taught them in many different ways. They teach that the Divine One is unknowable, although we know the Divine Mother and Father for they are in our lives every moment of every day."

It is each individual that must have that knowing within themselves.

"We are building the new collective consciousness. The acceptance of the Oneness has to be a pivotal part in the shifting of the consciousness because everything else stems from that understanding and balance. When this understanding, these truths are known, then people will see the walls they have created and desire to change them. Is this understanding the turning point where everything that has been falsely created begins to collapse? Yes, it will be because the walls of the current collective will be present right alongside that which the new collective is beginning to build. This new understanding will be built up and over the old existing walls. Those who choose to remain within their own created walls will continue to do so. Their experiences in their incarnation will continue they just will simply not be aware of any changes. As we said before, all will be as, and where, they should be depending upon their choices."

How will the universal acceptance of Oneness impact life upon the earth?

"Once there has been a majority acceptance, war or disharmony cannot exist. There will be no 'need' for drugs, for to what or where would one need to escape? You will be living in total unification with each other and with the One. If there is nothing but peace and happiness, what would drugs serve? There would be no ingesting of that which is unhealthy, various foods, cigarettes, drugs, etc. There will be a greater concern, and helping, for those who grow that which is healthy. This will enable them to grow in a cleaner, purer fashion. This will also help in lowering the many problems regarding your economy. Money will be treated in a different way than before, and there will be no more gouging, no more need to be at the top of the rung. Once everyone recognizes that all others are equal to themselves, all will be on a level playing field, so to speak. Everyone helping to care for one another, all achieving their desires.

"We understand that hearing this, it would seem to be quite impossible that this could occur. In your current thoughts, actions, and deeds, this will not happen. It will take a majority of all to truly understand Oneness and who you truly are before this could take place. It all begins with baby steps and the sharing from one to the other of what you have learned and been taught. We know that this will take an amount of 'time' and what that may be we do not know. It will be up to the choices of those who hear, who share, and who walk the path to this understanding."

It will be wonderful when the old collective shifts to the new and people begin to believe that all you have told us is possible.

"It is beginning it is just that in this moment there are only small sections of the new collective. It will take the efforts of all to spread this understanding to others, but always remember that it will be others' choice to hear or not."

I know that the people who are awakening will be a tremendous support group for those who are yet to awaken.

"Each will give a hand and Love to support those who are hearing."

We understand that this is a principal reason for The Light Alliance.

"Yes, for not all people are in the same geographical locality. It will be the joining of all who resonate to the same understandings that shall share all they know with those nearest them. Everyone speaking as One Voice."

Will the Utopia that earth once was be the end product of the renewal? Will it be a process, a product, of the Awakening?

"Of course it will. It will take much of what your 'time' to accomplish, but it shall happen. We believe you now have enough information to understand separation and that man came in to this incarnation in forgetfulness. It is that forgetfulness that allowed man to experience and create the false belief of separation. It is through remembering your true essence that you also begin to regain the understanding that in reality there is no separation, it only exists because it has been created and believed by man.

"We see your planet as something that you call Disneyland. It is full of man's created experiences and this was the choice for all who chose to incarnate upon earth. It is quite a fanciful place. Please understand that the earth plane is not for every Spirit. There are some who will choose never to come into it because they choose not to forget who they are and their connection to the One. There are other planets to incarnate into where you do not go in forgetfulness of your true self, but maybe other things are forgotten so that you may experience them. It is altogether and ultimately about the experience. Life, whether it is in the physical or Eternal, is an experience. Each day there should be no one who, at the end of that day, cannot look back and say this is what I experienced and learned this day. For if you go through your life not experiencing, or being aware of your experiences, then your purpose for being here is not being fulfilled."

It reminds me of so many people who before, or by, the end of the day are so bored they wonder why they got up that morning.

"Or they find themselves at their bedtime simply going to sleep, getting up the next day and going through it all over again. Not stopping for a moment to look back upon what they did in that day. What did they see? What did they have for lunch? Who did they have a meaningful conversation with? We are amazed there are so many people on your planet who cannot even remember what they ate for dinner the night before. They go through this process of eating, and most of their day, in a stupor, if you will. They have separated not only their thoughts but their actions as well. With the Awakening will come the removal of these blinders of separation, and then you will begin to see real connections being made with themselves and those around them."

I believe that there are a tremendous number of people who will follow the development of these Teachings and this wondrous journey from start to finish. This is not only my thinking, but most importantly my strong desire as well.

"Yes, Little Brother, it is our desire as well. Little One asked us about our answering of questions from people. We will be most happy to answer these questions for them. This will be another source of learning. We would say to have someone write down their questions regarding the Teachings or other matters of a spiritual nature. We, of course, would not answer questions of a 'fortune telling' nature for that is not our purpose here. There is no one who can foretell anyone's future as it is dependent upon what choices they make in that Now. There are those who can give guidance in personal matters, but ultimately, it becomes the created experience of the one making the choices. Our desire is simply to teach and to help all to awaken to their true essence and nature."

We would present all pertinent questions to you. I remember always how you have told us that it is by our questions that you know where we are in our awakening and how much we understand about a particular subject you are teaching.

"We would be most pleased to see how our Teachings are being received and understood by those who have chosen to hear them."

This really is a very exciting time.

"Yes, and we are most pleased that there will soon be a time of reunion for all of you to once again be together. We are with you, Sister of My Sister, and Light Sister whenever we are needed, and wherever you are. We are excited for the time when all will be reunited, for there is energy that flows when you are together."

Thank you. So many things have been placed into an understanding that is most illuminating.

"We are well pleased. If there are no further questions for us in this meeting, then we shall depart in Love and Blessings."

The "Girls" have spoken many times throughout this book about Oneness and how understanding it is a principal objective of the Awakening. With each session, it seems as though we are given, and grasp, a deeper understanding of what it all means and that this is for our continued spiritual development. This session was no exception.

The subject we really enjoyed was the discussion of our planet being seen, from their point of view, as a kind of Disneyland. We already knew, from their Teachings, that we had all agreed to forget what we knew in the Absolute in order to remember who we are through our experiences while on earth. It was interesting to find out that our planet has one of the highest, if not the highest, degree of forgetfulness. It seems we pretty much forget everything from the Absolute when we arrive and obtain our physical body. This choice completely allows us a multitude of experiences that can eventually lead us to remembering that which we first chose to forget. I know that there are varying degrees of forgetfulness with those who incarnate and that some of our greatest teachers have incarnated with more memory of who they are and of the Absolute. Take for instance, Yeshua (Jesus), Buddha, Krishna, Mohammed, just to name a few. These men came to teach us so much, but for the most part, our ego's kept us from really "getting it."

This whole lesson paints quite an interesting picture for us as to how challenging we can choose our incarnation to be. From each of our experiences, we can most likely agree that this journey of remembering can sometimes seem to be a difficult one. Fanciful is not a word we would necessarily choose to describe our journey, so it was interesting to see our earth through the eyes of such highly evolved beings. It creates a whole new perspective on all the things we may choose to experience, and we are here to be enlightened through those experiences and not scared witless by them. It was never intended for us to live out our lives in constant fear or worry about the past, the present, or what may be in store for us in our future. Live every moment in the Now and make every choice in the Now. Every breath is an opportunity for remembering, for joining with the Oneness of all things.

Chapter Three

February 2, 2008

The next session was about the importance of always being aware of everything happening both within yourself, and around you, in each moment of your life. This ability to remain alert and focused in the moment is what we refer to as being in the "Now." It took a little while to arrive at this understanding as there are a number of voices out there addressing this subject. Our first ideas on the "Now" had included terminology commonly used by others to describe this state of being. Through the "Girls'" comments and suggestions, we finally arrived at a better understanding of its true meaning. Being in the "Now" actually has two meanings. First, the word "being" is the conscious awareness of who you really are. It is not existing singularly in the moment, but it is being fully aware of everything in that moment. It is being the eternal spiritual being that you are and reflecting this understanding in every moment of your life while you are on earth. Second, we use the term "Now" in two ways. The first is used in terms of the "Now" or moment you are in, and the second is the spiritual understanding that there is "no time" and that everything that you could ever choose in your life is present in every moment. This may or may not seem somewhat confusing to you but is explained in detail in this next session. So here we go.

"We do greet thee. How is everyone on this you're evening? We have come for your questions."

May we discuss a subject that has been written about before but may not always have been understood? My knowledge of this is not extensive, so it is just as much for me as for others who are awakening. This is the subject that Sister of My Sister refers to as the Eternal Now.

"Little Brother, may we ask you a question? Where and by whom was the expression 'Eternal Now' heard?"

Yes, of course. That is a very good question. Sister of My Sister uses it often, and I think she may have read it somewhere.

"This is not a phrase we would use. *Eternal*, of course, means forever, but 'Now' in your terms is a fleeting moment. These words together would seem to be somewhat of a dichotomy, if you will. You have something that is forever being a part of that which is momentary. What we would say is there is an 'eternal now' only in the aspect that all is eternal and each thing repeats with each 'now.' It is a continuum. From your conception, your expansion within the Divine Mother and Father, you have been and will always be eternal. It does not matter how many incarnations you come into, how many various physical bodies you may inhabit and leave, for you are and shall remain eternal. That is to say your true self, Spirit, is eternal. The physical, of course, is simply left behind once it has served the purpose as your vehicle. The 'Now' simply means to be observant of all things around you whether it be a sight, a smell, a texture, a sound, or any number of things you may sense. Everything that is existing within your moment of 'Now' should be appreciated. You should be conscious of all things and join with them as the Spirit you are.

"Being in the 'Now' is the understanding of Oneness. It is with each breath that one 'Now' passes into another. You cannot move back to that which has passed nor can you push ahead into that which has not occurred. You make your choices within the 'Now" you inhabit, and you make them in the awareness of who you are."

As Sister of My Sister explained it, it meant that every conceivable and possible choice was present at the same time and, for all times, in that one eternal moment.

"It is the continuum of life. It is a circle. There is no beginning and there is no end All things within this continuum, this circle, exist, have always existed, and will continue to exist. The potential and the possible are held within that continuum."

If you are being in the "Now," you are living in the "Now." In essence, as you have taught, you are living in Oneness. I see that in every potential moment of our lives, there are an infinite number of choices we can make.

"Yes, and each choice is made in that which is called the 'Now' for that moment is all you have at that point of your 'time.'"

So would it be appropriate, or accurate, to say that every moment contains all the potential choices anyone could ever make in a physical "Now"?

"That would be well said. For example, there are sixty seconds within your minute, therefore there are sixty 'Now's.' If we view the 'Now' as occurring once in every second, then each second broken down into nanoseconds would yield an equal number of choices within the 'Now' in which they could take place. You can see how many then that there are. We do not expect that each person should think of each breath they take, but to know that each one is taken in a 'Now' and exhaled in a 'Now.' That is what the 'Now' is. It is not a grouping of 'time', but a passing of 'time.' When you are making choices, it may take many seconds, or minutes, of 'Now's' to make your decision."

We should be more consciously aware of every moment of our life.

"Yes, and if you are truly awake, that is what you will be truly experiencing. Let us explain the continuum of eternity for this is something that mankind in general seems to have difficulty grasping. First, it must be known and understood that there is no end, only continuance. You shall never not be, shall never cease to be. At times you may be Spirit and at times you may be Spirit encompassing a physical body, but you will always be Spirit never ending. Every cumulative experience you have ever known, in every incarnation, remains with your true self. It is your choice when you incarnate to temporarily forget all you know in order to experience and remember.

"Within the Spiritual realm, each 'Now' is also within a frame of context. This is not necessarily of time, for there is no 'time' in the Absolute. 'Now's' exist within a frame, a context, a sequence, but there still remains an endless stream of 'Now's' that are all within the Absolute."

Is there anything else that is important to say that will help the reader to understand this concept of "Now"?

"Let us give an example. If a person puts their hand upon a stove, they feel the heat, the pain. They, of course, will quickly remove their hand, but that awareness of that pain was conscious. It is much like a conscious decision, a conscious awareness of a decision. In the 'Now,' you will 'feel' that choice, for to be consciously aware of something is to feel it. It may not be a choice you are 'feeling', it may be a sensation, a sound, a taste, but all will be 'felt' within that 'Now.' So we say that being in the 'Now' is being consciously aware of your actions, your choices, and your 'feeling.'"

Thank you for that explanation, it is very much appreciated. How then can one incorporate the concept of "Now" in the physical world of time, space, and form to the "Now" that exists in the Absolute where there is no time, no space, and no form?

"This may be hard to grasp for some. You know only of time within your earth. So we do not necessarily want to take you out of that for that is what you are used to. It is your choice to come into this physical world knowing that you are going to be bound to a physical 'time.' It is important that you understand that within this 'time' is where your decisions count. It is where your choices count. You are not going to have an endless supply of 'Now's' upon this earth during your incarnation. They are limited and bound by both the earth and your physical body. We know not what your limit or that of any who incarnate may be, but it is not ongoing, it is not continuous as it is in the Absolute."

Is being in the "Now" where the physical and spiritual realms meet?

"Yes, it can be very much so, for if you are truly in the 'Now,' a part of the tapestry of life, then you will be One spiritually, mentally, and physically. This is to 'Be in the Now.' To have all three parts, the body, mind, Spirit as One and in harmony. You are using the term 'Now,' but what you are asking is not the 'Now' of a passing moment, but the actuality of 'Being in the Now.' So there is somewhat of a difference. Every moment, every breath, you will be in a 'Now' of a passing of 'time,' but sometimes you will 'Be in the Now' in a spiritual sense."

Yes, for us this "being in the Now" is where spirit and matter unify in Oneness. It's like you have one foot in the spiritual realm and one in the physical realm. You are unifying the two into wholeness, Oneness.

"Yes, and you will be more aware of things. You are more aware of the light, the colors around you, the sounds, and for some, this may only last for a fleeting second. It is hard to hold 'being in the Now.' It is not yet a physical possibility for there is too much interference, if you will, within your earth. When you are in the physical realm, things pass you by without you actually noticing them. You are caught up in many other things and your mind is elsewhere while your body is doing something else. You are in the 'Now' of physical time but you are simply just there. You aren't noticing what is around you, what is passing you by. When you are 'Being in the Now,' in the spiritual sense, you are completely in harmony. All parts, body, mind, Spirit, are in total awareness and harmony of all that is around you in every single moment. You may not, at this point at least, be able to keep and hold this awareness, this harmony, but when you find peace, and joy, within it you can, and will, bring this understanding to other people. These times will give to you a greater awareness of your own existence and the lives and connections of those around you."

Thank you for this excellent guidance. The collective consciousness seems to be a repository for all thoughts, feelings, and behaviors. The New Collective that we are building is also going to be a repository for the new, positive, higher-frequency energy. This will expand with each experience of each awakening person.

"Little Brother, it is as the layers of an onion. The outer layers, or the skin, protect what is inside. You must remove these layers to reach the center. If you see the outer layers as the old consciousness and the center as the new, then you begin to understand what must occur as the new is built. The old layers, or walls, of the passing consciousness must be peeled off. These layers keep the truth from penetrating, and all the Love and energy of the Divine Parents simply cannot be felt. As these layers are removed, the energy is able to reach within and the Love that the parents hold for you is 'felt.' The final removal of these layers is the Awakening, and for each who chooses to awaken; this energy and Love is now able to encompass as well as fill you."

That is a beautiful way of explaining this.

"When you incarnate, you bring with you, in your spiritual form, all that Love, that energy, but you chose to forget it. In order for it to be rekindled within, you must take off the outside layers. Consider the center of the onion to be all which you have forgotten. With the peeling back of each layer, you proceed with your Awakening. The beliefs of the current consciousness has held tight and has created layers, and only the new consciousness, in Love, can begin to remove those fast held layers."

We understand that the residual of past and present choices has to play out in our lives. How do these residuals affect us when transitioning

from that which we are not to that which we know we are? In our lives, it is the residuals that are the anchors that seem to hold us back. It is certainly our desire to be cut loose from them.

"The residuals will affect you according to the time and effort that you give them. If you are in the awareness that residual effects are playing out, do not put your efforts, or energy, into stopping them, for you cannot. Simply allow them to play out for that is what they must do. They must be allowed to run their course and then leave you. It must be completed. Do not forget that it was your choices that created not only the resulting experience, but also the resulting residual."

Do we need to give residual effects more emphasis?

"It would be important for people to understand about their choices. We hear so much of 'Why me?' 'I'm such a good person, why is this happening to me?' 'I didn't ask for this,' and on. It has nothing to do with your value as a person, for your value is that which you identify with, or believe in. It has to do with the choices you made and the choices you were involved in. Sometimes people think it has to be the choices they made, but if you were with someone who made a choice you did not agree with and yet you went alone with it, you, in essence, also made that choice. Whether you believe it or not, the fact that you did not leave the situation, or try to stop whatever it was, you still are participating in what was chosen, even if it was by someone else. If you are a passenger in a vehicle and three people within that vehicle go and rob a store, even without your participation, you are still a part of the choice that was made by the others. You also will deal with the residual effects even though you may believe you had nothing to do with it. Making no decision is a decision. It is a yes, a cooperation. When you allow something to continue, you have participated in that choice."

This will be hard for many to accept. Once people understand they have a responsibility to voice their own choice and if they see something happening, or about to happen, yet do nothing, they have, in essence, condoned the action and have participated in it.

"Your responsibility is indeed to voice that which you feel. For instance, if you observe someone mistreating another person or an animal, you have the choice in that moment to either stop the action, or walk away from it. Leaving is not a nonaction, it is the condoning of the action occurring. People will almost certainly not listen to you, nor agree with you in that moment, but you have stated and stood up for your belief. Do not get involved to the point where you may experience bodily injury, but your belief can be stated by shouting for help, calling the authorities, or by making the action known to others. You then have taken a stand and made a choice. Do not participate in the act by not voicing your choice. The residuals then will be completely different for the one who conducted the action and the one who voiced their stand against it. This is an important teaching."

Thank you so much for all the important teachings you have given us in this session.

"We have taught this day on many things and have given you much to think upon. For now we shall depart in Love and Blessings."

Some of the Teachings on "Being in the Now," and the word "Now," I introduced in the first Teachings from the Heart book. These current Teachings helped to expand and deepen our understanding of their meanings.

With all the challenges we were facing, and all the focus on the books being written, we seemed to have little time left for meditation. There were many nights when the lights in the library were still on in the wee hours of the morning. It's always easy, especially when facing something major in your life, to find every excuse to not do something you know you should be doing, and this is exactly what we did. The "Girls" always gently remind us to remember our meditations. We knew it was time to restore our balance of energy. We used to meditate for at least one hour every evening when we were in Happy Camp, and the results were always very calming and centering. So we once again set aside a portion of each day to find our "place" within the stillness.

Meditation is an excellent way to begin the process of peeling the layers of the onion away. I loved the way they had shared this Teaching with us by using the analogy of the onion. It is the peeling away, layer after layer, of the debris that both your ego and the collective consciousness has covered you with that gets to the core of remembering of who you really are. As you peel away these layers, you begin to get glimpses of your true self and these glimpses fill you with such comfort and understanding that you keep peeling away. I think that for some people maybe it also gets a little scary. There's a lot of "stuff" down there that we don't want to look at, whether we put it there with our beliefs and experiences, or it was put there by others. I know for a fact that with time and dedication you can, and will, one by one, get rid of those layers. What you will discover is who you really are, where your happiness, peace, and "knowing" come from, and how this will change the rest of your journey on this earth.

I was very intrigued by the subject of residuals. They explained it in such a simple manner and I could really see how they affect your life. It really makes one understand how important the choices and decisions we make, not only in the moment but for a "time" afterward, can and will create experiences in our lives. This understanding has helped me in making my choices as I want the residual of them to be something I desire and not something I have to "live through."

I never know for sure when the next session will be. It all depends on the questions we begin to formulate and if the "Girls" have something in particular to share with us. I just do my best to remain centered and be open and ready for whenever they do happen. My greatest desire is that as you are reading them, they will give you answers, help your growth and journey, and most of all, that you would feel the Love that comes from these Teachings.

February 10, 2008

The next session followed a couple of days after the last one. Amazing how one day from the next can bring such changes. Our special kitty Sarah had once again taken a turn in her health. The "Girls" had helped her once before, but I didn't know if this time they would, or if it was Sarah's decision that the time had come to leave her ailing body.

"We do greet thee."

We greet you also. Today, may we discuss a subject that perhaps not everyone has heard of before—this is Universal Life Force Energy, or ULFE? We know this, of course, to be the energy of the One, but the questions are designed for the individual who will hear of this for the first time.

"First, we would say to understand that ULFE is a term that has been coined by mankind. It is just a name given to that which is simply the One and only energy that exists. There is only One energy, but it fits to call it Universal Life Force Energy."

Energy, in general, has already been discussed in some detail, but what, at this point, can be said to help people understand how to define it and what it is?

"It is difficult to define something that in undefinable. There is only One Energy and there is only One Source of that energy. Energy is Spirit. It is what Spirit emanates, if you will. It is the emanation of the One Spirit that creates all energy. Therefore, all energy that exists within your planet, within the universe, within all that is, comes from the One Energy, from the emanation of the One Spirit. It comes in the form of masculine and feminine energy as directed by the One, dependent upon where it is needed and its purpose."

What would be the best way to explain this to the person who is just awakening?

"It would be difficult for us to give an analogy for there is not just one thing upon your earth that is the source of creation for all things. Things on your earth are made from parts of other things. For example, you do not have just one source for heat. Heat can be produced by gas, by electricity, and also derived through the power of your waters. So you see there are many ways to generate a thing on your earth, whereas Universal Life Force Energy, which is everywhere at all times, is generated from only the One. This energy is directed in many courses, but there is only the One Energy."

A lot of people do not understand their animation, or what gives them life. How do we help them understand that there is only the One Energy that animates them, gives them life, motion, and breath? At all times, they are breathing the Energy of the One and their heart beats with this same energy.

"They must understand that they came from the One, have always been with the One, and shall return to the One. It is the sustaining of you as Spirit, in the Absolute, that is done by the One and by the Love and Energy of the One. The energy of the One is the One Spirit at all times, whether it is in the Absolute or in an incarnation. You come into the physical, as you know, in forgetfulness, but you do not come in without that energy. Maybe that is going to be difficult for some to understand, for each spirit is a part of the whole of the One Energy. You may not remember this, but it still powers your furnace, so to speak. It is that energy that allows your heart to continue beating, your blood to flow, and your mind to continue working. It is the energy you brought from the Absolute that is always with you, for it is you."

That is good. People will relate to that since it has been put into such simple language.

"Generally we have found that the simpler the language, the more complete the understanding."

What we are talking about is the Universal Intelligence.

"This energy, being as it comes from the One, certainly has the intelligence of the One. It may seem simple to us, though difficult to explain it, that you are the expression of the One. It is to what extent you learn to use that energy and to understand it that will help you with your creations along your journey. Once you understand it in its entirety and how to use it in its entirety, there is nothing that can block or bar your way. It is this learning and using that takes what you call 'time.' There are very few who have ever controlled this energy, so to speak."

What can we say to help people understand the universal ramifications of the use of this Energy in their life?

"Everything is an echo. That which you put forth will come back in a myriad of ways. It can come back as a sound if it is a voice you have put out. It can come back as a reaction if it is an energy you have put out. Everything that you do, say, and are will come back to you."

As we, or others, awaken, are there any steps, or sequences, that would help us to understand and be able to use ULFE? Is this a process?

"It will vary with each one. As you are awakening, you have learned how to draw energy into your body and how to properly release it. As the awakening is increasing, others will understand how to use this, how to put forth energy where it is needed."

I am sure that this understanding will create a heightened awareness combined with more knowledge.

"As you are awakened, you will feel the energy. It will be a vibratory humming of Spirit. It will also be with you. You cannot walk down the street, you cannot greet another person, you cannot sit in the sun without 'feeling' this energy around you. It will take 'time' for many to get to that point of actually 'feeling' the energy within themselves, as well as around them.

"They will understand that not only do they contain this energy, and that the energy is available, but they will also begin to 'feel' this energy. You will also 'feel' the energy that comes from others. This is part of what we have spoken about—the 'gut reactions. It is the energy that is sent off from another and encompasses your 'gut,' so to speak, and from that 'feeling,' you will know if that person is someone you desire to spend time with, experience with, or if it is someone you simply bless and allow them to go their own way.

"We hear your creature and she is not quite feeling well."

No, since she had her surgery in January, we have been hoping, wrapping her in Love, and giving her energy to help her little body get stronger.

"She has a very strong willing spirit, but we are not sure that this will be enough to guide her through the issues occurring with her physical body. She is not yet ready to leave. We do see a small blockage across her area of breath."

Yes, her windpipe. We had a tumor removed about a month and a half ago, as you know, but they were unable to remove all of it. We don't know how fast it is growing, so we do not know how much time we have with her. We were hoping that it would allow us another year or two.

"We are not sure of her time. It will be when her spirit realizes her body no longer desires, or is able, to go on. We will send energy to her body."

Thank you so very much. I would like to ask you whether the rise of the vibrational frequency on earth, as a result of the Awakening, will by nature allow doors to open to advanced gifts or abilities.

"Yes, there will be more awareness of one's abilities. As one awakens and the vibration rises, you will open the pathways to many things. There will be those who desire to be healers, to travel in Spirit, to 'see' beyond the physical and communicate with others, and many other gifts to which one will become aware."

What happens with any "extra" energy that results from this rise in vibrational frequency?

"It is simply stored in the solar plexus. There is an unlimited repository there. It is cellular and it is here we know it is accumulated, although it can never be emptied."

How does each individual cell store energy?

"It simply 'expands' to accept all that it is given. There is intelligence within your complete cellular system, and it is to this intelligence that one would speak. You can request health and regeneration while envisioning a healthier body and mind. This massive network exists outside of what is considered 'normal' body function, so had become one of scientists' unexplained phenomenon."

So that intelligence within each cell, which altogether makes up the whole of the physical, connects with the Awakening? Therefore, is there a higher unity within the body itself at the cellular level? The cells are then communicating?

"Yes, though many who are awakening have not necessarily chosen to speak with their physical bodies to make them healthier. They have chosen a part of their journey to experience conditions within their bodies. Although the physical body may not necessarily heal, Spirit and mind will awaken. This may confuse a few for now. Later we will endeavor to explain it in more understanding."

We have talked before about the humming and vibration that is going on, and being felt, with the physical body. For the individual who feels this for the first time, it may be unnerving. It is good to understand it so that it does not become a misunderstanding on the part of those beginning to experience this.

"There will be many who will suddenly begin to experience a physical reaction to their awakening as well as a spiritual reaction. It is something to be aware of should it occur although it may not be noticed by all. If you begin to feel these vibrations, this humming, within, do not fear it for it is a part of your awakening."

Thank you. In regards to the energy centers, or as they are commonly called "the chakras," what are they? Not everyone is necessarily aware of them.

"There is much which has been written about them. Your books are complete with information. The energy centers, as we know them, are simply energy transmission centers within the physical body. It is that which spirit put into effect before you entered into the physical. Spirit came with the centers, so to speak. As Spirit entered into the physical vehicle, it simply put them in place."

How do they function both individually and collectively?

"When the energy centers are working completely open and collectively, then you are awake. You are then totally open to all experiences and to the understanding of these experiences. You understand why the experiences are occurring and why they have occurred. You know what to do about, and with, them. Not all people are totally open like that. If you would look at people with illnesses of the stomach area, the intestinal area, most often one or two of the energy centers in those areas are blocked or closed. This does not allow the healing energy to flow. When the energy centers are open, the energy flows from the head to the feet, or the feet to the head, depending on whether you are drawing energy from the Absolute directly or drawing energy from the earth. Know that all energy comes from the Absolute, but energy that has been given and absorbed by the earth contains within it the aspects the physical realm as well. It is just two ways of receiving the energy to accomplish the intent of the one who is receiving. So if there are certain energy centers that are not open, this can result in physical, emotional, and mental problems. It is important that all centers are opened, which is why in your healing sessions, you must address all of them before beginning the session. It is the cooperation and participation of both the recipient and the practitioner that aids in the opening of the centers."

Most of the books we have read number the energy centers, or chakras. These are numbered from one at the base to seven at the crown. This would perhaps suggest that the energy is only to be drawn from the crown to the feet. What do we do as far as numbering them if we draw energy from both the crown and the feet?

"We would advise you to stay away from numbering the energy centers. It is something that man has done. Even the word 'chakra' is man-made. We simply know them as energy centers, but you may use whichever you desire. To number them would depend upon the way you were receiving the energy. One could be seven, and seven could be one. It is important not to get focused and tied up with numbers."

That is important. With this information, the healing modality book that we are being inspired now to write will introduce chakras as energy centers.

"The physical body is kept moving by the energy that is within Spirit. It is the energy of Spirit that encompasses the human body. These energy centers within the body are the points of Spirit. It is much like a mother ship docking with its space station. It sends out an arm, if you will, to dock with the main station to give it what it requires. Imagine that Spirit is docking with your physical vehicle at each of these energy centers. As you awaken and these energy centers are opened, then each center flows one to the other, allowing Spirit to soar. When one or more remain closed, know that Spirit will work upon those areas to open and awaken them."

It is an endless loop, with the energy flowing back upon itself. It is a continuum of flow when all energy centers are open, a flow that is never ending and never ceasing. Everything is open and functioning.

"If you would visualize Spirit as having a tentacle going to each and every energy center and constantly giving and receiving of energy, the areas that are not yet opened simply do not disperse, or allow, the energy to flow. There is a one-way valve, if you will. These closed centers may receive limited energy, but because they have not fully opened, they cannot give energy to the next center. So the circle, if you will, receives back energy from only those centers that are opened."

So that would describe the way the energy is entering and circulating throughout the body.

"Yes, it encompasses the entire body, but it may only circulate throughout the body by using those energy centers that have awakened and are open."

Should we talk about names or just locations of the energy centers?

"We would say to just speak of locations because, again, the names are just something given by man and can add confusion to something which in actuality is quite simple."

We can discuss both entrance points of the energy whether it is from the Absolute or the earth and that way not get confused by numbers or names.

"If you think about it, when Spirit comes into its physical incarnation, it has brought with it not only forgetfulness but has also brought with it all the tools to awaken. Some of these tools, if you will, are the energy centers. These centers are placed within the physical, and it is this joining that will awaken Spirit and help in remembering who you are."

Are there any minor energy centers, and how important are they?

"The hands, actually the tips of each finger and thumb, are what we call sub-major centers. The soles of each foot are the second sub-major centers. It is the soles, not so much the toes, as the soles of the feet are what remain in contact with mother earth. Little Brother, there will be much more taught, learned, and written about concerning this healing modality. You will write a book for those who will desire to be an energy practitioner. In the application of the energy will also come many of the teachings we are sharing with you. This energy, of course, has always been it is just this particular application that is new."

This is wonderful. As people awaken, they are going to desire to know more about their bodies, the energy, and how the energy works in their bodies.

"There will be much more revealed to you that you will write of in the modality book. Besides the major and sub-major energy centers there lies meridians. These meridians are simply pathways. They are much like your highway systems and are different ways of getting from one point to another. Your blood has a way that it flows throughout the body, it has its direction, and so energy has its own flow as well. The meridians are the pathways for the flow of energy both inside of the physical vehicle as well as for the exterior, and they connect you to all things."

If there is a blockage in an energy center, would there then be a new pathway formed to move around it until it can be cleared?

"Yes, just as the physical body would create its own flow around a failing organ, the meridians would move around an energy center that is blocked. The body has its own intelligence to compensate for a lack within itself and so there is also intelligence within the energy system.

"People have put things into the atmosphere that are not healthy. They have put things into their bodies that are not healthy. They simply have not taken very good care of that which allows them function in the world. Have most been taught from a young age to take care of their bodies? Do they eat the right foods? Do they get plenty of rest, exercise, fresh air, and clean water? If the answer to all these questions was yes, they would not have the problems that your people are now facing. They have put unhealthy foods into their bodies, they overconsume alcohol, they smoke, they have taken mind—and body-altering drugs, and most do not do any continuous form of exercise. Your youth of today are going to have a myriad of problems as they grow because of what they, and their parents, are allowing to be put into their bodies. They do not use their bodies in exercise daily for they seem to be 'plugged in' to some device most of the time. Even though many of these devices bring entertainment, they have also brought much deterioration of the physical."

Are you referring to the diseases that stem from a sedentary lifestyle?

"Yes, and you can choose to change this at any point before your body reaches the point where changes would not be sufficient for its continuance. Through many abuses, or misuses of the body people create a condition, or conditions, that they may not be able to correct. It is sometimes to the point where, even if they were to awaken, Spirit would not be able to help correct these conditions. If one can find within themselves that spark which tells them they are loved, special, and deserving of a healthy body, they can, and do, find the ability to come from behind the walls they have created with food, alcohol, and drugs, to begin creating the physical body that will carry them through their journey. This spark of desire many times also fires the awakening of who they truly are, and it is that understanding of their true self that gives them the strength and determination to create and follow a new path. The experiences they now are creating will take them away from the habits that were destroying them."

Returning to energy storage for a moment, does the person who is not yet awakened store energy within the energy centers?

"Those who have not yet awakened spiritually are simply not aware of the energy at all. We don't know if storing is the proper term, for it is actually the remembering of the energy. As you awaken to your true nature, there begins within the energy centers a remembering as well.

As they remember their purpose, they can draw upon the flow of energy with conscious intention. This energy is of course unlimited."

Is *aura* the correct term to describe the energy field around a person, or any living thing?

"It is a proper term. *Aura* is fine. Some look at it simply as a 'glow' that outlines the body, or any other living object, while we look more deeply at the colors that are present within this 'glow.' Because we deal so much in colors and what each one means, we can tell by viewing the colors which come from within, how a person is feeling, awakening, and opening. This energy field fluctuates with all that is occurring within, emotionally, mentally, and spiritually. It ebbs and flows according to the individual and their place along their journey."

In addition to reflecting the feelings, the moods, and the health of the individual, what else do the colors indicate? Do they indicate the frequency the body is vibrating to at that very moment?

"The distance to which the colors extend would indicate the frequency, or vibration, of the individual at the moment you are 'reading' or seeing their aura. Sometimes people will pull their aura in close to themselves, and this generally means that they are guarding or protecting and they are not sending much energy. There can be many reasons for this guarding or protecting, but it is generally done by those who do not understand either who they truly are or their connection to all things in life. Sometimes the energy may be pulled in when there is illness present and their energy is quite low. At these times, color would be your means of understanding whether an illness is within."

Sometimes when you are showing your colors to us, there seems to be a language of spirit, or a "feeling" associated with the colors. Is this something that can be explained?

"It would be hard to describe, but we will attempt to do so. As you know, we 'speak' and express ourselves with color. The colors we present are also with 'feelings.' We know how, and what, another is relaying not only by the color they are emanating but also by the 'feeling' that engulfs us in that moment. Our colors indicate questions, Love, observations, and many of the things that you express in verbal terms. The one difference is that when you express with words, you may not be saying what you truly feel. Colors always tell the 'truth.' An analogy would be your stop lights. You know that when you see red, it means to stop, yellow means to use caution, and green means go. There is no other interpretation of those colors. Where words can be misinterpreted or used to deceive, colors cannot. When we see the color of another, we know what the 'feeling' is and the true thought or questions being relayed."

When we look at this in that way, then you must have a vast array of colors to express every "feeling" and every possible expression of those "feelings." You must incarnate with the knowledge already within yourself of what all the colors mean. This is your way to communicate with each other.

"Yes, this is a knowledge we are born with. We bring this understanding with us to our physical vehicle. It is our communication system, and we would not expect you to completely understand or comprehend. Yet you do have the capability of looking at a person and seeing their color, their aura. Your planet has not awakened to this level of communication for it is not what the intent is for this world and incarnation."

I understand that when you read an aura, you may see many different colors, but does Spirit come in with its own color? What about the colors of the Divine Parents or Yeshua?

"Spirit does come in to this incarnation with its own 'core' color. You will have many colors that will also occur within your aura, depending upon where you are in your awakening and where you are physically, emotionally, mentally, and spiritually. You will always be 'known' in the Absolute by your color, and those colors will also be recognized between people who are opening and awakening to this understanding.

"The Divine Parents also have unique colors, and it is by these colors that you will recognize them during times of meditation while conducting healing sessions and when being given inspirations. Yeshua also has a 'core' color just as you do. It is for you to know and remember that he is Spirit who entered into the physical with less forgetfulness, therefore having greater knowledge to impart and teach to those who chose to hear. All were created with the expansion and intention of the One, which makes everyone a part of the whole and connected one to the other."

As we continue to awaken and express ourselves as who we truly are, Spirit, will our colors become more intense?

"Yes, as one awakens and Spirit remembers, your colors will become brighter, more vibrant, and will extend further out from your physical body."

Thank you for all the wonderful information on colors. One more thought about meditation. Is it best to focus on a particular program, or ritual, or is it of more value to simply reach that place of silence?

"You do not need programs or rituals, simply sit, breathe deep, and find your focus. When the chatter of the mind interferes with the silence, the stillness, simply refocus upon your breath. People think that they must follow a program or ritual to obtain the stillness, and this again makes something which is simple, become complex. If you are thinking of all the steps you must take, and in what order to take them, then you are not 'being' in the moment 'being' in the silence."

We understand that there is an upper limit to the vibrational level the physical body can receive.

"If you try to go beyond what your body can contain, then it must try to 'expand' in order hold all that you are attempting to give it. At some point, when it can no longer 'expand,' it will be rejoined to that which is the Absolute and no longer be of the physical realm. The body would cease to be. As long as you are aware that there is a point that your awakening can no longer be contained within your physical body, while you are still intending to experience in the physical. Spirit, mind, and body know what that point is and will protect you from going beyond that point. If Spirit, mind, and body choose to continue with increasing the vibration, then they would do so in agreement and with the 'knowing' that it will end the physical experience. The goal of the fully awakened person is to reach the level of what is now possible for the full attainment of Spirit within the physical body."

Thank you for this wonderful, informative, and very important teaching.

"You are most welcome, Little Brother. This has been a long session for Little One, and so we shall now depart in Love and Blessings."

This session was long and so very interesting and informative. It really gave us so many things to talk about and understand. I particularly loved the portion on colors. I had been seeing colors around people from a very young age, but this helped me to understand so much more about them. I have read many books on color interpretation, but now I know that those colors are not going to necessarily mean the same thing for each person. It really does depend on what is going on with them.

Sarah, our kitty, had been restless again for about a week. We knew that her surgery in January (which I wrote about in the January 17 session) did not completely remove the growth that was slowly blocking her vocal chords and was so very difficult to remove. We had received some encouragement from the surgeon that although it may grow again, it was benign and very slow moving. We took this as hopeful news. Sarah almost immediately had returned to her old self, and her meow was no longer as distorted or gravelly sounding. We were really happy when she actually began to like the special food for her kidney problem.

She had been doing really well until a short time before this last session. Her meow was still normal, but we noticed she was becoming agitated again. The "Girls" told us during the session that it was now Sarah's choice (or rather her body's) as to when she would leave. They did say that they would endeavor to work with her, which they did. We also knew from their explanation that it was Sarah's desire to stay with us but that her physical body was not cooperating. We had learned that animals do not always have the same expression of the recuperative power, influenced by Spirit, that we as humans have been given. Still it was her spirit's desire to go on. So the "Girls," in their own way, removed the remainder of the tumor so that Sarah could continue her journey with us. This was truly a miracle of healing. Even her vet could not explain it, but we knew. She desired, in spirit, to remain in her physical body. We have been and are forever grateful for the "Girls'" outpouring of love. There is more to Sarah's journey, which I will tell you about later on.

This whole lesson with Sarah led us to a greater understanding of the healing modality as well. We had been told that when we joined with the Spirit of the person we were sending energy to, we would be able to "see" if it was still the Spirit's desire to continue even though the physical body was experiencing difficulties. We learned that not every person who is experiencing physical ailments would necessarily be healed in a session, or sessions. Sometimes Spirit has chosen to experience certain conditions while incarnated, and if that is the desire, then healing may not occur. On the other side of the coin, if it is the desire of Spirit to experience the healing of the body, but the body is not in harmony or unity with Spirit, it may not respond as desired. It is a joining, or comingling, of desires on both the part of Spirit and the physical body. This is why all energy centers are opened prior to conducting a session and we speak to the recipient regarding their intent and desire for the session. We have seen healing occur in so many ways, from mental, emotional, and spiritual, as well as physical. I never try to second-guess the energy as I know and believe that it will do exactly what it is intended to do. The practitioner acts as the "funnel" for the energy, but it is the intent and desire of the recipients that disperses the energy.

We speak quite a bit on the energy centers, meridians, and the attributes of Universal Live Force Energy. I did leave out some of the more detailed aspects as Bruce was going to be writing a book on the healing modality. This book would contain everything we had been given and taught. As of the day I am writing this second Teachings book, that modality book has been written and published. We have already trained many practitioners and will be speaking with and training more this summer. I don't want to get ahead of my time line, so I will leave more on that till the end.

February 17, 2008

This next session was a short one to discuss what it means to be unlimited in our potential as Spirit in physical form.

"We do greet thee. As always, we are ready for your questions."

What do we need to know at this point concerning unlimited potential?

"Unlimited potential is, as you said, unlimited. When arriving at the awakening stage of one's journey, they should be aware that they are unlimited, that there is no limit for Spirit. Potential is unlimited, but it is just potential. The actualization of acquiring physical manifestation from that potential, in its unlimited form, is an unknown while one is in physical form. There are so many inhibiting factors to achieving full potential, such as vibrational frequency, density of the collective consciousness, limits of your physical vehicle, and the 'time' on your earth that it would require to accomplish this. Spirit is unlimited in all things while in the Absolute but once incarnated is bound to those vibrations."

Would it be correct to say that this is our "birthright" as an individual expression of the One?

"When you came from the Absolute, you had all the understanding of yourself as pure Spirit, and of your connection to the One. Now that you have entered into the earth's vibration, it is a matter of remembering. The amount you remember as to your unlimited potential will be dependent upon those things of which we have already spoken."

Is the knowledge of unlimited potential then a by-product of remembering?

"Yes, for until you begin to remember who you truly are, you will be unable to grasp the understanding of unlimited potential."

People will ask about the process of transformation, within humanity, that will occur with the elevation of the vibrational level of the earth.

"As your vibrational level, your frequency, upon this earth rises, your physical ability to grasp or to understand different levels, different dimensions, is very possible. It will be a matter of whether or not this particular remembering was a choice you made before your incarnation."

Another facet is for people to take a very honest look at themselves as far as what abilities they now have versus the abilities they would desire to have and what they are going to with what they have.

"You may choose to be a ballerina, yet you have no coordination. This lack of coordination would indicate that this was not an ability you chose while in the Absolute. Once you realize this potential, as a ballerina, was not part of your 'blueprint,' you can do several things. You can take dance classes in the desire to improve, or to encourage changes within your inability, and with practice, you can improve. To say that you can take it to its fullest potential is not necessarily so, because it is not an ability you chose to come into this incarnation with. We say necessarily so because if one has a strong desire, they may modify their 'blueprint' in order to experience this desire. Your full potential, as unlimited Spirit, allows you to remember the possibility of making this change or modification. So much depends upon your awakening to this fact, your choices along your journey, and the vibration and frequencies you currently move within."

Are we talking about the restrictions of the lower vibrational frequency as it affects the body and brain? Is there an upper limit as to what can be accomplished even though we may aspire to a higher level of development?

"If you chose, in Spirit, to come in with the ability to dance while physically incarnated, then you can easily increase that potential. You must realize that many have come in with potentials that they never use because they never awaken to become aware of them. Maybe it does not serve them for some reason to pull out, or develop, those potentials. Many times they choose other experiences along their path."

Can the individual, once they begin to become more adept at meditation, use this to discover potentially untapped, or unknown, areas in which they have abilities?

"It is a matter of listening to your 'gut,' if you will, and you must have the desire. Spirit may have desired to give the physical body, that it chose, four different potentials. Yet once you actually incarnate into the physical and begin your journey, you may chose and desire to experience only one of them. It does not mean you lose the others, it simply means that for some reason, some choice, Spirit decided it did not resonate with all of those potentials it arrived with."

All those potentials would be a part of the "blueprint," wouldn't they?

"Yes, they would, and it is your choice upon your remembering your true nature as to how many, or any, you desire to experience."

From time to time, we have talked about geographical areas that have higher vibrational levels that were left for this very time we are now in. Within these higher vibrational areas, can we tap into the higher degree of energy to raise our potential? I understand that the lower frequencies of other areas may not allow this potential to be utilized in the present moment.

"It stands to reason, of course, that if you are in an area of higher vibrational frequency, and you are aware of those frequencies because you have awakened to your spiritual potential, you will increase with that energy level."

Perhaps a good piece of advice for people is to allow Spirit to lead. Spirit will always know what the maximum level is at any given time.

"Yes, Little Brother. We have followed your people and understand that the one thing they do is to 'run wild' with an idea. They do not take the time to really understand the concept behind the idea and what its purpose is or what it is meant to do. They run wild when they hear the words 'unlimited potential' and immediately think they can run out and become a millionaire or multimillionaire with very little, to no, effort. If this is not something that was in your 'blueprint,' then you must modify it to begin with, and then there must be an action to create such an influx of monetary compensation. It is not going to just, *poof,* occur. You have not gotten close to that expression of creation, feeling/ occurrence. You are still in thought/action and this is how many, many are creating their experiences. Some are ever so slowly coming out of thought/action and into thought/manifestation. This does not mean that just because you think something that it will instantly occur, but the difference between the two thoughts is the action. In both instances, you will take an action, but in thought/manifest, the action you take will be aided by your understanding that your desire has already manifested and is complete within the spiritual realm. Your action is then aided by this knowledge. Those who are strictly in thought/action are generally those who have also not awakened to who they are."

This is very good advice. We realize that there are things that are our potentials if we choose to act on them, but there are also matters of more practical concern.

"There have been many books written regarding manifestation. We see them all of the time. What many of them do, unfortunately, is make a person believe that all they have to do is believe. When this manifestation does not occur they begin to think something is 'wrong' with them, or that there was something 'wrong' with the book they read. Therefore, they become disillusioned. The unfortunate thing is not only that they become disillusioned to that particular writing, but they put all writings of this sort into the same category. When they dismiss everything, then that which will resonate with them may never be found. We caution to not run out thinking that anything you want, or desire, is immediately yours. As always, there will be an action to accompany the desire. We do not wish for people to become disillusioned with something they have read because it did not work for them in the way they were told that it would.

"People are told to simply put your desire 'out there,' believe and concentrate on it, and it will happen. There must, at some point in the process of 'putting it out there,' an action taken for every thought. For instance, you desire a better job. If you, day after day, go to the job that you already have and do nothing except continue to go to that job, the percentages of acquiring another job are quite low. But if you go to your current job every day and in the meantime you are also sending out resumes to other places, other potentials, then the percentages of receiving another job, one you desire, are considerably raised. The desire for the intended purpose fuels that acquisition, but the action works hand in hand with that desire."

So if we were going to give, in Love, a word of caution to the reader, what would we say to them at this time?

"We would say to go slowly and to understand that what you desire may be achieved. That desire, seen as completed in the Absolute and with true understanding of its spiritual completion, will go along with the actions you take to acquire it. Once you have taken all action that you can, then you must in complete trust let it go and allow it to find its way to you. Continue to create and experience your creations while you wait, in trust, for your desire to manifest. Know that there is 'no time' in which this may occur and that sometimes there is something so much more than that which you envisioned. Spend your 'time' not in waiting but in creating, experiencing, and living your life to its fullest."

Little One read an article about an opening of Divine masculine/ feminine energy, which would aid in remembering, from the fifteenth to the nineteenth of this month. She explained to me that the understanding you gave her was that this remembrance would be like peeling off a crust. Could you please explain what you meant?

"This opening, as we explained to Little One, would be as if you were holding a balloon and you wrapped a layer of cotton around it. Imagine that there are people within this balloon, yet even if you popped the balloon, they would not be able to get out due to the layer of cotton. The people on your planet incarnated in forgetfulness, and the earth, to a degree, is also in forgetfulness. Although Spirit never really 'forgets,' it simply agrees to enter in forgetfulness. This layer, or crust, of forgetfulness also surrounds your physical universe. What will be happening on the dates you mentioned is much like a flaking, or peeling, of that layer. This peeling will allow the influx of a stronger surge of energy from the Absolute to come into certain areas."

Can this be equated to the analogy of the onion that you gave us earlier? Is this just a peeling back of layers so that we get to the point where the crust is more and more transparent and allows more energy to flow?

"We do not believe this occurrence will allow a continuous flow, it will happen on and off in a period of 'time.' For example, if a dam had a very small crack and small amounts of water were able to seep through, this would be acceptable and manageable. If this crack was not repaired and sealed, the entire dam could begin to crack and be destroyed. This dam is much like the crust of forgetfulness around your earth and the energy that is allowed through that small flaking. If too much energy was released, it could actually destroy the earth. It would be too much, too quickly, and much too strong. The forgetfulness is part of your journey just as the remembering is. From time to time there occurs the allowance of these small openings. This energy is utilized by those who are awake to help heal the earth, give energy and love to everyone, aid in healing, and begin the balancing of Divine masculine/feminine energy on the earth."

You mentioned these openings can be used in healing. Is this also true for receiving inspiration?

"Yes. It is for the healing of self, of your planet, for inspiration, for growth, and for awakening. As this energy settles down upon each one who is awakening, it will help them exponentially upon their journey and their growth."

So it is to be drawn by intent?

"Yes, once you are aware of it, you can intentionally draw it. For many who are awake may not have heard of this opening, but although they did not know of it or how to draw from it, they will certainly 'feel' something from it. They may not be aware of where that 'feeling' is coming from, but they still share a part of this energy. Those who have yet to awaken will simply not know or 'feel' anything."

Thank you so much for this explanation and for all that you have taught us.

"We are most joyous to do so. For us the 'time' of rejoining of the council comes quickly. This will be wonderful of course. We are looking forward, in Love, to this 'time.' We are busy and doing many things with several others at this time. We are not bringing the Teachings to others, but we are giving energy to those of our planet who are working with others. It is certainly a time of growth and change. Be aware during the next four days of your 'time' of all climatic changes that occur. There will be many changes in the form of earthquakes, several big storms at sea, and a possible volcano that has been quiet. There is nothing to worry about for this is simply a stretching of the Mother. These changes will increase with 'time.' These are earth changes and are not associated with the energy openings."

Thank you for this information.

"You, as always, are most welcome. For now, Little Brother, we shall depart in Love and Blessings."

This session, while short, was very interesting for both of us. Unlimited potential, and how we express this within the finite physical world, was quite fascinating. We understood that the earth's vibrational frequency, and our own which is aligned with that of the earth, would directly influence our ability to manifest advanced abilities. We would begin to become aware of these abilities as we continued to awaken. It was very clear from this teaching that raising the earth's vibration would, in turn, open the door for a transformation that could affect all of humanity. This would occur, providing everyone chose to embrace such advancement. This would mean a massive shift in the current collective consciousness, allowing the new one to unfold. In the meantime, the best we can do is search out those specific areas on earth that have the highest energy frequencies known at this time. At least that would give us a head start on this process, and earth changes will bring about an elevation in these frequencies.

The opening spoken of was one that both Bruce and I felt strongly about. I had a basic understanding of it from what I had read on the Internet, but their explanation made is so much clearer and they "connected the dots" for me. Our experience with this energy was felt quite strongly during the opening. We even continued to "feel" the energy that was left from this for weeks to come.

February 23, 2008

A rather remarkable event had occurred the day before, in the afternoon. So before this next session, I will take you to that event first, and then on with the questions and answers from this evening session.

"We do greet thee. We have come because you have called."

Greetings, Dear Ones, I called because we wanted to ask about what occurred with Little One yesterday afternoon. This was quite a remarkable thing.

(Author's note: I was a little reluctant to even share this experience with anyone as I didn't want to, in any way, seem less credible. The "Girls" have always stressed the fact of credibility, which is why they don't answer many "fortune telling" types of questions. I decided to share this story because it is so remarkable and I hope will be enlightening to all who read it.)

"It is because of the close relationship we have with Little One that we were able to do this. We simply did this to discover what was going on in Little One's body, and how she could be helped. It was discovered that there is a blockage, if you will, but we believe that this can be worked upon. We will attempt, with Little One's help, to remove this blockage ourselves with the help of the one that Little One has chosen to call 'Dr. Mike.' We believe this blockage has been built upon stress and therefore can be corrected. It is much the same as when you put stress on your gallbladder, by directing your stress toward it, and caused it to be diseased. Little One is also doing this to her body even though she is not consciously aware of it. Her stress is being directed to her stomach area and this is where it is accumulating and acting out. We will send her much calming energy, and with her meditation, we will break down this buildup of stress. 'Dr. Mike' did an 'examination' to see that most things are working well and functioning efficiently as they should be. It is just this one blockage. We 'know' that healing sessions will also greatly aid in the correction of this blockage. It would be beneficial for there to be no stress, but we understand that this is not an easy time. This is where the choices of how you accept and allow things to affect you can be strongly seen. Once you have left this area and the stress that was allowed from your circumstances, this blockage will also dissolve."

Would it be a very good idea if we just took her up to northern California now?

"There is much to be accomplished here, and it would be whether you believe that you could accomplish everything on your own. There is the sale of your items to be completed and much rearranging of things. There will be two trips required regardless of when you go, so it is up to you to choose, if you desire, to accomplish things on your own."

I am fine with doing the things myself. I will leave that decision up to Little One. Normally I would have stayed with the plan to go up on the fourth or fifth of April with the first load, come back and sell off everything, and then go back to Happy Camp after that. This seems to be the most constructive use of our time.

"As always, it will be up to you and Little One to make those choices."

Thank you. I am fascinated with "Dr. Mike." Is he from your planet?

"Yes, he simply appeared in a particular-looking 'feeling form' to make it easier for Little One. It was for her benefit to take a form with which she is familiar."

She said she really enjoyed the green scrubs, white mask, and blond hair.

"Yes, for this is the familiar way your physicians cloak themselves."

Should we focus healing energy on her abdominal area?

"We would suggest you work from the heart center to the base center. This is the area she is retaining the most stress in and it is, of course, the biggest section of your physical body as well."

Very good, we shall focus on that. Should this be done on a daily basis?

"We understand your difficulty, in the moment, of doing anything on a daily basis. Do this as much as you choose to do."

We will definitely incorporate it into our daily activities. Is there anything else that Little One and I should know in regard to "Dr. Mike's" examination?

"Only that she should listen more closely to the urgings of her body as far as the foods she is eating. She knows what does and does not work. It seems that the things she ingests with higher cholesterol are not necessary and are not working well with her body. She can do a rearranging, if you will, of the things she eats."

I know that you are helping her with a clearer understanding of those things that serve her body and she is greatly appreciative. She has mentioned that she feels the "humming" now.

"She has had the humming for quite a while, but it is just that she did not recognize what it was. Now that she is recognizing it, for what it is, it is right."

I would like to ask you a question today about spiritual expression. What exactly does this term mean?

"It is simply the expression of your physical body that is blending and mingling with Spirit. Spiritual expression is what which you show outwardly for it cannot be seen within. It can only be seen from without. Spiritual expression is living your life in a way that comes from Spirit, loving, caring, compassionate, and truly finding your joy and happiness. When you are 'being' who you know you are, then that expression and knowledge is then presented to others for their understanding. You allow Spirit to be 'seen' encompassing the physical."

Other than "feelings," what are the other ways, or means, of spiritual expression that should be exhibited by the awakening person?

"It should be, above all else, love. If you are truly awakening, then you cannot help but give Love to all those you encounter. If you find that you are unable to do this in all instances, then you realize you still have some awakening to do. Spiritual expression is expressing Spirit, because we know that Spirit is complete energy and Love. It would be the expression of this energy and Love that is the ultimate for the awakening person."

People may ask if there is a limit to spiritual expression, or is it unlimited?

"Limit is only that which you put upon yourself. It is through your idea that there is limit, that limit exists. Spirit is not limited therefore the expression of Spirit is not limited. You can Love and show Love to many. You can give to many. Of course, we understand that while you are in the physical you may anticipate, or believe, that your ability to give is limited to your financial position. If you only give of what you are able, your time, your guidance, and your commitment, then in that way, you are not limited. Share your time, give as a volunteer, mentor someone, or just be there in times of someone's reduced energy. There are numerous ways you can express this giving."

Is there a progression in your spiritual expressions that could be used as a yardstick to measure your degree of awakening? Many will ask how do they know they are awake.

"At this point within the Teachings, they should certainly know if they are awake or not. If they are not awake by now, they would not be reading this that is being written. As they continue the journey, along with the Teachings, the awakening will come through spiritually understanding who they are and what they have now become. They 'know' they are not a physical body alone and now are beginning to see through the eyes of Spirit."

Is the level of their spiritual expression also giving them an understanding of their level of awareness and consciousness?

"Yes, for if they are still caught up in ego, if they are still finding themselves with moments of anger, moments of fear, then they know they still have work to do upon their awakening path."

Thank you. We have spoken on this term "feeling" before, but could we speak a little further on this topic?

"Feeling is something that is not only of thought but is physical as well, and it all comes from Spirit. It is difficult to explain, or to understand, for 'feeling' just is. It is something that you know within yourself to be truth. People know when they are about to do something that is not being Spirit. They have a warning, they have that 'gut' reaction. The mind may get involved and say this is not the way to go, but sometimes they ignore this and continue on their own way. So 'feeling' is that which will talk to you. It is that which will lead you if you would but listen to it. It is part of Spirit, it is Spirit expressing itself. Because Spirit is in, and encompasses, the physical body, this 'feeling' will express itself in a physical way."

People will ask how to develop this "feeling" as they awaken. Perhaps they are not quite sure as yet because they have been ego-based in the feelings until they began to awaken.

"As you are awakening, this 'feeling,' this 'knowing,' is also awakening. It is growing along with your awakening. If you walk hand in hand with it, you cannot help to notice it, for you will feel differently. Some people, at the thought of something joyful, may get a quickening of the heart. Also, when they are about to do something they know is not expressing who they truly are, they may get a churning of the stomach. The physical will speak to them. As they progress upon the path of awakening the 'knowing' of this 'feeling' will become stronger. It is to follow this 'feeling' that will guide you down the path of spiritual awakening."

Is the "feeling" then actually cellular?

"Yes, because Spirit encompasses the physical. The physical body is composed of cells that move with and without the physical body. The complete understanding of this cellular level is known only by a few, but they are sharing this knowledge with others. So you can say, of course, that 'feeling' is indeed of a cellular nature."

Is there a difference of "feeling" within the body, mind, and Spirit? Are they expressed each in its own way, or do they combine for a full expression? In other words, will each begin "feeling" something and then combine for a total body, mind, and Spirit experience of "feeling"?

"It will be a total involvement. There will be, for example, feelings that relate specifically to the physical. If you break a leg you will feel pain, but that is a different type of feeling. The 'feeling' we speak of generally will occur within the gut region, or solar plexus, or within the heart energy center. These 'feelings' are not caused by actual physical pain, but by your 'knowing.' They are the system of guidance as you make your choices and create your experiences. Trust in what your body is telling you when making these choices and know that Spirit is in the lead."

People will want to know how do they begin to recognize these "feelings" for what they are.

"They will just know. These will become a part of them. The sensation of these types of 'feelings' may make them uncomfortable at first, or be perceived as uncomfortable, but once they begin to get in tune with their purpose, they will settle into their understanding."

For people who are still ego-based in their feelings, this is going to be difficult.

"If they are still ego-based, Little Brother, they are not very far along on the Path. The dropping, or shedding, of the ego is necessary for them to continue walking the Path. They must be aware of these types of feelings as they occur, that they are ego-based, and drop them. They no longer serve them."

So we can say that they begin to develop this spiritual expression of "feeling" as they awaken and as they raise their awareness and consciousness.

"Yes, before they were awake, they were not aware of anything which is of Spirit. They are certainly aware of pain, for this is physical pain. They are believing and aware of limit, this causes them fear. They are aware of all ego-based emotions. They are not aware of spiritual emotion because they cannot yet see or understand that concept."

In regard to spiritual communication, "feeling" is going to be new. What can we do to help others in the understanding of this?

"Each must find their own mode of expression. Joy expresses it best in order to get to that which we are feeling and trying to communicate. The example we would give is this: you walk up to someone you haven't seen for a while, and without any words, you engulf them in a hug. They now 'feel' that you have missed them. You do not have to verbally say, 'Oh, I have missed you.' It will be your expression of Spirit that will enable them to 'feel' your emotion. This is much the same way that we communicate we simply touch to be understood. We do not have need for words. When we come here to 'speak' through the physical voice of Little One, we are required to use many words because that is your way of communication. Where we are from, we simply 'feel' another's joy or question. This is the best way that we could explain this to you."

At our level of evolution, words are all that most people believe they have to communicate. Much is made about expressing oneself in words, especially between two people in a relationship. One is always wondering why the other one does not share themselves in words.

"Yes, we have seen this. It is because there still is the 'need' to be reassured of another's interest and intentions and this 'needs' to be expressed in words. A touch, a smile, commitment, a wordless sharing does not seem to be sufficient for most, and this is because of where they are and who they believe themselves to be. They are still bound by ego and do not understand their true essence. This can all be changed by those who are growing in the understanding of who they are. Try it yourself. When you greet someone, look them in the eyes, smile, engulf their hand in yours, and then say the words 'It is a joy to meet you.' Let your 'feelings' speak first, before your words.

"Your little creature has entered and senses our presence. We feel that her energy has weakened since we last spoke with you. However, she is not yet ready to leave. We will again see what can be done for her. We have 'spoken' with her and she knows that when she makes her decision to leave her physical body, she shall go in her true essence, Spirit, home with us. We are joyful to have her as a part of our family. She will always be with us until she may decide to reincarnate once again. As you know, there is no beginning, no ending, and if her choice was not to be with us, then she would simply return to the Absolute. We have all chosen and it is agreed she shall come be with us. She knows that she is already a part of our family."

What can we say about the relationship of "feeling" to "knowing" in spiritual expression?

"Once you understand that 'knowing' is a spiritual intellect, then the understanding of 'feeling' cannot but help go with it. You cannot have a 'knowing' without a 'feeling.' You will 'feel' the 'knowing,' for one cannot be without the other."

Is there a point of origin for "knowing"? Is there a point in the body? Is it also cellular?

"It is Spirit, that which encompasses you within and without. This point of origin begins with, and continues with, Spirit. It is felt on all levels, spiritual, physical, mental, and cellular."

How does "knowing" differ from thought?

"The 'knowing' comes from spiritual intellect. Thought comes from physical intellect. To have a physical thought requires the input of knowledge; you could not have a thought if you did not have words. Speech occurs with a physical thought and all the words you have acquired within your bràin appear to you to be your only true means of communication. This is physical intellect. Spiritual intellect, or 'knowing,' which is what we prefer to call it, is simply part of who you are when you know yourself as Spirit. It does not require speech, or words. It is not a thought, it is a spiritual way of 'being' that reaches far beyond physical words. This 'knowing,' hand in hand with 'feeling,' is the ultimate expression and communication of Spirit."

Is this a process that will become automatic at some point with those who have awakened?

"Exactly, it is like learning anything. You start from point A and think about each step. Once you have learned it, when you have understood and learned all the steps, it becomes the accumulation of all the training that gets you to the point of not 'thinking' about it. It just simply is."

Thank you. Is it only possible for us to have a unified experience when body, mind, and Spirit are as one?

"Yes."

If it is coming from somewhere else, then we are still in ego?

"Yes, Little Brother, you have it well."

That is an excellent guideline for people who desire to know. This is how you "know."

"If it is not from the unified body, mind, and Spirit, they have more work to do."

Can an individual intend that this ability will increase as they use it?

"It is as any ability. The more you exercise it, the more you will learn to use it. If you were to take up tennis, you would need to learn how to get the ball over the net and deliver it to the spot you desire it. This is minimal at first. As you go on, and with time and practice, the ability grows. This ability then becomes second thought."

People often look for landmarks to enable them to see if they are progressing in their understanding, and use, of spiritual expression. As they continue to awaken and journey on the Path to Oneness, these mileposts along the way help them to gauge their progress.

"One day they will simply stop and say, 'I'm happy.' I have no perceived problems. They will know that this is another sign that they are achieving what they desire. They can wake up every day in joy of what will occur that day and will go through the day sharing joy with others. They will 'feel' and 'know' that they are an integral part of everything and everyone around them. They are awakening. They are well on the path to awakening."

Awakening is like a tunnel with many offshoots, each offshoot having its own door. Behind all these doors are abilities that can be used once the choice is made to open the door. As they open these doors, one may discover new abilities that they never realized they even had.

"This is truth. They may suddenly be able to paint, or write music. They may discover many new ways to creatively express themselves. These doors open spiritual pathways to remembering that which you chose while in the Absolute, that which you created in your 'blueprint.' With the process of Awakening comes the opening of these doors to discover who you are, why you are here, and how you create all your experiences."

The wonderful thing about this is this is the way we learn to express ourselves as eternal spiritual beings. There are a lot of people who think they have to go out and do something that is extraordinary. They do not realize that this is the expression of who they are. It is a spiritual expression and every expression of Spirit is equally important.

"How can someone, for instance, be in a concert listening to the music of your composers Mozart or Bach and not 'feel' the spiritual feelings this music gives to them, even without their knowledge or understanding that they were expressing Spirit through their music? If you listen to a concert violinist or pianist play, you will see that they are simply expressing Spirit through music. If you watch a painter who puts upon the canvas colors that bring physical tears to your eyes, how can you believe that they are doing anything but expressing Spirit?"

Thank you. Is there anything else on spiritual expression?

"Just simply to be aware of it. To be in knowledge that it will happen as you continue along the path of your journey. You cannot help but express spirit when you truly understand that you are Spirit. For now, Little Brother, we do depart in Love and Blessings,"

This was the end of a very interesting and informative session. I would love to share with you the whole "adventure" of Dr. Mike.

I had gone into take a nap, and a short while later, I "felt" a presence in the room with me. Of course I had felt the "Girls" with me many times before, but this was different somehow. I could actually see a figure standing by the side of the bed, and although I could see through it, it was nonetheless very clear and fully formed. If it hadn't been for all the time spent with the "Girls," I probably would have gone screaming down the hall. Instead I just laid there and received an "examination" that was both fascinating and entertaining all at once. Before me was a figure dressed in green surgical scrubs, blond hair hanging out of a surgical cap, and wearing green latex surgical gloves. Somehow this struck me as hilarious. I had a highly evolved being dressed in soap opera–style doctor garb. What a great sense of humor these loving beings have, I couldn't help but laugh. I understand now that this was the purpose for the "getup," to relax me and put me at ease. The "exam" was not uncomfortable at all, just the tickling sensation of things being moved around somewhat. Most of this I observed to be happening in my stomach area, but again there was no discomfort. "Dr. Mike" introduced himself, not with words but with "feeling," and "asked" permission to proceed. Well, how could anyone refuse that request? Afterward, the "Girls" explained to me what had been found. They answered all of my questions so that I completely understood what had happened and how I could now take steps to improve my health and well-being. To follow their suggestions would of course be my choice. There were other important things that I learned as a result of this experience. Even though they have the ability to "see" our true state of health, there is also a density, a blocking, due to the current lowered vibration of our planet. So a "physical" exam was necessary to gain full knowledge of my health. However, as time and reflection brings clarity to any subject, we feel it was actually genius in action. The reassurance I felt from knowing that "Dr. Mike" had literally seen me from the inside out gave me a confidence that I had not experienced before. My trust in him and the "Girls" was enough for me to lift myself out of a stressful and difficult period in my life.

At this point in our lives, we were under quite a bit of stress. The telephone rang incessantly from early in the morning to late at night, and weekends were no exception. The calls from creditors came, and came, and came. We really tried answering them all at first and explaining our circumstances, but after some downright and very ugly conversations, we simply stopped answering the phone. They didn't care, not about us or how hard we were trying to stay afloat. We had been gradually selling off our furniture and belongings to try and survive, at least until we could find that open door to financial increase. It seemed as if all the doors were shut tight and bolted. I submitted hundreds of applications for jobs, but never received an answer. I know there were so many in that same boat and our vast numbers were slowly sinking it. We seemed to be running out of lifelines. The stress level was to the point where Bruce and I weren't sure how much more of this particular experience we could endure.

All of the past months had taken their toll. As I look back, it was a miracle we were able to write any books during this phase. Even though there was much more to come, it seemed as though things just could not get any worse. We thought of just packing it in, selling out everything, and shutting up the house. We really had both had enough.

In looking back, there was a period of relief which began with this "examination." It was indeed a direct intervention in our lives, for I strongly desired some help, just a little help. As usual we had no idea of the incredible events that were about to unfold. I will share these as our journey continues.

Spiritual expression is a very important one to spend some time reflecting on. It takes time and effort, but the peace of mind you find from developing these abilities will get you through anything you will face in life. Since the source of this level of knowledge is Spirit, you are completely removed from the biased emotions of the physical mind in ego. You begin to see and understand the true significance of what you are experiencing in life, not just what you can physically see and hear. These things of the physical are not reliable and will only send you down a roller coaster of fear-based emotions and completely stress you out. We know we have been there. Learning to develop these natural abilities of spiritual expression in what was such a difficult time was beyond hard. But in looking back, it was well worth the ride.

The "Girls" have such an ability to "know" how much we can endure. When we seemed to be at the end of our rope, it was "time" to reveal these incredible abilities so that we could continue. Over the years we have known them, they have been a constant source of love, guidance, and inspiration in our lives. It is the outpouring of their energy, and Love, which has enabled us to, as they would say, "continue" to this day.

Just as the story with "Dr. Mike" was a remarkable event, little did we know that the next ones were only days away.

This experience is one I am not likely to ever forget. This may sound a little "out there" too many, and believe me, I don't blame you. If I hadn't already experienced the "Girls" and many other unexplained things along my journey, I probably wouldn't understand or believe it either. This was still an experience I had to share regardless of any less-than-positive feedback.

February 28, 2008

In this session, we began to learn more regarding "earth changes," what they are and why they are occurring.

"We do greet thee. How are you on this your evening? You have questions for us?"

Yes. We haven't really talked much about earth changes. What should our response be toward them as they unfold?

"You should be aware that they are to come. We believe we have touched somewhat upon these happenings. Simply do not be frightened by them, but observe them and understand they are necessary for growth and evolution. However, these changes can, and will, bring about those exact feelings of fear in your people, even for those who are now awakening. If you live in an area that is being affected, know that this is ultimately for good. Not all changes will occur from natural sources, some of these are created due to the choices that mankind has made. It is what has been put into the air, the water, and the ground. These choices are changing the air quality, the ozone layer, your drinking water, and many of your natural habitats. The things done, or not done, will bring about many of the earth changes. These can be corrected by those who are awakening and understand their connection with, and too, the earth and everything and everyone upon it. New choices can be made and new conditions created."

Many "doomsday" advocates speak about this subject, but destruction of the planet is not the purpose of these changes.

"No, we do not desire anyone to be thinking of something like what has been spoken of, an apocalypse. This is certainly not something like that. These changes are just something to be made aware of. Be observant and know how some of these changes are happening. If possible, do not put yourself in an area in which 'natural' changes are occurring. If you reside in one of these areas, then stay alert and be prepared.

"Even we do not know of all that will transpire. We are not privy to the understanding ourselves exactly when earthquakes, tornadoes, floods, or droughts will appear or where they will appear. We cannot know in this 'time' what the severity of them may be. Therefore, as we have cautioned, be prepared as much as you are able to be, especially if you live in an area where these may present themselves."

**Thank you. On a different subject, many people will wonder what the
next stage is for their physical and spiritual development as a result of
their awakening.**

"As it is in all things, from the time you entered into the physical,
there is growth. Your physical birth was the beginning of your journey.
The awakening of your true self began when you no longer saw yourself
as separate but as connected to all things and all people. Your continued
awakening is the result and growth from that recognition. It will become
a deeper understanding and a deeper 'knowing.' You shall be reaching
out more to others, with this understanding and 'knowing,' and guiding
them in their journey."

**How do we know when the new collective consciousness will overshadow
the old one?**

"You will see changes. Changes that will be within your government
and choices made that will aid all people, not just those in power. They
will make these choices based upon their understanding of who they truly
are and the total connection of one to the other. You will see changes in
your educational system. For those who are already awake and who are
preparing to become educators, they will give their knowledge to those
they are teaching. It will be through their example in living their own
lives that others will learn. There will be no more of what you call 'road
rage.' How can one rage against the very ones they know themselves to
be a part of, to be spiritually connected to? There will not be the anger,
fear, and separateness that is now your experience. This will take much
of your 'time' for your current collective is quite thick, quite dense, and
it holds its beliefs and ideals closely as the only 'truths.'"

**There are many people who ask, are they where they should be? Is it
correct to say that each person is where they should be?**

"Everyone, where they are in the moment, is where they should be.
They are in that place due to their choices, their decisions. If they were
not supposed to be there, they could not be. They simply should look
at their situation and ask, 'How did I arrive here?' If where they are is
not serving them, then they should begin making the choices to change
that. This is something to be consciously aware of. If they are not happy
with their circumstances, if they are not satisfied where they are, they
can change it by making new choices. This is not to say that this will be
'easy,' for there will be residual to pass through, it may require Love and

aid from others. New experiences can be created with new choices and sometimes one must let go of all that was previously created to truly find that which they seek."

People who are awakening may wonder about how they can meet, and network, with others who are awakening, how do they find them?

"Let people know they can go on to your communication system [Author's note: They are referring to the website] and they can find out about The Light Alliance. There can also be information leading them to other groups who resonate with the same, or similar, teachings. It will be for them to discover where they resonate the most. What is important is that the understanding of who they are, why they are here, and how they create their lives is available. It does not matter the messenger if the message is constant. We have chosen to be with and instruct The Light Alliance."

There are many people who believe that one person cannot make a difference.

"Everyone is the sum total of the whole, of the One. So each portion of the One is important in and of themselves. Every person, whether alone or with others, completes a picture. If only one person walks down a dirty street and begins to clean it, that makes a difference. If only one person feeds a homeless family for a day, that makes a difference. You must know that if you are out there, helping in Love, then you are putting forth the energy of change. By putting your hand forth to help others along, you have made a difference. A single smile can make a difference. Picking up a flower to give to your neighbor, who is homebound, or making them a meal, makes a difference. It is those things, big or small, which begin to raise the energy. So as you can see, one person does indeed make a difference."

Since we have already discussed where some of our guidance comes from, there will be people who wonder what other forms of guidance they might be receiving as they continue to awaken.

"The guidance will be fit to the one receiving it. There has been, and will always be, guidance for each and every spirit on this planet. You came into this experience with guidance and it now is a matter of becoming aware of this guidance. As you awaken and gain understanding of who you are, you will begin to 'see' this guidance in many aspects of your life."

Are there additional spiritual "tools" we have not yet discussed?

"In regards to the 'tools' of which you speak, we have given you guidance on meditation, on energy centers, on seeing beyond what you currently know, and on making choices and creating experiences. In this 'Now,' that is sufficient."

This is good. The desire is to be in step with all you have previously said and not to go beyond your current recommendations. I would like to know how everything looks with Little One physically?

"She is much better. The acidic output of her stomach has decreased with the pills that were recommended. Her meditations are giving her more focus and aiding her in centering her energies. Her diet has improved and she is now eating more in tune with the suggestions and guidance given by us and 'Dr. Mike.' We would like for her to have more physical exercise, but we know this is an area that is difficult for her and not yet her choice. She is doing better than previously."

Is "Dr. Mike" doing any more?

"He has given his observations and guidance, we have taken his suggestions and are helping Little One to implement them."

Wonderful, and there has been a noticeable change in her and she seems to be feeling better.

"This is as it should be."

Thank you so very much for your help. Little Sarah seems to be doing a lot better. She sleeps so much better now. Thank you for all that you are doing for her.

"It is our joy and purpose to help you in all things as we are able. For now, we do depart in Love and Blessings."

The journey we are taking together through these Teachings is a deeply personal one for me. If I did not truly live and understand the material I am sharing, then I could not expect others to gain a full understanding of the Teachings or the reason why they are now being given.

I had begun to feel better almost immediately after "Dr. Mike's" examination. Whatever he did, the results were noticeable right away. I not only felt better but my entire outlook had changed. It was apparent that much help had arrived and definite steps were being taken to improve my health and well-being. Bruce helped me to implement all the suggestions I had been given with notable results. We did not know, at the time, how much of this was due to diet, exercise, and medication, or the direct intervention by "Dr. Mike" and the "Girls." Over time we gained enough information to come to the correct answer that first was their intervention followed by my heeding their suggestions.

Sarah, although still weak, took a turn for the better. She wasn't constantly meowing and restless. She was even able to rest for periods of time where before she would be in a constant state of agitation. We were very hopeful.

The telephone still rang off the hook, but somehow we developed an inner peace that lifted both of us up and over the difficulties we were still facing. We were able to focus more of our attention to our writing. I was rapidly finishing the first volume of Teachings from the Heart. We had found a calm place in the center of the storm.

March 16, 2008

Between the last session of February 28 and now, Sarah had taken another turn for the worse. In fact, it was strongly felt by both of us that her time had come. We were so grateful for the comfort she had received for the past three weeks. Naturally we were very concerned and asked the "Girls" if we could please speak with them.

"We do greet thee. You called for us to come?"

Yes, Dear Ones, we desire to speak with you. We are concerned for Sarah and would like to know if she has made her decision?

"We feel that her choice will be based upon how her body is reacting to that which grows within her. It is getting to the point where she will make a choice. It would be advised for your pet doctor to take a look at her and allow his guidance to aid you in making your decision."

I have a very strong sense that she wants to continue her journey.

"Spirit is strong within her, but as you know, the body does not always follow in this strength."

We just wanted to know if she had made her choice. The rasping sounds are once again being heard and she is acting in a frustrating way. I feel that her body is not working in the way she would desire. We are so happy that you will be there for her.

"We are with her always."

She knows that when she makes her choice, she will be going with you? Will it be possible to know or feel her presence after she goes to be with you? Will she come with you sometimes when you come to speak with us?

"She knows that we are ready to enfold her spirit and that she will live with us. You may always feel her presence if that is your desire, for connection of Spirit is never lost. When we come to speak with you, she may certainly accompany us."

This is wonderful and very comforting, and we are very grateful for this. Thank you for giving us important answers to these questions. I do have a few other questions to ask at this time. Is there any additional advice or guidance for us in this Now before we leave and head back to Happy Camp?

"Go as you have been. We realize that in your physical environment, things are not going as you would desire them, yet things are continuing. Circumstances come along as you need them and things fall into their place. If you continuously keep your eyes focused, and do not look back, you will continue creating in the direction you desire to go. Looking back on Now's which have been sometimes allows the creation of experiences that you may not desire."

There seems to have been a change in the attitude among some of the creditors. Some now seem to want and work with us.

"We believe that at this point in 'time' your earth is undergoing a transformation in economics. We have been observing and we see that there is an implosion, if you will, in many aspects of the financial world and outlook. People will begin to see that taking a 'hard' approach will not succeed and that if they desire to gain any of their projected losses, they must cooperate or lose all."

Yes, we see that too and also see signs that things may get a lot worse.

"It will get considerably worse before it is able to get better. This will go on for much of your 'time.' Many jobs will be lost, companies closed, homes deserted, and volatility in your stock market. It is a balloon that is overinflated yet there are those attempting to put in more air. From moment to moment you will see air released to try and achieve a balance, but none shall be achieved. It will be like one of your roller coasters, up and down, and will keep many people nauseous."

This is what we have thought. Particularly for this nation as people are so focused on money.

"Not only focused on money, but think of all who are still spiritually asleep and go through their days with only the intent of getting more and more money. They do this to the exclusion of all else and physically and mentally make choices that create experiences that do not, and will not, serve them. When they are unable to any longer fulfill that purpose of getting money, they will find themselves reevaluating their choices. This will be difficult for many because this is how they have identified themselves. How much money and possessions they have acquired and how much more they can acquire. In some cases, it will allow the awakening, but for others, they will simply feel anger, frustration, fear, and desperation. In so many ways this is what we see is now occurring but we are 'knowing,' as we have said, that this will only increase. Many of the financial problems have been created by the big companies that have allowed, and given, credit to those who were unable to meet those commitments. The companies kept extending and extending credit and therefore leading people to believe that all was okay. At some point they would have to reach a limit, but even when that limit was reached, they continued to extend. We do not understand how the results of this extension were not foreseen. There also became the limit where people were unable to continue paying upon this extended credit. As jobs were, and are, lost this inability to pay becomes monumental. Just as something built upon a false foundation, all will crumble and fall. These companies are only a portion of the problems that your planet will face."

Yes, even in our financial situation, we receive weekly offers for credit.

"It is quite remarkable that you have a society that lives upon that which no longer exists, it is all now just play money."

You know it really is because there is nothing to back it up. Here comes little Sarah. We will take her in tomorrow. Her veterinarian will be there, so I suspect we'll be making a decision then.

"It is getting more difficult for her spirit to be in this body that is not cooperating with her, but as to whether it is 'time' for her to leave, that will be her choice. We will give energy, Love, and all else that we are able to give."

We are delighted that she can go and be with you, and other than having her physical presence, we will always be connected with her. She is in capable hands.

"Yes, you will always be connected as you have always been. When the 'time' comes for you to leave your physical vehicle, you will simply be rejoined as the Spirits you are. Until then, we will watch over her. She is greatly loved by all and we are in joy she will be with us."

Is there anything else that we need to know at this point regarding decisions or choices?

"Just to continue the way you have been going. We would like to see, of course, more 'time' for meditation, for communing with everything around you. We understand, of course, your involvement with many things at this 'time' in your Now. Make your choices in complete awareness and spiritual consciousness. These will be the stepping-stones toward that which you desire, or the steps toward that which will be more than you have imagined and will serve you best."

Thank you for all of this information. These are all the questions I have for now.

"If a decision is made tomorrow about your Sarah, either by her or yourselves, then we will be there to take her with us. We ask you not to worry. We know there will be emotions, but understand that she is with us and that she is fine. She will be running, playing, and being a kitten again, if you will. We will let you know at all times how she is doing. We understand that you do not want her fighting Spirit against body, for that does not serve her journey. Go with the recommendation of your pet physician. It may be to let her go to prevent any further discomfort, or to try something different for her care. You will have a difficult decision, but you will 'know' which will serve best."

We thank you for these words of encouragement and comfort.

"You are most welcome. For now, we will depart in Love and Blessings."

We didn't sleep much that night, nor did Sarah. She was so restless. We tried to comfort her, but she would not lie still for very long. She walked through the house crying the most mournful meow and it almost broke our hearts. We both were awake and stayed with her the rest of the night. When morning finally came, Bruce wrapped her in her favorite blanket, carried her out to the car and my waiting arms. We drove to the clinic that was only about five minutes away. We didn't say much on that short trip, but Bruce knew my heart was breaking even though I was trying to hold back the tears. I knew he felt the same. We had already lost so much of what we had worked so hard for and now it seemed as if our little cat was next on the already-long list.

We looked at Sarah thinking of all the joyous times we had shared with her and realizing that her journey may now be ending. However, beyond all hope and for a reason I can still not explain, we clung to the desire for help to arrive from our highly evolved "family."

We arrived at the clinic and took Sarah in to be examined. We had no idea that something had happened to her during the trip from home to the vet's. As I lifted her up out of the car, she seemed different in some way. Call it a "feeling." She suddenly wasn't laboring as much in her breathing, had settled down in my arms, and was no longer agitated. I had completely missed the changes as I was so caught up in sadness. When our vet examined her a few minutes later, she noticed a slight rasping sound but didn't seem to be very concerned about it. It was nowhere as loud as it had been. Her urine specimen confirmed what we already knew, and that was that she was at the beginning stages of kidney disease. The vet saw no reason to put Sarah down and suggested that we take her home, make diet modifications for the kidney problem, and observe her behavior. If things worsened, then we should return. We were stunned and didn't know what to think. When you have put forth so much energy in hoping to hear good news and then you hear it, you have trouble believing it. I remembered all the good news days that quickly were followed by not so good news day. We decided to just go with this news and trust its continuance. We took her home and watched her carefully. Over the next few days, we noticed she was her old chipper self, much like she had been after her surgery in January. We were definitely encouraged by this and supported each other by remembering that the "Girls" had told us they would work with her. We just had to find out if it was their energy she had received, so we asked for a session and the following is what they told us.

"We do greet thee. You have questions for us regarding your little cat. We can already 'feel' them, so we will answer them for you. Yes, it was much energy she received. We simply helped her to keep her wind, if you will. We simply removed the veil that was restricting her wind. We joined our Spirit with hers and helped her with her choice to continue. We are pleased that she is better and much happier now."

We are so grateful for what you have done to help her. Words cannot express the joy, Love, and gratitude we both feel at the wonderful blessing you have given to Sarah and to us.

"We were most pleased to help for it was not yet her decision to leave. Had it been her choice to go, then we would have honored it for she too has the freedom to create at will. She will let us, and you, know when her time has come and her decision to leave has been made. She knows that you are in great desire for her to continue with you and it is her desire to be here for you. This choice of hers enabled us to help. Little Brother, there is a Teaching in this that you will come to understand in 'time.' This lesson will have much more meaning for you when you have awakened to the awareness of what has occurred and how it occurred, especially in respect as to what is to come into your experience. You are a healer. It is in 'knowing' the intent of the one you aid that allows the energy to flow and find its purpose. Know that as a healer you always follow the intent of the one receiving the energy, in that way, there is no pushing against another's will to create their own experiences."

Thank you, Dear Ones. I have the strong feeling that this will have a profound impact at some point in what is to unfold as the Awakening continues to strengthen. For now I will hide my thoughts and impressions from within with the strong desire that what I "feel" will manifest in the not-too-distant future.

"Yes, Little Brother, know that what you are feeling will, in 'time,' be your created experience. For now, we do depart with much Love and Blessings."

We were absolutely astounded by what the "Girls" revealed. Sarah continued to grow stronger and was again her usual self. We would have her with us for many months to come. This was also a high point that enabled us to overcome, somewhat, the stress and challenges of our financial situation. In a way, it was like being lifted up and over the "nasty stuff" that had been our experiences for almost ten months now. We really did feel lighter and more optimistic about the future no matter what it might hold for us. Sarah's recovery, as a result of the "Girls'" love and intervention, was like a candle in the darkness. It enabled us to see our way more clearly.

March 27, 2008

We were now just days away from leaving for Happy Camp. We were excited about being reunited with Annie and Teresa. We had decided to sell most of our belongings, leaving only our bedroom set, books in the library, and some southwestern art pieces that we had collected. After the three-day sale, we locked up the house and made the trip north. Originally we were going to put our remaining items in storage and just let the bank foreclose on the house, especially since we couldn't find a source of income to support the payments. The final decision not to do any of that wasn't made till the last minute. We had looked at storage units, obtained prices, but something just did not feel right. As the moving sale began, we had the feeling that somehow we were going to return to our home. We chose to go with that feeling.

"We do greet thee. You have called us."

Yes. I wanted to tell you that Sarah is feeling much better. We are so grateful for what you have done for her. We have no words to express our joy.

"We simply helped her wind by removing the obstacle that held it back. This was the remnant of the tumor your physician earlier removed. We would say that we 'talked' to the cells of her body and they worked together with the energy in removing this."

There was such a noticeable and quick improvement in her ability to breathe easier.

"We believe that she will not have any further difficulties with her wind."

Wonderful, and we have the feeling that things are beginning to move.

"It has been decided that when you, Little One, and Sister of My Sister are reunited, it will be the 'time' to begin reviewing the Teachings and understandings that you have been given. You have been receiving

Teachings all along, even when they came within our conversations. We desire to review so that you will not miss what has been given."

I thought maybe it had been more difficult for you to "get through" to us because of all that we have been going through.

"We could reach you no matter what is going on in your life. We are connected and 'in tune' with you. Here is something for you to think about, Little Brother. The mind, when in ego, sees the physical body as being solid because of the way it is constructed. It does not grasp the fact that it is not a solid form. In truth, it is part and parcel of the atmosphere around it and as such is in constant motion. While the mind remains in ego, it will not acknowledge this fact. Once you awaken to the understanding that you are Spirit, that you are pure energy, your mind will also awaken to its true purpose, being connected in Spirit for your continued journey. This understanding expands with your experiences and you begin to diminish the ego's hold upon your mind and body."

I am at the point where I truly understand this fact.

"This is good. It is important that you understand so you may answer questions from others and for your own continued journey."

One of the main purposes for the Awakening is to help others and to aid the earth in her renewal. We have all signed on 100 percent for this project.

"You all would not have been chosen if we did not know you would make this commitment."

We feel honored. This is a wonderful privilege that we have been given.

"There have been others throughout your ages who had been chosen to receive, but did not accept. They also did not accept those teachers who did choose to come and share their Teachings. We are in a quandary as to why someone would turn away from hearing and knowing the truth of things. Perhaps it has been the fear, or the belief of created separation. Once again the messages, the Teachings, are being given. Once again they have the choice to accept."

There are no words to explain how I feel about this. It makes me understand how imprecise our language is. Feelings are so very hard to

explain, so it is best just to let them happen and not be concerned with the actual words.

"Words are only needed to be there when you find yourself in the presence of those who are still only in ego. The only way to reach beyond their ego is with words, and many times even the words, if they differ from what ego has taught them, will not be heard. The words you write in your books are for those who are searching beyond what ego has given them and are searching for answers to the questions they ask. Words have their place, but once an understanding of who you truly are is reached, the 'need' for words diminishes.

"We will be with you during your sale and your trip north. Know that we are with you. For now, we shall depart in Love and Blessings."

This was our last session before we arrived back in Happy Camp. In looking back over our time spent in Las Vegas, we saw it as not only one of the most challenging times in our lives, but also one of considerable growth and incredible Teachings.

We had scheduled a three-day house sale to sell off as much of our furniture and belongings as we could. We were left with several bare rooms and only our bed to sleep on for the last couple of nights. We felt a little relief as the money from the sale would help us to continue for several more months. We were really hoping to find some temporary employment in Happy Camp.

With the sale over and the house prepared for our absence, we loaded up the truck, got Sarah comfortable in the backseat, hooked up our small mining trailer, and headed off to Northern California.

Chapter Four

April 2, 2008

We were happy to be out of Las Vegas. It was nice to breathe a little after everything that had been our experience for the past five months. The financial storm was not over, but for at least a little while, we could rest and recover while in Happy Camp. We were at least away from those incessant telephone calls and the daily harassment of creditors. We knew we would have to face it when we returned in the fall, but for now, this was a very welcome time of relative calm.

On the trip, Bruce and I talked a lot about all the Teachings we had received while in Las Vegas. There was so much to fill Annie in on. Our weekly telephone calls did as much as they could to keep her up to date on what we were learning, but it is always so much nicer to talk face-to-face. We were very curious about all the new things that would be given now that the three of us had come back together. Many of our questions had been held through the winter waiting for just this time to ask them. The trip to Happy Camp was smooth and uneventful and passed quickly. We arrived there on the second of April. Our old work trailer would not arrive until the fourth from Washington State, so we drove straight to Annie's. After greetings, hugs, and a quick catching up on events, it was Annie's desire to speak with the "Girls" as soon as possible. I freshened up a bit, relaxed a little, and the "Girls" joined us.

"We do greet thee. It is such joy for us to all be in one place again. We are quite pleased to be here and it is wonderful, Sister of My Sister, to speak with you again."

You know how I feel.

"Yes. This is the way as was intended. What are your questions?"

I do not know if this is the time, but I would like to know about the significance and value of the Reiki system.

"As in all things, the value and significance is with the one who resonates to its teaching. We can share with you that the symbols are those which were inspired by the one who first brought it to the attention of all, Dr. Usui. The symbols meanings were based upon his traditions, his education, and of course, upon his ethnic background. They are important because as he was inspired to this energy modality, that which is called Reiki, he formed these symbols and sayings for each movement. The significance was given by him for his inspiration. All this inspiration was given for his 'Now,' but you have reached a new 'Now' and you shall be inspired as well. As you know, and have been taught, energy is constant and there is only One energy. It is the transference of that energy from one to the other which is the variable. There are many energy modalities upon your earth and this, which shall be inspired to you, is another way. This is a more direct, if you will, approach to the delivering of this One energy. There will be those who will resonate with the simplicity of this modality and will understand how in its simplicity it is given from one to the other. It is for those that this energy healing modality is given. You will learn, share, and teach. It will be for others to choose if this resonates for them as well."

Thank you so much for that explanation. We are joyfully awaiting that inspiration. May I have your explanation of the names Astrid and Shiloh?

"It is simply that they are the two essences of the One Spirit. It is a balance of masculine and feminine energy that together create the Divine One. These names were simply given to identify those essences, for we understand your way and the desire for having identifying names."

I have read that there are people who claim to be channeling the feminine aspects of the One Spirit.

"The feminine aspect of the One comes through only those who she has chosen. She never remains, or resides, in one of a physical nature, she only 'speaks' through the chosen one's voice. We understand that there are those who have claimed that the spirit of the feminine resides within them. What we believe they may be speaking of is the 'feeling' of Mother Earth, of Nature, rather than the Divine One. For neither the masculine or feminine essence of the One would reside in that which is physical. The 'voice' may be heard through the physical vehicle, but the true Essence of the One only resides within the Absolute."

I feel that there is a great significance in Her union with Little One. Would it be that Her essence resided in Little One during specific times on the earth?

"It is more that the essence of the Divine Feminine and the Spirit, called by us as Little One, were together in the Absolute. They 'knew' each other, if you will, there. That is their connection. It is not that She would reside within a physical incarnation. She does certainly come through Little One to share a message or Teaching. To actually reside within a physical body would not be possible as the total essence of the Feminine would be too much for a body to bear. The Divine Mother has chosen Little One as her channel due to the connection of one to the other while in the Absolute."

Could you speak on the interaction of the body, mind, Spirit, especially the role of Spirit?

"Spirit is who you are. You are Spirit encompassing a physical body. The role of Spirit, as it has always been, is that of leading body and mind in the remembering of who you truly are. Spirit forgets only that which it chooses to forget when it incarnates. When it comes into the earth plane, it has agreed, and it has chosen, to forget in order to experience the remembering. It is the opportunity for Spirit to help the mind and body along in the journey. It also experiences this remembering of itself as the journey is created through choices. There would be no reason for Spirit to come in if it was not to encompass and occupy a body, to journey to the place of remembrance, and experience all choices and residuals along the path.

"In the Absolute, Spirit knows who it is and that it is eternal. When it chooses to come into this earth plane, it also comes in with the agreement that it shall forget all that it knows. There are those who will choose to come in with more remembrance of their true self, and those that have remembered have, and are, your teachers. This forgetting is what one may call amnesia. Spirit comes in knowing that it will no longer have the memory from, or of, the Absolute. It chooses this in order to remember through chosen experiences. One of the purposes of Spirit when coming into this earth plane, this physical incarnation, is so the Infinite, the Divine, can also experience through Spirit. If Spirit was to come in with total knowledge, there would be no reason for it to come, for how can you experience that which you already know? It is not that Spirit experiences alone, for Spirit experiences with the body and mind in remembering."

So Spirit itself actually chooses to forget?

"Yes, and this is why we call it an Awakening for not only are body and mind, with the help of Spirit, awakening, but it is also the awakening of Spirit to that which it has always known while in the Absolute.

"On our planet, for instance, when we incarnate, we do not come in forgetfulness. We choose those things, those memories that we desire to bring into our planet, this is because of our particular evolution. There are some things that we come in not knowing so we can also experience, in our own way, those things. On your planet, because of the vibrational level and because of the desire of Spirit, as well as the Infinite to experience completely, Spirit agrees, and chooses, to come into the physical body in forgetfulness."

So how then does Spirit remember?

"It is exactly as you are now doing. Spirit begins to awaken, and as it goes along its journey, it comes into contact with people, places, and books. It begins to remember. It is important that Spirit, mind, and body always work in conjunction with each other. It takes all three to work together. It is three in one. Spirit has chosen to experience fully that which it can while in the physical, therefore it enters in forgetfulness."

I have a sense that my body, mind, and Spirit are waking up quickly now.

"This is why we are so pleased that the council is together and that, at some point, Light Sister will also be here as this is the 'time' of the joining. Some awaken in less 'time' and some take more. We understand this, and we teach you, that your body may lag behind or your mind may lag behind. Once Spirit begins to remember, to understand, and to live that understanding of who you truly are, then both body and mind cannot help but follow. This Awakening occurs at different paces for each who is experiencing it. Little Brother, do you have a question?"

Yes. Since Sister of My Sister has not had the opportunity to speak with you, I felt that this should be her session. I do have one question though. When Little One and I were talking today, we discussed our shared

feeling that a book was to be written explaining the Awakening for those who have a religious background.

"It is something that you will do, for it is important for people to understand that they can be in any faith they have chosen and still Awaken to the understanding of their true self. Once they begin to awaken, it may be somewhat uncomfortable, or difficult, for them to continue in the direction they were walking while in their faith. They begin to understand that it is they who create their lives, it is their choices that create their experiences. They begin to live unconditional Love. They do not have to feel that they must leave their faith in order to awaken. This understanding of Spirit simply allows them to make the choices and create the experiences they desire in their walk. They will no longer look at others as being separate from themselves, but that all are connected to the One Divine Spirit, an inseparable part of the whole."

Thank you. Will we see the completion of this project, the Awakening, in our current incarnation?

"You may not see it in this incarnation, in the physical body you now encompass, but you will be present at its completion."

We are doing what we can to prolong the lifetime of the physical body. We know you will give us information that will aid us in extending our physical lifetimes and that we may reach the highest vibrational level that is possible in the current "Now."

"As you take care of your physical vehicle and the new consciousness rises, we will see how much the vibrational level can be raised. We are beginning to see more now of people looking toward the long physical lives, caring for themselves, and understanding that it is their choices that prolong their experience on earth."

I have been feeling for the last several months a warmth, like heat, within my heart area.

"Sister of My Sister, this also is part of the Awakening."

There is a strong feeling among us that the Teachings are about to go to a whole new level.

"Yes, Little Brother, we will begin with more Teachings, but we may not necessarily do much in the short time you are here. After you have picked up the remainder of your items, and have returned, we will begin. We would like to then meet several times in your week to begin these new teachings. There will be an understanding and all will be upon the same page. It is important for those who come into the council to also be aware that they are Spirit, pure energy, unconditional Love. All have come in for the purpose you have put into your 'blueprint.'"

Then it is Spirit, body, and mind that choose what is the best way to fulfill what is in our "blueprint"?

"Yes, Sister of My Sister. It would be, if you will, an understanding of Spirit, a 'knowing.' Spirit may not necessarily have remembered yet, but it has a 'knowing' of the purpose that it came to accomplish. It is led through its direct connection with the Divine. It is the Divine always that works with each Spirit, for that connection is never broken. It is just forgotten until it is remembered."

I don't think that we need to tell you how much we appreciate you and Love you.

"We are feeling overjoyed that we are here. It is coming home, if you will. The energy here is completing. It helps us to be able to project ourselves more. We enjoyed, of course, being with Little One and Little Brother in their home and lending them our energy and Love. We are with each one at all times even if our 'connection' may vary. Now we are back together where we can continue with the Teachings. Are there any other questions or comments?"

I have no further comments, I am just so happy we are all together again.

"Little One is also quite pleased. We understand that she mentioned this evening that she is beginning to choose to hear what we say during our session with you. We have always told her that it was her choice when she would desire to do this. She may not choose to hear every time, but she may listen to the tapes. Her immediate hearing enables her to share with you in the discussion afterwards rather than taking the 'time' to listen to the tape. For this we are quite pleased."

A lot of what we are all going through is just a whole sequence that we had to go through. There are things we all had to understand, and experience, so that we could share our understanding with others in order to help them begin to awaken.

"Yes, everything the council is going through is first for your remembering and then to be able to enlighten those who come along."

You have previously talked about the integration of the council together.

"For the council, it is important that you be integrated so that in your thoughts, in Spirit, you are in the same place. Some that come to Council may be a little further behind in their remembering. They will continue their awakening because of who you are being, because of where you are in your understanding, and because you will be sharing with all the Teachings that we bring. They will quickly catch up. Everyone will not be at the same place of Awakening when they enter and this is fine for it is where they should be at this 'time' on their journey. This is the way it is intended for it is through Spirit and your teaching, of our Teachings, that all will eventually be at the same 'knowing' and understanding. Do you have any further questions?"

They can wait for another session. We are all just so happy to be together with you.

"We are most pleased as well. We are with each of you at all times as you know, but it is much more enjoyable to be able to sit and converse with you like this."

I would like to ask about the possibility of my going to Las Vegas for the winter when Little Brother and Little One return there.

"We believe that if this is your choice and desire, it would be excellent to remain together. We are not yet of the knowledge as to whether this will be cohesive, if you will, with the keeping of the home. We have asked, but as Little Brother knows, the decision is now in the hands of those in the banking, and it is their decision whether this can or cannot happen. We do know that regardless of what occurs that you will be together. We do feel the intent Little One and Little Brother have put forth to remain in their home, and it is our desire that the books they have written would produce the means to do this. At this 'time,' we are not in the 'knowing' as to what 'time' this would occur. We are not always privy to all things for it is beyond the scope and reason for our being here. Our purpose is to give the Teachings. We simply are in the way of 'knowing' that the council will remain together and that we, of course, give you our energy and join with you in the desire that what you have created in the spiritual shall come to pass in the physical."

Thank you. With all the discussions regarding manifestation of finances that we have had with you and with the Divine Parents, it is interesting that when this subject arises, they come "over the top" at that point and begin to communicate.

"Yes, this is so."

We know that you are very interested and desirous for the finances to be acquired, as this is important to the project, but we also understand that this is the Divine Parents to unfold.

"This is as it should be. It is our desire also for you to remain together in an area where you may experience your peace."

There is definitely continuity and peace at our home in Las Vegas. Annie will feel the energy that is present in and around the home itself.

"Yes, your home, in particular, is of energy turned up, but the area itself is an example of energy turned down. Your home, and the area you have created around your home, contains high energy. The council is family, as will all be who come together and resonate with the Teachings. Know that your path to this Awakening began in other lifetimes, other incarnations, this is simply a continuation, with this incarnation, of that journey."

So we know that we are going to be physically together now in one place?

"Yes, we do not believe there will be another separation."

The only separation will be temporary when Little One and I return to Las Vegas to bring some things back and possibly find out more of our situation.

"That is necessary for this trip to tie up loose ends, so to speak. You may also have forthcoming information to you about your home."

Thank you, Dear Ones.

"You are most welcome. We know that you are desirous of remaining a part of this home until the 'time' to move on to the next part on the journey. We will ask the Divine Parents but we cannot guarantee, of course, that we are to know the answer. This may be for you to choose and experience. Know simply that we are with you, for the Teachings are our goal and our purpose. We are also here for all who have questions and it is our desire that others may come to hear and ask as well. Little One may conduct sessions for others so they may begin by asking their spiritual questions, it may also increase finances toward the project. As always, it is to be energy for energy."

You would come so that others may speak with you?

"Yes. At first we were not sure, but we have been told that this now would be a possibility. We do ask that those who come would have questions of a spiritual nature regarding their journey, or their awakening. We are not fortune-tellers as you know so would desire that the questions be spiritual in nature. If we can be of assistance in helping the finances to be gained for the project, then we are most pleased."

We had decided to leave this matter up to you, so we are very grateful and excited to hear of this. We are absolutely dedicated to the outcome of this project.

"Yes, Little Brother, we are quite aware of this and we, of course, have always known this. It is most pleasing to hear that you are also in this knowledge."

Very definitely, we are totally committed to the project and to receive your Teachings.

"It is as we said, Sister of My Sister, we understand that there are many teachings and many spiritual writings out there already. All in their ownare perfect. There are many who will resonate with other teachings and other writings that is as it will be. It is simply an indication to us that those people must go on with what is fulfilling and resonating with them. The ones who our Teachings resonate with will be with us. All that you have previously known and learned was for the stepping, if you will, to that which you are receiving now. Those were inspirational teachings that you heard. They were perfect for you in the 'time' in which they occurred, for they allowed Spirit to begin to understand and grow. It was for the completion, the next understanding, that we have come Teach you."

I absolutely understand that now and I am filled with so much gratitude, Love, happiness, and joy.

"Sister of My Sister, we will continue to give that and to lend all of our energy to that which happens. If there are no more questions, we shall simply depart in Love and Blessings."

It was nice to have the three of us together again. Even though we had been away for five months, it was amazing how quickly we got right back into the swing of things. In some way, it was like we had never left. We decided to return to Las Vegas and find out for sure how long we might be able to keep the house and to pick up things that we could not fit into the truck on the first trip. At the end of this session, the "Girls" were informed, and in turn informed us, that there might be some information for us regarding the house when we returned to Vegas. Naturally we were very curious as to what that information might be.

We had been taught by Annie to place a lot of emphasis in the symbols we used for Reiki sessions and practitioner certification. It was interesting to learn that the energy would flow whether we used these symbols or not. Little did we know at the time that in a matter of months, we would be given inspiration for an energy healing modality that would greatly expand upon what we currently knew.

Bruce and I were surprised to hear Annie asking whether she should go to Las Vegas with us for the winter. We had talked a little over the previous winter about how lonely she had been and that it might be a wise decision for us to be together on a long-term basis. We all were pleased to hear that the most desirable circumstances would be for all of us to remain together. What was even more interesting was their "knowing" that indeed we would not be separated. No matter if we lost the home, or not, the desire was for us to be together so that the Teachings could continue. We talked about this subject, after the session, for quite a while.

When we first began receiving the Teachings from the "Girls," they cautioned us that these channeled sessions were not for entertainment, or as they said, a "free for all." This was a very important understanding and not to be taken too lightly. We understood that some of the information we received would be shared with others at a "time" designated by the "Girls." This pertained to both the written books and the information given to the council. The council family would, if they chose to be, be present at channelings and would be able to ask questions pertaining to their own spiritual journey. For the council, there would be no fee involved; they gave energy with their participation in moving The Light Alliance and the Teachings out to all who desired to hear. Others who desired a channeling in order to further their own journey would be able to also meet the "Girls." We were honored and grateful that permission had been given to hold seminars, or sessions. As we had been told, energy is exchanged for energy, so it was okay to receive some monetary assistance to keep us and the project afloat.

The "Girls" seemed pleased at our renewed commitment to the project. It was now the perfect "time" for us, collectively, to express our desire for this project and put it out into the spiritual realm. We could see our desires as complete and simply allow their unfolding into the physical world as directed by the Divine Parents. This meant to let them go, in trust, and continue to create and experience. No matter the "when" of their unfolding, we knew that whatever occurred would be for the highest purpose of everyone involved and the movement forward of The Light Alliance and the Teachings.

April 3, 2008

We got a good night's sleep and were feeling refreshed. Tomorrow our fifth wheel trailer would arrive and we would begin the process of "settling in." Today our thoughts were already on receiving our next session.

"We do greet thee. Good morning. How are you on this your day, Little Brother and Sister of My Sister? We have come today for several purposes. We will speak this day on a subject that we heard you speaking of in one of your discussions. This would be the progression of Spirit once it has chosen to leave the physical. This is an important concept to grasp. It is one that we would have touched upon eventually in our teachings, but we feel that this, due to your questions during your discussion, is the 'time' to speak on this.

"As you know, when you come into the physical and you encompass and inhabit the physical vehicle, it is yours throughout your journey and throughout the 'time' here that you have chosen. When you are through with the physical, when you have chosen that it is 'time' to leave, either because you have fulfilled your purpose for this incarnation or the body has chosen to leave, then you shall move on. What occurs with the physical shall be up to you or to your loved ones. It is not an important issue for the physical will simply, in one way or the other, return to that from which it came, which is pure energy. It will return to the earth in either a burial, as you call them, or a cremation. Either way, it is returning to the energy which it is. As to Spirit, it is of course complete in and of itself. The mind, as you know, is an integral part of Spirit that chooses, during your incarnation, to either remain with Spirit or be influenced by the ego of the physical body. Spirit, at its moment of leaving, will perceive what you would call a blinding presence, or light. Many have seen this. That light is the energy from the Absolute as it reaches towards Spirit. That moment of leaving the physical is also the moment of recognition as to your true nature. Many will already have discovered this during their journey, but for others, it will be their 'time' of awakening. It is that moment of going home, if you will.

"Once Spirit is lifted by the light from the Absolute, by the essence of All That Is, then it is simply home. Once it is back in the Absolute from where it began, it has total recall, total memory, of all that occurred in its previous incarnation. This becomes an integral part of Spirit, a part of its 'cellular' memory. This memory is held by Spirit and may be drawn upon, in many ways, during any other incarnation. We will speak more on this particular thing at a later 'time.' Once you have returned to the Absolute, you may again then choose to incarnate, either to earth or other planets. This choice would not be for the continuance of a prior experience, for each experience in and of itself is unique and completed. You may choose to come in with less forgetfulness in order to teach or simply to experience different things that you desire. It will all be chosen again in the Absolute just as it was for your very first incarnation. Which would you choose? It may be that you do not choose any incarnation, but choose to stay awhile in the Absolute. This is what Little One has done many times. Her physical incarnations have been but a few.

"Once Spirit is back in the Absolute, then you begin to formulate, if you will, a new 'blueprint' that shall encompass your new incarnation. At that 'time,' whatever that 'time' may be, you simply will reenter wherever you have chosen to enter. You certainly do not have a 'reliving' of what your previous incarnation(s) had been. You would not base your return upon what you had just experienced, for as we stated, each incarnation is complete in and of itself. It would not be so much that you wish to continue an experience but possibly elaborate on a desire that occurred at a later time in the physical life. Let us say, for example, that at some point in your experiencing, you began to desire to be a doctor. Your previous incarnation may not have included this because it was nearing its end when the desire was felt. Upon your decision to reincarnate, you may choose to experience that particular desire in your new physical life. This would be a choice you enter into your 'blueprint' for your next incarnation."

You have a "blueprint" before you come in, and so if for some reason you don't really fulfill that "blueprint" as you had first desired, can you come back to fulfill it?

"You do not come back in, Sister of My Sister, with the same 'blueprint.' You enter every time with a new 'blueprint.' You simply may take some aspect of the old with you and incorporate it into the new. As you know, the 'blueprint' is something that is flexible, modifiable. You have desires about what you wish to see, to experience, but once you have incarnated and begin the journey to remembering your true self, you will also remember parts of your 'blueprint.' You may then choose to modify it depending upon your desires of your current 'Now.' It is not as if there is a destiny and that everything that is written down must come to pass. As you grow and as you become aware, you may have the desire to change some aspects of your original 'blueprint.' You may decide to say, 'Oh, I am not going to go in that direction,' 'I'm going to modify my blueprint,' 'I now desire to go in this direction.' It is important that you understand there is a 'blueprint' to begin with and that you may modify or change it as you are creating your experiences."

What I understand right now is that everything that has happened to the three of us has brought us to the point where we are now ready to receive more pure truth. I'm seeing the necessity of clearing my mind of everything that I previously knew, setting aside old beliefs, and listen to what you are teaching us.

"We are most pleased to hear this. Little Brother is going through his current incarnation to understand various created religions. This was his stepping-stone for awakening to who he truly is, it is the way he intended it for himself. You started your stepping-stones when you started to become interested in channeled messages that were being brought to you. It is for people to understand that each learning, each written word, each belief, can be either a stepping-stone for awakening, or it can be where you may choose to remain. It is simply your choice. We desire, of course, for those that are Light Alliance family to be moving from stepping-stone to stepping-stone and not remain idle upon only one stone. If you would, imagine that you are walking across a wide expanse of water and upon this water are stepping-stones to carry you across. You can choose to remain on any one stone, which is how it should be if that is where you are comfortable and where you resonate, but for Light Alliance, we are desirous that you would step, with awareness, to the other side of that stream. Once you arrive, then you may begin creating those next steps that will carry you on the water up the stream. This creative progression, as you are awakening, will enable you to not only 'know' yourself as the Spirit you are but to live and be that understanding. Are there any questions on what we have spoken regarding the progression of Spirit when it leaves the physical?"

No, I understand. It was a big help and I "know" that Spirit understands what is truth and what is not.

"Yes, we know that you do, Sister of My Sister. It would be interesting for you to know that the one who was called Edgar Cayce, during his incarnation, had chosen at one time to incarnate into our planet. When he chose to come to your planet, he chose to bring much knowledge of healing with him, he was in less forgetfulness regarding that subject. He shared much of this knowledge with many, but not everyone was ready. It was not a 'time' in your history that people were able to understand and grasp his concepts. He did indeed have those who understood and learned from him, but what he chose not to do was to share more of the actual healing practice, its application, rather than doing the healing himself. This was his choice and his experience. We can share with you that he has since chosen to be back with us once again and has been known by many who have channeled him as Teacher."

I went to a channeling session once where Teacher was being channeled and he greeted me by saying that if I continued to eat heavier foods, my body would have difficulties.

"There indeed are things that are better for the human body than others. This is perhaps a good time to have a discussion regarding foods. There is not any living food that is not good for your body. That is not to say that all living plants are good for eating for some have other properties, but all that have been identified as being for consumption are going to be proper for your body. We have spoken before of the importance of taking in pure water without chemicals or additives. We have spoken about the foods that are living, pure. You know of the body's requirement regarding red meat and that this is fulfilled with consuming it only once in your week. This is because you require that iron that is present in the red meat. Staying away from those things that are chemical or have many additives is proper for your physical body. Staying away from dead foods, those overly processed, which have had all their nutrients stripped from them, also serves your body. If possible, of course, grow your own foods or the next thing would be to consume foods that others have carefully, lovingly, grown and not used chemicals upon. Even when they are organically grown, wash them thoroughly before eating for there is much in your atmosphere, from other sources, which can settle upon them.

"We also would like you to know that a body gains weight because of its perception of food. If you perceive that a certain food is going to cause you to gain weight, it will indeed cause weight gain. That perception begins with and lies within the collective consciousness. If all things are done in moderation, then it is not harmful, unless of course your physical body has chosen to have an allergy to certain food items. If this is the case, then you would stay away from them. If you have an allergy to something that will cause you to have a breathing difficulty, or a rash, then of course we would say to understand where this allergy is coming from and why this is occurring. You would stay away from that which causes and creates these problems.

"Wheat, in its purest sense, is nutritious for you. We suggest that you stay away from anything that is white, for it has been stripped of its nutrients. Stay away from canned foods. Frozen foods are fine especially if they went from their fresh state immediately into a frozen state. These have then not been processed in any way. We would suggest that you not consume pork because there are elements present within this meat that causes energy centers to be blocked. Although as in all things if it is only occasionally partaken of, then there would be no long-term effects. You simply would not choose to have a healing session, or in Little One's case, do a channeling on that day.

"As we have said before, eat when you are hungry. Do not tie yourself to a moment or schedule. If you awaken and feel that hunger, then eat. If you do not feel that hunger for a length of time, simply wait until you do. While you are eating, remain aware of your food, its taste, its texture. Taste every bite. Take a moment between each bite to savor that which you are consuming. Chew slowly in order to break down the nutrients so they may be passed quicker to all parts that require them. Taking your time will allow your brain to signal you are full. It does not matter if food still remains on your plate, save it if you are able or simply take less the next time. If your hunger returns in several hours, get something to eat. It is through this understanding of hunger, its signals, that allows you to make choices that will serve your physical body with optimum health. Many times people feel what they believe is hunger when it is actually thirst. Most upon your planet don't consume enough water. They are able to consume twice or three times what they are consuming. If you first believe what you are feeling is hunger, then drink a glass of water. If the hunger continues, then get something to eat. Your body will establish its own rhythm. It will tell you the same way that your 'feelings' inform your gut what is happening. Your body will know when it needs its nourishment and you, in turn, will put into it that which is whole and living. Do not deprive yourself of those things you enjoy, for life is about enjoying and experiencing. Simply do those things, which may not serve you, in moderation. Your incarnation here is to experience, and if you have a list that says NO, NO, NO, then how do you find your joy within that experience?"

What about those who are overweight?

"There are many overweight people who will remain that way because they starve themselves. Every time they look at food, they think, 'I can't have that.' Instead of eating when they are hungry, and stopping when full, they just do not eat. The body will retain that which it holds on to. Some are overweight because they have yet to understand the physical emotions, and identifiers, behind their overeating. The eating is done to mask an emotion or identifier, which they believe and have attached as their reasoning for overeating. Many may not be consciously aware of any reasons until someone comes who can share with them and aid them in recognizing these identifiers and emotions for themselves.

"It is important that you are getting exercise each day and that you spend 'time' outside to breathe in the fresh air. Commune with nature, and greet the Oneness. It is not the one oneness of the physical, but is of Spirit. You actually blend into that which you experience, you become as One.

"It is also important to be aware that ego will choose, at all times, to lead you. That is the physical reaction to identifiers. The allowing of ego takes you from the true understanding of yourself as Spirit and continues to present you with identifiers, which you then choose to create your experience. Part of healing and caring for the physical vehicle is to begin deflating ego and understand who you truly are. When you have this awareness, and you live that understanding, your physical will follow suit with Spirit and will 'be' in a healthy state. The council has come to understand this, and although ego will pop up its head from time to time, if you remain within the awareness of who you are, it is not allowed to rise very far before you once again deflate it. You understand that you are always in the 'Now," for there is nothing but each moment of each 'Now."

When I do my meditations, I'm sending energy to form the new collective consciousness to eventually override the old one. Would you please comment on that?

"We simply are always within the new consciousness. We don't expend our energy within the old collective for it shall be only for those who choose to not awaken. Its energy will be depleted as more and more become aware of their true essence. We send our energy, and Love, to those awakening and to those who are creating the New Collective. We do not focus our awareness of what has been, only on what 'Now' is. We do not give energy to your political system, nor to your educational system, for those are part and parcel of the old collective that has been. Do not dwell on this old way for you cannot tear down the walls that support it. Your energy will reach those within these walls who are awakening to who they truly are. This focused energy on the New Collective will lift those of like mind and bring them on their way, their journey, to the path you are now beginning to understand. It is to understand that we, and you, cannot change a person's experience, for that occurs within each as they begin to question and awaken. Always send out your energy in Love, for this is the true motivator behind all that is or will ever be."

One thing I have found to be very helpful with this movement toward the integration of body, mind, and Spirit is the natural fallout, the release, that occurs from being aware of cravings, or obsessional eating. For me this is especially true for chocolate.

"This is what happens, Little Brother, as your body begins to ingest the live foods. You will actually begin to feel differently as you look at certain foods. Follow your 'gut' instinct for, as we have shared with you, it is that 'feeling' that alerts and allows your body to be in awareness. It is much like your choice to no longer go through that which you call 'fast food.' It is no longer something that your body chooses to experience, for there is no more joy in that eating. We know that this type of food is dead and has been processed to the point it is no longer real food. It contains additives to prolong its existence, which can be for a great length of your 'time.' Some of these establishments are now offering foods that are fresh and living for they have seen the decline of those who have chosen to eat there.

"There are many who believe that cheese is not a 'good' food. Cheese comes from a living source and is processed in a live way. It is not that it is not a good food, but because it is higher in its fat content, it should be chosen and eaten in moderation. The body does require a certain amount of fat to assimilate that which it ingests. To put an over amount of fat into your body does not serve it, it does not deal well with it and stores it in areas that can cause other issues for the physical."

When you were speaking of pork, it reminded me of my previous studies that included the laws of kashrus. The reason pork was prohibited, for those of the Jewish faith, was because it would spiritually deaden your sensitivity to things of Spirit.

"This is quite true, Little Brother. This is one of the foods we would say to avoid, but if you must, only do so in moderation. All things in moderation will serve you. We suggest that while alcohol, on the whole, is not meant for the human body there are those who enjoy it occasionally. This also should be consumed in moderation. Red wine has shown to aid the body in several ways, but not if abused. Beer is a natural product because it comes from hops and yeast. This should also not be done to excess, but an occasional glass of wine or beer will not harm your body. However, distilled alcohol is not something that should be ingested. This would be what you refer to as your 'hard liquor.' They not only kill brain cells but they also block the energy completely in the body. This same understanding goes for drugs whether legal or illegal. We understand that there are times when a drug may be appropriate for pain, or other conditions, but we would desire to see the body overcome these things through the understanding of Spirit and through its own intentions."

What about vitamins?

"Vitamins that are derived naturally are fine. We know that food which is grown, because of the environment, does not always have completely what is required. It is also difficult to ingest enough of one thing to obtain a desired level that particular vitamin. To supplement the things you are eating is proper if that is your choice."

Are there other things that we can do?

"Yes, continue with juicing the living foods. These are assimilated within your body much quicker and more thoroughly than eating may be. Soy is a product that has been viewed in many ways. We would share with you that your soybean resembles very closely a nutrient that our own planet produces. In some, you may need to be aware of eating too much, but it is a complete nutrient in and of itself."

It is absolutely correct what you say that the more you are led by Spirit, the less you desire anything that is not in line with Spirit's intended outcome for the unification of body and mind.

"When you are Spirit and you are living as such, the body can only desire and choose that which completes it. There are those foods that were created by the One for the continuance and spiritual growth of the physical body, but as always, it is your choice as to what you consume.

"For this 'Now' we send you our energy, and in much Love and Blessings, we do depart."

The explanation the "Girls" gave us as to what happens to Spirit when it leaves the physical body, and returns to the Absolute, was really amazing. The "Girls" call this the progression of Spirit and it seems a very appropriate term for the process that takes place.

There are so many opinions and, in some instances, doctrines that address this subject, and there is a great deal of differences in those opinions. A lot of controversy exists among not only those who address this issue, but also with those who sincerely, and earnestly, are looking for an answer to this timeless question. The explanation we were given is a basic understanding of this process. We understood that we were to be given a more in-depth understanding that would enable us to build a stronger foundation.

We had been given our first dietary, exercise, and lifestyle guidelines in our very first session on October 2, 2007. It is nice to be reminded of them from time to time as it can be so easy to slip back into old habits, especially when you are first awakening. Once Spirit has unified itself with the body and mind, it then guides both in bringing about optimum health and well-being. This occurs in order to fulfill what you desired before you took on a physical form. The more you are Spirit-led, the happier and healthier you will become.

April 5, 2008

Since our plan was to drive back to Las Vegas, pick up supplies for the fifth wheel, and consult with our attorney, we really wanted to have one more session with the "Girls" before we left.

"We do greet thee."

Greetings, as you know, we just finished a wonderful meal and are pretty much stuffed. Perhaps we should not have gone back for seconds.

"We can sense Little One's fullness. Possibly there was some overindulgence, but we know that the food you ate was appropriate for your bodies. It was living food, nutritious food. What are your questions for this evening?"

The circle breathing exercise you have taught us is quite effective.

"You can do this anywhere you choose. It is a simple yet very uplifting form of energy movement. There are many benefits that you will 'feel' from not only this breathing technique, but from the healing modality as well."

Would you elaborate on channeling a little bit? I have felt that you have delivered me messages through someone else I was listening to before I met Little One and Little Brother. Is this correct?

"When someone is channeling or doing a clairvoyant reading, it is possible for a message to come through from another entity, besides the one being channeled, in order to deliver a message to someone who is present. Simply said, at those times, Sister of My Sister, you did receive messages that were inspired by us, if you will, and intended for you alone. It was knowledge that you should be aware of. It was before our presence was known by you. We often went to people who were channels for others and through them we delivered a message that was to be given to someone. It is much like your communication system. It is simply done through a channel. Sister of My Sister, we have been giving you messages, in one way or another, since your birth. We have always been with you, although it took much of your 'time' for you to be aware of us as you had other choices and experiences to complete. We knew there would come the 'time' for us to connect."

I thank you for waiting with all of my heart and soul.

"This is our project, our purpose. You are most welcome. We have now covered information regarding your physical body do you have any questions on this?"

No, everything you have presented is quite clear.

"We desired to make it simple, for it need not be a complicated thing. This we have stated many times that something need not be complicated to make it truth."

It does make it easier when the three of us are doing this together.

"That is the purpose of the council. It is to listen to that which is taught and to discuss, to formulate, if necessary, the questions. It is to understand the Teachings and to be able to pass them to others. The next thing we would speak of would be the emotional part of the physical body, that which is created from birth. We know and we understand that it is actually formulated within the womb. This emotional body is attached to the physical body. It is a harder body, if you will, to care for. Before you are spiritually awake, you allow the hurts, the anger, the fear to stick to you and define and identify who you are. As you grow in your awakening of Spirit and become aware that these identifiers no longer serve who you know yourself to be, you may still hang on to them. This is why many have difficulty in truly awakening. It is a comfort for them to be able to say, 'I would not be this way if . . .' It is easier to do that and blame it on someone, or something, in a past 'Now' than it is to face what is the situation in your current 'Now.' It is not seen as something that no longer serves you, or where you desire to be. We have great challenges with those who continually blame who they are upon what occurred to them as children. We understand that it has its impact in that moment, in that 'Now,' but it is not an impact that you must carry with you, unless you choose to do so. This is very hard for most to understand or believe. They would be well served to do so, for to shed the old emotional body and create a new one with the understanding of who you truly are will be life-changing. Are there any questions regarding this?"

This is very clear. I don't have any questions. I'm so looking forward to Little One and Little Brother returning here in about a week and a half. Then we will always be together.

"Yes and forever is in this 'Now.' This being apart is only a short interlude, if you will."

I have felt different ever since they walked in the door.

"That is because this is meant to be. It is the final pieces in the puzzle of this Now. It is as if pieces were missing and now they are complete. It will continue like this as the project, the council, and The Light Alliance grow."

We are greatly appreciative. Thank you.

"You are most welcome. We have now spoken about the physical body and touched upon the emotional body. You are aware of the mental body, the intellect, and the ego. There is also the attachment between Spirit and the physical body. Both the emotional and the mental 'bodies' are part of the physical body. It is as if the physical body is wearing several coats, if you will. The Spirit, which encompasses all of those, is connected to the physical by a thin layer, or covering. This covering is with Spirit at all times. It is that conduit between them that allows the energy of Spirit to pass within the physical. We do not have a name to give you for it, but it is important that you are aware of it. Its complete purpose is to be that connector between Spirit and the physical body. Its completeness, its ability to be at its highest energy is dependent upon the nourishing of the physical body. Not only nourishment as related to eating the proper foods, but also that the emotional and mental bodies are in alignment and harmony. This harmony, this nourishment, strengthens this connection. If you could see this, it would appear transparent and would be within and around the physical body, just as Spirit is. It is the buffer from the higher energy of Spirit to the lower energy of the physical body. We will speak more on this at another time."

As Spirit continues to remember its true nature, and as the physical vibration rises, is there a natural tendency for the physical to be at a higher frequency and therefore drawn more into the "knowing" of Spirit as it remembers?

"Yes, Little Brother, as your awakening deepens, you will be lifting the physical, emotional, and mental 'bodies' to higher frequencies.

But while you are in this incarnation, you will still be drawn to earth's vibrational pull. You will be able to achieve the highest frequency that is currently available within your earth.

"Sharing this knowledge with others will also help to raise your vibrations, as you will be fulfilling portions of your intended purpose for your incarnation, which is to help others to awaken. We are very pleased that we have heard many conversations where discoveries are being made, and felt, about the Teachings. You understand them within the 'level' you are in your 'Now.' They are not too overwhelming to those who receive them. We are pleased to see that you have held back your knowledge when you realized that others were not quite to the moment of understanding. It is as we have taught, proceed with baby steps. You give them just enough to think about by understanding where they are on their path. All this helps you to also strengthen your vibration."

It seems that the mental body, as Spirit remembers, would actually unite with it. Even though it is of the physical, it seems to be the link that unites the two.

"What it does, Little Brother, is to move your thoughts, actions, and intentions from the mind based in ego to the mind based in Spirit."

This would then become a comingling of the two?

"This certainly can, and does, occur. We know that it does take trial on your part, but it can happen. It is what we have taught about being in Spirit mind, or ego mind. This is what we have meant by this."

It is like a shift in awareness?

"Yes, and the awareness is shifting greatly right now. Unfortunately, there is also a movement by others to shroud or stop the Awakening. We are not concerned for we know that the Awakening will continue and that this attempt to stop it is by those who are still in an ego consciousness. An example would be men in business who see only their own gain, or it could be anyone who thinks of themself first and then of others. It would be those who are more aware of profit and less of what caring and giving can accomplish. There are still many who think like this, but these are their journeys, their choices. There resides fear within them of anything they view as new or different, and this allows ego to generate this fear within many others. This same mindedness, this ego, has affected many Teachers who came, and come, with a message of Love and truth."

Then those who are ego-based will not understand the Awakening?

"If ones ego is allowed control, then it will not even be aware of the Awakening and will simply remain spiritually asleep. You are either choosing to be Spirit in all you do, or you are allowing ego to be in control. You cannot switch on and off like a lightbulb once you are awakening and awake. You may experience moments within your 'Now' where ego will attempt to reestablish itself, but it is quickly recognized by Spirit and squashed, if you will, in its attempt. When these moments do arise, do not fall into ego blame, simply recognize, refocus, and put ego behind you."

This heightens the understanding that in order to awaken, you must shift from being led by the ego to being led by Spirit. There is no way one can stay in ego and awaken.

"This is quite correct, Little Brother. You understand, of course, as we stated, that as you are awakening, there will be moments that you may transgress and go back into ego. How long you remain there will be your choice, but this shall be less and less with your continued awakening.

"We have told each of you that your knowledge shall be deeper as now is the time to accelerate the Teachings. We are looking forward to questions for us to gauge where you are in your understanding. No matter what the questions may be, we encourage them, for it will give us the opportunity to see where you are. We will put forth things from time to time for you to chew upon, and then will anxiously await the questioning that results from them."

Is it the emotional body, as the person awakens, that is most susceptible to the influence of the ego? Is it this "body" that pulls the person back into self, or ego?

"Yes, for it is the emotional body that is the feeling part of the physical and it has always been that which can easily be led in many ways. For example, children that are abused can become tough, if you will, within their emotional 'body.' It can either implode by creating many physical problems or many emotional problems. If they are not yet awakened to their true nature, then they may make choices based upon this experience because this experience has become an identifier. Once they awaken to the truth, and the source of all things, then they realize they can begin to let go of those identifiers and choose to create in the 'Now' and let go of what no longer serves who they know their selves to be. So, yes, that emotional 'body' is certainly one that is swayed the easiest."

It seems to be the body that is most effected, or the easiest to be effected, by fear.

"As you know, your physical body itself is simply that. It is composed of tissue, bone, and the organs that continue you on. The emotional 'body,' even though being led by the physical body, is also greatly influenced through Spirit."

It is clear that it is so important for them to shift to the understanding that they are Spirit. It is not just a partial shift; it is the complete shifting for the total awakening of a person's being.

"For it is the shifting of the mind, and once mind goes to Spirit, the emotional also goes."

How does fear affect the emotional body?

"Fear, which is ego-based, keeps the emotional body grounded where the ego is most comfortable. This is why we have said many times that sometimes you simply need to get outside of your comfort zones."

The thought came that this is kind of a cyclical thing; when the emotional body, being influenced by the ego, is expressed through the physical, many people will arrive at a point where they may think that they have gained control over ego. This actually is nothing more than a self-preservation action on the part of the ego to try and convince a person through use of the emotions that they have reached a certain state of awakening. In actuality, they have not awakened. In order to maintain control, the ego must continue this pattern.

"It is as if the ego is able to erect a cloaking device that can actually make the emotional, mental, and physical body believe that it is going on to the next Spiritual step. Actually, it is trying to stay where it is most comfortable. Ego wishes to always be in control and it needs to do things to convince the physical body and, in particular, the emotional 'body' that 'No, this is where you need and should be.' 'You are moving forward, you are advancing.' Actually it is simply keeping you where it is most comfortable. You will go outside the ego by becoming aware of who you are and living that awareness and truth. You must choose to hear and to shift from ego mind to Spirit mind."

I see that the created belief, by ego, then creates an emotional attachment that the person feels they cannot let go of, but this is only an illusion of support.

"Yes, Little Brother. You know how your starfish clings to a rock. You know how difficult it can be to remove them. That is much like the emotional 'body.' It simply takes someone, or something, to pry it off the rock. The rock is the ego. Sometimes it takes a shock of some sort to remove it, or maybe it can be done through a gentle peeling. It is the intent of Spirit at that point to keep what has been peeled back remaining peeled back. So it becomes somewhat of a tug-of-war, if you will, between the ego-based mind and the Spirit-based mind. Once you know the truth, once you take that step, you truly will desire to take the next step, whatever that awakening step may be."

Each of us has come to understand the power of forgiveness. Is there a deeper awareness that we can convey to others?

"You should always forgive in Spirit and not with the mouthing of words by ego. It is difficult to say 'I forgive you' if you do not feel that forgiveness, if that forgiveness does not touch you. It is very easy for the ego to say whatever is necessary to be said. If the ego feels that to say 'I forgive you' will help maintain its control, then in the long run, that is what it will say. It is Spirit that 'feels' that forgiveness with unconditional Love."

For my own experience, it was reaching this state of forgiveness that made it possible for the unification of my body, mind, and Spirit.

"Yes, once you have truly, in Spirit, forgiven a person, a circumstance, or an event, and once you understand what it was, that it is no longer serving you and that it is no longer present in your current 'Now,' you begin to unify. Do not dwell upon past 'Now's' that no longer exist, nor look toward 'Now's' that have yet to arrive. Simply 'be' in the moment of your current 'Now.'"

This is surely a pivotal point in the process of awakening.

"As you truly awaken, you will know that everything that occurred in a past 'Now' is to be forgiven and forgotten if you are truly to move forward with the knowledge and understanding of who you are. Spirit knows life as experiences that are created either by ego or Spirit. If you have been in another's created experience, do not let it become your identifier and know that you can now choose those experiences in which you desire to be a part of. If you find yourself not being who you are, or in situations that no longer serve you, then choose to leave those behind you. Move forward in the understanding that you create your experiences through your own choices, and there is always a choice. Ego may desire you to think differently, but know within the Spirit that you are that you always have the choice for your desired experience. Only you allow ego to make those choices for you.

"Are there any other questions? If not, we would suggest that you begin formulating questions for when we meet again. At that time, we will be bringing more for you to learn and understand."

Thank you so much for these sessions. They have been very beneficial.

"We are so pleased to touch upon those things that are so foremost upon your minds and hearts so that you may see them clearer. As we have said, it is all part of the Awakening, for now you can understand how to present these Teachings to others as well. For now, we shall depart in Love and Blessings."

It was a wonderful teaching the "Girls" had given to us on the emotional, mental, and physical bodies, and their relationship to themselves and to Spirit. We were particularly interested in the spiritual body and how it is connected to the physical as well as emotional and mental bodies. In Bruce's book *Now That You Are Awake*, this is identified as the spiritual membrane, or spiritual essence, and it protects the physical body from being damaged by Spirit as it awakens. It also protects it in the presence of higher frequencies. This coating, or membrane, expands to protect our physical bodies when we are in the presence of higher energies. It is extremely durable and enables us, as eternal Spirit, to encompass a physical body during our incarnation on earth.

We had so much to do that afternoon. We dropped off our mining trailer, got the fifth wheel opened up, and made a list of all the things we needed to bring back with us to set us up for the summer. We decided to leave Sarah with Annie. We knew she was left in the very best of care.

That evening we talked about all that we had learned over the past three sessions and then retired for the evening.

The next morning, we left around six to get as far down the valley as we could by late afternoon. We arrived back in Las Vegas around two the next afternoon.

Once we arrived home, we began to pack up everything on our list to get ready for the return trip. I can tell you I was getting really tired of that drive and was looking forward to being in one place for a little while. We had been thinking about getting an attorney for some time, so we made an appointment to see one before we left. We really needed to find out where we stood rather than to try and second-guess how matters might unfold. The meeting we had was very helpful and we found out that our imagining had painted a much dire picture than was actually the case. We were only a few months behind on the house and we had every intention of trying to recover. We were anywhere from one to six months behind on some of our bills. Our savings had helped to keep several bills current, including our fifth wheel. This was a very good thing as that is what we planned on living in during the summer mining season. The attorney's advice was to do nothing for the time being, as it would take months before any foreclosure proceedings would be started. He informed us the same thing would be true for the bill collectors. The phone calls and collection notices would continue of course, but the situation was, in his opinion, not as pressing as we were making it out to be. I sure trusted him and hoped he was right. I still continued putting out applications for jobs and would look for something in Happy Camp as well.

The news from the attorney was like a breath of fresh air for us. We now felt that we had time to turn things around. We were definitely uplifted by this information. He said that if and when we were ready to possibly file for bankruptcy, just give him a call and he would help us with everything. Of course at this time that would be the very last choice we would desire to make. We figured that this news from the attorney was what the "Girls" had mentioned in the session right before we came back to Las Vegas.

We ended up spending a week at home. It was a very special time for us. The feeling of actually being able to relax in our home was not one we had enjoyed for many months.

We arrived back in Happy Camp on April 17, and naturally we were all interested in learning what the "Girls" had in store for us in their next meeting.

April 17, 2008

"**We do greet** thee. We are most pleased to be together this evening. We are so happy that all are back safely. We understand that there are questions."

There are questions that I formulated while Little One and Little Brother were gone. When Spirit travels during sleep, does it remain in forgetfulness?

"This would be the time, as Spirit is traveling, that your ego is not present or active. There are moments then when you are not in complete forgetfulness. This 'time' of travel would create the most vivid dreams, or visions. It is because Spirit, at those moments, is in more of a clarity of remembrance than when you are consciously awake."

Some mornings when I wake up, things come in that are what I call understandings. Could that be from Spirit traveling?

"Definitely it could be that while your physical body was asleep, or unconsciously aware, that Spirit was traveling and regaining the memories of who it is. It could be that as you awoke, these memories would for a short while remain with you."

How is Astrid connected with your planet?

"Astrid, the Divine Mother, is One with the masculine essence of the One Spirit, therefore, she is our Divine Mother as well. You know, as we have taught, that they are two in One, masculine and feminine aspects and essences, and it is that One Energy that is for all universes and all planets. Her connection with us would be somewhat different than with you, for you have not yet remembered or awakened to the truth of who you are. Of course you are now remembering and awakening, but there are many on your planet that has yet to choose to remember. Our planet did not come in with the same type of forgetfulness you chose, it was not in our blueprints. We chose to incarnate on our planet with less forgetfulness in order to experience the Divine in a different way, a somewhat more intense way, if you will."

Please explain what the Divine Mother meant when she came to our session and said that she felt as if she had come home.

"The term 'coming home' simply means that for so long upon your planet there has been very little remembrance of the Mother. There has been forgetting of that which was given to you in the beginning by her. This would be the nurturing of the earth, the compassion of one for another and the joy of living as One. This has been forgotten. This has been abused. It would be much like a person whose home was made uninhabitable, and therefore, they must not remain there. She simply withdrew, but now she feels as if she is 'coming home,' returning. She is coming back to that which she was the primary creator of, as far as the environment, the feminine essence. It is the return of the Divine Mother's Spirit, if you will, to that which she was cocreator."

She also said that she had been looking for a channel.

"It has been quite difficult for Her to find one who was willing for Her message to be pure, for not many upon your planet are able to do that, either by choice or by the fact that they are not yet awake enough. It has taken 'time' to find one who was willing to stand aside and allow our voices to be heard, with the use of her voice of course, and this is what the Divine Mother desired to bring her message through."

Thank you. Let me ask you, are there nature Spirits?

"Everything upon your planet has a vibration, if you will. Yes, *spirit* would indeed be a good word to describe the attributes of all living things. All things have a spirit of sorts. The wind has a spirit, the rain has a spirit, but it is not a spirit in the sense of your Spirit. It is more a quality, an essence."

Are all Spirits in the Absolute in the same level of knowing?

"When in the Absolute, all Spirits have full knowledge, recollection, and knowing of themselves. There are no levels, only the One Truth, which is for all to understand."

Is there any difference between the answers that are given by guides and by those Spirits that have passed over from their physical life but not yet returned to the Absolute?

"Yes, there is, for a Spirit who has not yet passed onto the Absolute may agree to meet with what we call a 'learned one,' or what you call psychics. Before you return to the Absolute, you may choose to stay within the earth's physical vibration in order to aid someone on their walk, to deliver a message of Love, or just stay close to those you shared your journey with. You will still retain some degree of forgetfulness but you will have full memory of your previous incarnation and those you shared it with. Your frequency, although raised from what it was while in the physical, has not yet risen back to what it will be upon your return to the Absolute. Your knowing of who you are is complete at the point of leaving your physical body, and this total remembering may help others as they continue their journeys. These Spirits can only come to you with the knowing of who they were while in the physical and it is to that incarnation they give you answers, and those messages are sometimes passed on through psychics or mediums. There are many out there who claim to be able to receive these messages, but sometimes they filter what they believe they are hearing through their own perceptions or ego. By doing this, the message is not always delivered as was intended. We would caution those who would seek out these psychics. Be aware of several things. If they tell you what you will be doing or where you will be in a day, a week, a month, or more, then we would suggest you walk away. For no one can tell you these things, these are things that shall happen from your choices, your desires. You create your future through these choices, and since you have yet to make them, they cannot possibly know what your choice may be. You may also receive messages in dreams, visions, and things you see or hear.

"As to guides, these are Spirits that you know from the Absolute and they agreed, before you entered the physical, to come along with you to give you guidance. They are the small voices you hear when trying to make a choice; they are that 'knowing' that comes over you at certain times. These guides shall remain with you until you leave the physical. They are always available to lend you energy and guidance. Once you know of their presence, then 'communicating' with them is the next step."

Would you please explain what is meant by the phrase "In my Father's house, there are many mansions"?

"This is an interesting saying, if you will. Simply what it means is in the realm of the One, there are other 'homes,' or 'mansions,' meaning other planets and universes. So this saying would mean that there are many life-forms within the Oneness. For instance, your planet, our planet, and other universes. They all coexist within the One."

I'm really learning to begin from scratch now.

"This is sometimes the best way, for if you go into any situation with a preconceived idea, whatever you hear in that situation will be filtered through that conception. It is necessary to be as a newborn babe, learning, discovering. When you do not bring with you established beliefs, then you are learning and not filtering. We never ask one to discard current theories or beliefs, simply to set them aside as you hear. If it is your choice to pick them up again after hearing, then you shall be blessed to continue that journey, but if what we teach resonates within the part that 'knows,' that part being who you are, Spirit, then you shall continue your journey with a new understanding and begin creating a new experience. Little Brother, do you have any questions?"

I'm quite interested in focusing energy where it would be most productive.

"Energy is always productive wherever it is focused. It is through the intent of the one pulling the energy, for whatever purpose it may be, that allows the energy to flow to the desired conclusion. This is why we say to always be aware of utilizing the energy at its highest, or 'turned up.' Energy surrounds and encompasses all things, but there are those who 'turn down' the energy when making choices and therefore create experiences that do not serve in Love. When you focus energy into any one direction, be sure that you are creating, in Love, those things that are for the highest. Once you become aware of who you truly are, and live that awareness, then all the energy you draw upon will be for the highest good of all who receive it, or all created desires."

Little One and I realized, when at home, that it was time for us to focus on what we can do and no longer be focused on what others are doing.

"Yes, for to be too focused upon what others may do is simply to be choosing to be in their experience and this is not what you are choosing. You are choosing to be in your own created experience. You simply let them do what they are going to do."

Would you please comment further on how we manifest our desire?

"Sister of My Sister, when you are in the stillness, in the silence, and you are being who you truly are, Spirit, and you are not in physical mind, ego, then you are making that connection with the Absolute. It is at that moment that Spirit understands that all that has ever been, or will be, exists already in the Absolute. When you create a thought, which becomes a desire, you put your energy and focus into it and release it into the Absolute knowing that it is complete and manifested within that realm. Then through your continued created actions, and choices you live your life with this 'knowing' of completion and trust in its unfolding. Whatever occurs shall always be for your highest continuance. When you await a destination, or a particular manifestation, then you are not continuing in the 'Now.' Live each moment of every 'Now' creating, choosing, and experiencing."

Also it is not to expect it to happen immediately?

"Yes. Much can also be accomplished with 'feeling' also. The Divine Parents 'felt' into reality everything that shall ever be. They did not think things into reality, they 'felt' them.

"We would now like to say that we are ready to begin the Teachings again. They will be, as we have always said, through the questions you ask so we would like to have you think about your questions regarding what we have spoken about prior to this session. We will, of course, be bringing up new things as well in order to encourage more questioning. We do believe that you have the foundation quite well regarding the teachings on Awakening, so we shall now move beyond the foundation. Knowledge of the walls are beginning to go into your 'knowing.' So we will continue along that line and much will be imparted as you formulate your questions for us. If there are no further questions for this evening ,we do depart in Love and Blessings."

This turned out to again be a very interesting session. We had a number of questions to clear up before the newer Teachings were to begin. These questions came about from past sessions after we had some time to digest the given material. We were well informed in regard to free will, which we understood to be the freedom to create at will, but we had some remaining questions as to how much involvement the Divine Parents exercise in our lives where this is concerned. We knew that, in general, their desire is to experience that which we choose to experience, but that there are times when direct intervention may take place. These are more precisely termed as "appointed times" as we later learned. Still, it was very important for us to gain this information to add to our growing understanding.

Normally we do not learn much about future events other than that they are part of the Awakening and that earth changes are part and parcel of it also. We also understood that the economic upheaval, which was just getting started, was also a part of mankind's wake-up call.

The teachings we received on Spirit, and manifestation, added still more information to help us understand all we could about this process. There are so many voices out there discussing manifestation today and we really wanted to obtain a clear understanding of this subject.

Bruce and I were looking toward a profitable year gold prospecting. We had worked so hard the year before with only minimal results. We knew that residual effects from past choices must be allowed to run their course and we were completely accepting of our situation, but really desired to do much better this year.

When it had been mentioned that this was the time for new teachings, we were really excited. We joyfully anticipated the next session that was to follow two days later. As the weather was damp and very cold in Happy Camp, we decided to stay temporarily at Annie's home. This proved to be a good decision as the weather turned really bitter and our fifth wheel was not equipped for this type of cold.

April 19, 2008

"We do greet thee. How is everyone on this your evening? Do we have your questions?"

We are all wonderful, thank you. Yes, we do have several questions. In regard to the emotional, mental, and physical bodies, what can we say about them as we teach others so as not to confuse them?

"We feel that the important thing, of course, would be to explain that the only thing that has form, and therefore is an actual body, is the physical. The mental and emotional bodies are simply essences of feelings, thoughts, and choices that are based either upon Spirit or that are leaning toward the physical, which would be ego mind. It is up to the individual and their perceptions of things as to which way those bodies, or essences, if you will, will be directed. It is important to understand that your emotional and mental 'bodies' may be directed by either Spirit or ego. These bodies are attached not only to the physical but to Spirit as well."

We talked before about a membrane. May we go into that at this point, or is this meant for some other time?

"No, now is fine. It is simply that this membrane is not something that is seen, only known. It is somewhat of a protection, if you will, between Spirit, which is pure energy, and the physical body. There was a buffer needed, for if Spirit was to encompass the physical in its entirety, its pure form, its full energy, the physical body would not have been able to absorb and contain it. There was this transparent layer, this membrane, created to protect the physical body. Whether it had ever been detected we do not know, but it is just that protective layer between the full force of Spirit and that of the frequency and vibration, or density, of the physical."

Does this membrane get thinner with awakening?

"No, if anything, it would get thicker for with the Awakening comes more energy. It is not that the physical body will not rise in its vibration, for it certainly does. As Spirit begins to remember, the physical body will also begin to rise in its frequency, but it will never achieve the same vibration and frequency as Spirit."

With attainment of higher evolvement, there is no more need for the membrane, is there?

"The evolvement may only be of Spirit awakening to its truth, so the physical body would still be somewhat protected continually as the vibration of both rises. It is important again to also understand that your emotional and mental essence can be attached either to Spirit or ego. If you are in Spirit, the feelings, actions, and words you contain will be ones of unconditional Love, joy, and compassion for all things. If feelings, actions, and words are coming from ego, then they will be of hatred, anger, confusion, and all the energy will be 'turned down.'"

So this would be a good tool for self-examination as to the degree of awareness the person is experiencing?

"If your emotions are jumbled, so to speak, and you are feeling much anger, hatred, separation, or any of the other emotions that you have termed as negative, then you can be assured you are coming from ego. Your emotional 'body' is now coming from the physical, or ego, and not from Spirit."

Would it then be true that as you awaken, you shift your awareness from ego to Spirit when you are dealing with anger, hurt, or whatever your feelings may be that represent energy "turned down"?

"If someone is still coming from any of those feelings and emotions, then it is for them to discover where these feelings are coming from, find its roots, and look at it for what it truly is. Once you do this, you then deal with it and let it go so that it does not return. Be sure that you are truly letting it go and not retaining a portion, or portions, of that feeling and the cause for that feeling."

I am following up on what you told us about when Spirit leaves the body and goes immediately to the Absolute, where then would be what we call ghosts?

"Simply speaking, a ghost, which is a word created by man, is Spirit that has not chosen to go to the Light, or Absolute, yet. There are cases and instances where the 'blueprint' of a Spirit who incarnates into a physical body contains an agreement that says that at the 'time' of their physical passing, they shall, as you would say, remain earthbound. They wish to experience what it would be like to be here without the physical body although still within the vibrational frequency of the physical body. Once you have left the physical, you are in the understanding of who you are but are not in the total remembrance that you will have upon your return to the Absolute. They may also have chosen to stay close to someone and act as their guide, to deliver a final message, or just to watch over a loved one for a period of 'time.'"

What occurs to the emotional and mental essences once Spirit leaves the physical body?

"When Spirit leaves the body, it takes with it all emotional and mental essences. It may also keep those emotions with it while remaining within the earth's physical vibration, should it choose to stay, even though it is no longer in physical form. Spirit, of course, is simply choosing to remain in the physical realm for a period of 'time.' It is not in complete remembering because it has not yet returned to the Absolute. Basically what you have is Spirit no longer inhabiting or encompassing a physical body, but is still experiencing things that were a part of that physical body. There is a limit, if you will, on the 'time' spent doing that. We know that many have stayed for what you call centuries, but it is still limited 'time.' At some point, Spirit will simply choose to return to the Absolute, and so they do."

This would also explain the attachments of Spirits who have left the physical body but have not returned to the Absolute, to come as a guide to help someone who is going through similar experiences during their incarnation.

"Many times, that might be the case. If they left, let's say because of an overdose, they may then choose to stay beside someone they know in order to help them to avoid this same outcome. Generally if you are a guide, you have agreed upon that in the Absolute and so enter with another Spirit at the time of their incarnation."

We were speaking the other day regarding guides. We come in with guides, and we may acquire additional guides during our physical lifetimes. You just mentioned that this does sometimes happen, that Spirit once leaving the physical body may wish to be with another individual because they have something to give to them in order to help them along. Are you also saying that there is a higher degree of "knowing" for Spirit once it has left the physical?

"Yes, for at the moment of leaving their physical body, they completely understood what occurred within the physical to cause their death. They have the 'knowing.' They have the understanding that many times what they were doing, while in the physical body, may have not been the choices that allowed for continuance. They can then desire to be with someone who is having a similar experience in order to guide them and to help them understand their choices. Going directly to the Absolute is their choice as always."

So where would you say they are existing?

"This is a good question. They are certainly within your vibrational realm, your physical realm. It is not something of course that can be seen, but there are many who are able to detect the frequency and vibrations from within this realm."

Could someone stay in that state for a while?

"As we stated, that would be possible if that was the choice that was made. We find that generally that is not chosen, but if for some reason Spirit desires this, then it may be."

What about those spirits who need to have assurance from others that they are forgiven before they go on to the Absolute?

"Sister of My Sister, we do not believe that this would be a consideration for Spirit for it would know who it is and that there is no necessity for forgiveness. That is an emotion of the physical body and not of Spirit. If the ego was allowed to be in the lead during the lifetime of the physical and there were choices and actions that misused the energy, then this was a physical creation. Once the physical body has died, then Spirit is awake, even if it had not chosen to awake during its physical experience. Once awake and in the 'knowing' and remembering of its true essence, then it also leaves behind those misused emotions of the physical body."

In this realm where Spirit stays before returning to the Absolute, is there "time"?

"No, not as you know it. They do not know if they have been gone thirty, forty years or more. To them it was as if it just happened. When they see you, they see you as you were when they passed. To them, when they do return to the Absolute, it is as if their passing has just happened. The only place where 'time' as you know it exists is within your own vibrational frequency upon your planet."

Once Spirit returns to the Absolute, they may want to come back to visit, but is it under different circumstances?

"Once Spirit has passed into the Absolute, their return would only be through their choice to reincarnate."

The membrane that you spoke of earlier, what relationship is that to the veils that protect us from too much knowing, or remembrance before we are ready to receive it?

"The veils are in place due to the collective consciousness. The barrier, or membrane, we speak of is simply a precaution. It would be the same as if you were working with electricity and would wear rubber boots. You would not stand in water and hang on to electricity for it would be too much for your physical body to bear. It is the same with the barrier we speak of. It is simply your rubber boots, if you will, against the energy that constitutes Spirit. Yet the veils are those which are held by the collective, they are in place due to your experiences, creations, and choices."

In regard to the Energy, we understand that the Divine Mother's energy and essence will be present at the Centers and eventually the Sanctuary?

"The Divine Mother has chosen to give her energy and essence to wherever it is you create a place of Teaching, Love, joy, compassion, and remembering. This place shall allow those who are Awakening to be within the energy of unconditional Love and to begin creating their journey with their new understanding of who they truly are. The energy work and healing that is found within this place shall be extraordinary."

At one point in our previous discussions, we talked about miracles. These were not just miracles, they were "miracles."

"We know that as the Awakening continues and as the Centers and Sanctuary are created, the energy within them shall rise. This energy is the creative substance for all 'miracles.'"

At these places that we build, who is going to be doing most of the teachings?

"Sister of My Sister, we would be most pleased if you would decide to do some of this. It would also be those of the council who resonate with that aspect and who have that inclination, that desire, if you will, to teach."

Will there be channeling?

"Yes."

There is a lot for us to digest or, as you say, to chew on. We will have questions for our next session.

"That is well. For now, we shall depart in Love and Blessings."

There was more information given in this session that increased our understanding of the spiritual essence, or membrane, that protects our physical body from the full energy of Spirit. We now also knew that it protected the emotional and mental essences as well.

It was a wonderful discussion regarding what happens to Spirit after leaving the physical body and its choices, at that point, as to return directly to the Absolute or remain and continue to experience without the body. One may also choose to help someone still incarnated and guide them on their journey. This is an area of considerable debate with many different opinions and interpretations concerning Spirit's journey after the death of the physical body. This discussion really put matters into sharp focus for us. It also helped me to understand, and explain, past experiences with what I always knew, and referred to, as "earthbound" spirits. It was interesting to learn that they were still in a lower vibration than that of the Absolute and, as a result of this, did not as yet experience full remembrance. They have no concept of "time" as we experience during our physical lifetime. Their concept was the same as that of the Absolute where "no time" exists. Our concept of one who has "hung around" for centuries may seem to be only a day to their recollection. Even though they may stay behind, when they return to the Absolute, it is just as though they had gone directly from their physical body immediately following their death. This was eye-opening in so many ways.

We had just begun discussions regarding the first Center(s) and the eventual Sanctuary. It will be exciting when the "time" comes for the actual creation, on a physical level, of these places. For now we had been given some basic guidelines to build upon.

After the session, we talked among ourselves about all we had learned. We were truly feeling that the Teachings had begun again in earnest.

April 20, 2008

Once again we gathered for the next session, centered ourselves, and activated the recorder.

"We do greet thee. We have been requested by the Divine Parents to come this evening to speak with you on a couple of things. We would like to start at first with something we would like to see more of, if you will. It would be what you term on your planet as laughter. Of course we take this project quite seriously, but yet we think that it is possible that you are taking it even more seriously and we would like you to have joy in it as well, therefore we desire for you more laughter. Little Brother, you have a tendency to be quite serious, as you know, and we think that more laughter in your life is something that everyone would benefit by. It is something that helps to embrace others and is a wonderful conduit of energy one to the other. This was just something we desired to touch upon."

What if I tickle him?

"This may be helpful, Sister of My Sister, but we would suggest for you to stay away from his feet as he is quite sensitive there. Are you in the understanding that we are just a bit careful that these Teachings could become all too serious and that you may remove some of the actual joy that we have come to give? Although this is a serious project, it is not one to become obsessed with and lose the joy and happiness that this understanding will bring into your journey. Are you in the understanding of what we share?"

Yes, we will be sure to live this joy that the Teachings bring. I have a question. When we leave our physical body, we know that Spirit may choose to stay around longer. When they do decide to go back to the Absolute, would you please give us an understanding of what happens then?

"When Spirit passes back into the Absolute, they then have a full understanding of all incarnations past. They are able, if you will, to continue watching over loved ones, although not in the same way as when they were in the physical realm or even as Spirit within the physical vibration. In full 'knowing,' they may continue to observe, if this is their choice. While they are in the Absolute, they again may choose to experience life in another incarnation, and this is what we have taught as the 'blueprint' forming period. Many will draw upon memories from past incarnations that they may desire to experience again, although possibly in a different way than they had experienced it before. This choice is now made in full 'knowing' and of what occurred in that prior incarnation. So it is a reexperiencing, if you will. Most, we know, will remain in the Absolute for however 'long' they may desire. They may reincarnate into the planet they just experienced in, or they may choose another. It is different for each one. There is absolute contentment in the essence and presence of the One, and there is no 'time' limit as to when they may decide to either incarnate, or remain."

When they desire to come back, let's say, to earth, do they choose what level of evolvement they will come in with?

"Just as it is a choice to enter in forgetfulness, it is also the choice as to the degree of forgetfulness you enter with. If they come in, as Yeshua did, with almost pure remembering, then their physical bodies would be quite protected and in quite a different vibration, if you will. There have not been many that have been chosen, and who choose, to enter into the physical as Teachers. They have become persecuted by those they came to teach, and with man's ego and need to control, the true message they bring has been lost and only parts of the truth survive within man's creation."

How would you describe the Buddha?

"Buddha was an enlightened one. Spirit that decided to come in with more understanding, more knowledge, and therefore was awakened to the truth of who he truly was. He came and walked with man and taught. He chose what he would do, and be, before he entered the physical, much as Yeshua did. Much as Mohammed did. These were learned Teachers, but they were not allowed by the people and by the collective consciousness to teach all that they would desired to teach."

What about Einstein?

"Yes, Einstein did come into a physical body, of course, but it was chosen in his 'blueprint' that he would come in with more physical intelligence. This is not necessarily a 'knowing,' as we have taught, but more of a choice to use more percentage of the human brain than had previously been used. You can choose to come in many different ways with either a physical understanding or one of Spirit. You will always come with some degree of chosen forgetfulness in order to create, experience, and awaken."

This is a wonderful teaching for us and others. First of all, never judge anyone for you may not know who you are speaking with.

"One should never judge another, for this is not of Spirit but of ego. It is true that you may be speaking with one who chose to come as Teacher, but there are many who simply are announcing their own truths, from their ego, for the purpose of control. We would say to hear with your 'knowing' the words they share and to ask several questions. Are these things being said coming from unconditional Love and Spirit, or do they represent an idea of control or ego? Always 'feel' what you are hearing, does it resonate completely with who you know yourself to be? Is it given in joy and to enable you the freedom to create at will as you are on your journey? If something does not create within you the sense of Love, of 'knowing,' then you should look within yourself to find those truths that do represent who you are."

The experiences that the individual accrues in each physical lifetime, how does that affect Spirit in the Absolute? Through these experiences, does that increase the "knowing"?

"The 'knowing' is full and complete once Spirit returns to the Absolute. You can look at each incarnation as if you are reading through a diary. You then have a complete 'knowing' of each experience as you lived them and you may decide to draw upon any one of those experiences in future incarnations."

So we know ourselves through our experiences?

"Yes, once you return to the Absolute, you certainly know yourself in all of your experiences."

When you hear the term "old soul," what does that mean?

"It is simply referring to one who has incarnated into the physical quite a few times. You can be an 'old soul' on several planes from various incarnations, or you can be a 'new soul.' Some Spirits may choose to remain in the Absolute a great long 'time.' Some simply pop in and pop back out. It is simply a choice. We know that though many speak about reincarnation not many necessarily believe it. We do not understand, why wouldn't it be so? If you have made the choice to come in the first time, then why would you not have the same choice to come again?"

What about other incarnations? You have given us some knowledge as to our past incarnations, but are there others?

"We do not always know of people's incarnations unless the Divine One desires for us to know this. We can share with you that all who come to the council shall have been with each other several times. This is the way it has been chosen throughout different lifetimes. You are all now on this journey of sharing with others what you have been taught, and of bringing the energy work, the healing, to all who choose to hear."

Is there then an overall purpose to the shared incarnations of those who are, and will be, on the council?

"There is a flowing to every incarnation. Each incarnation, especially for the council, occurred for the purpose of this time, for this shared remembering.

"Next meeting, we will speak somewhat on the creation of Centers and of the eventual Sanctuary. We will also be bringing Teachings as well. Do you have any questions?"

Not at this Now. Thank you.

"You are most welcome. Remember to choose and to bring in more laughter. This is a joyful experience and need not be so serious. You will be reaching and speaking with many who are also on the journey to remembering. It shall be through your sharing of the energy and the Teachings that others shall know. If there are no questions in this moment of your 'time,' then we shall depart in much Love and Blessings."

We were a little surprised when it was suggested that there be more laughter in our lives. We knew that we were quite serious while in Las Vegas, but we felt that we had begun to feel lighter since our return to Happy Camp. Certainly there could be more laughter and we agreed to add more and find humor in our daily lives. There was no doubt that Bruce was the most serious of all. He, of course, had his reasons for this, but he did get the message and made an effort to lighten up. We were finally away from the incessant phone calls and this helped relax us and allowed us to take things in a more lighthearted fashion.

Just as we thought we were getting a good grasp on the progression of Spirit, more information came our way. This time regarding what Spirit can choose to do after it returns to the Absolute. What a beautiful understanding, not only of who we are but that we always have the freedom to create at will, no matter where Spirit is.

As always, we were eager for the next session. It may seem that this was all our days consisted of, but there was the work on the books, a job working five days a week for me, meditation time, and life. These Teachings were giving, and allowing, us to daily create our experiences with the understanding of residuals, who we truly are, and that it's all about our choices. What each of us had been given was so enlightening that it is no wonder we were always ready to speak with them again.

April 22, 2008

We all sat down for this next meeting and, as always, looked forward to all we would hear and learn.

"We do greet thee. There is one thing we would like to touch upon this evening. We would like to teach something that you were talking about at your mealtime. This is the subject of breathing in your meditation practices. We have taught this technique as circle breathing. In the evening, we would like for you to do as many cycles of this as you are comfortable doing. We would then like to have you work through colors. As you are doing your circle breathing, we would like you to bring colors into your breathing. See whatever colors you desire in whatever order you choose. We wish you to 'feel' as you are bringing these colors into your breathing. Actually begin to 'feel' the physical body and its response to each color. We would suggest that you begin to do that starting with this evening. You could start with six to eight cycles of the circle breathing technique and then bring in the colors. See them as brilliantly as you can until you feel you can reach out and touch them. This will not be a physical touching, it will be one of Spirit, a 'knowing.' If you drift off to sleep while doing this, that is fine. Keep aware of the 'feelings' that occur as you view each color. It will help you with focus and it shall be quite interesting to hear your reactions. There will be more breathing techniques in the future, but start with this. We will speak with you later regarding your experiences.

"We are so joyous. We are full of the color of Oneness. We are to the brim with the excitement, 'feeling,' and the Love of this project. It is our blessing as well that we partake in the sharing of this 'time."

In the experiencing of colors, will there be a feeling attached to them?

"There may be. We will be interested in hearing from you what your experience is. Once you have done this for, let's say, a week of your 'time,' we will come back to this subject. We would suggest for you to write down what your experiences this week are. It will be most interesting for us to see where each one is."

I feel the colors more strongly when I am near water.

"Yes, Sister of My Sister. The presence of water, particularly living water, moves as a ribbon of Oneness, if you will. It is the essence of one being in that movement of the water that shall rap around you, if that is understood. It is freeing when your meditation is done within moving water, whether it be the ocean, a river, a creek, or even water moving through a fountain. We would suggest that you have within your home a small fountain and that it be running during your meditations, or healing sessions. You will find that this energy of water can accomplish much."

Would you say that what we are doing is transforming our understanding of physical components to spiritual content?

"Yes, Little Brother, this is correct. This is the first step of all you will take, to move your understanding from the physical awareness to ones of Spirit. As we said, we will be most interested within a week of your 'time' to see what has occurred and what you have written regarding your feelings and experiences. It is by these that we will know when you are ready to go on to more advanced teachings.

"If there are no further questions, we shall depart in Love and Blessings."

We really enjoyed the exercise involving circle breathing and the drawing in of colors. This was quite an experience. Each of us daily would write down our experiences during this particular meditation. We knew that our individual results would be an indication as to when the next level of teaching on this subject would begin.

This was a relatively short session compared to some we had received, but I understood that there was an "understanding" of the meditation and the colors for us to arrive at. I have chosen to keep my commentary on this session short because it is for each one to experience and "feel" this, and it is your experience also.

April 26, 2008

After dinner, we all sat down to hear what turned out to be a most interesting session.

"We do greet thee. Everyone is well? What are your questions?"

Greetings to you also. My question is, do you have light constantly on your planet?

"We have what you here call twilight. We do have days of warmth that we create from within, and we can also have the intent and create sunlight. Our light is what we are desiring at any particular time."

Do you require rest?

"We do, as we still require a time of regeneration. These moments for us would be equivalent to your sleep."

What type of work do you do?

"We are for the Awakening of each and every planet. Our project, of course, right now is your earth. Our main job, if you will, is for reaching out with unconditional Love and helping others to awaken and understand who they truly are."

Is this the focus of everyone on your planet?

"Our children are also brought up to understand this and to know that this will be their purpose as well. Those Spirits who choose to incarnate on our planet do so with the full knowledge of what we are about, and it is their desire to join with us in bringing the Awakening."

Would you please speak on the effects of our words? Sometimes we say things that question what we have asked the Divine for. We put out certain requests but use the words "maybe," or "I hope I get it."

"Sister of My Sister, once you have put something into the 'hands' of the Divine, so to speak, let the Divine sit with its evolving. Know within yourself that you have created it, put energy and focus into it, and have 'let it go' to unfold in whatever way is for your greatest benefit. There need be no further speaking of it. Once you have truly released it and turned it over to the Divine, it is no longer in your hands. It shall be up to the Divine to create any adjustments, if you will, that will serve your purpose. When you use the words 'hope' or 'wish' or any others that indicate it may not happen, then you are unsure of the completion of that desire. Once you have released your desire, it is no longer yours to think about. Simply continue to create and experience along your journey."

I noticed today when doing the circle breathing that more energy was being felt through my feet than I have ever felt before.

"You, as you know, are always drawing energy from Mother Earth, but now you are beginning to feel that drawing, if you will. It is the feeling of the energy of all things of the earth. What have been your experiences with the breathing at night?"

The intent is to get myself to be conscious of breathing this way all of the time. The first night was interesting. I saw many colors but mostly orange and yellow and at times it was very bright. I also saw blue, white,

ultraviolet, and then purple. Some colors were very distinct while some were not. However, the more I tried to concentrate on the colors the duller they became. The feeling was that concentrating on the colors was something I should avoid.

"Do not concentrate on the colors for that will put you out of the Oneness and back into intellect. Simply allow the colors to flow around and within you and be one with them."

Thank you. Is there anything that we can do during the evening that will make our circle breathing more effective?

"We would suggest that you try this. When you lie down and begin your breathing, tighten your feet and then relax. Then tighten your calves and relax. Work all the way up your physical body until you reach your crown energy center, at that time be in the 'knowing' of yourself as Spirit. Then begin the cycle of the circle breathing. See what occurs. Sometimes it is the firing, if you will, of the nervous system of the physical body that can then also begin to fire the Spirit as well. This can aid you in your path of Awakening. Experience it and see what happens.

Remain in the Now and much will come.

"If there is nothing else for this 'time,' then we would like you to examine what being in the 'Now,' in the silence, truly means. When you are in the silence, you are in the One. We understand that this 'feeling' of being in the Now may not last for an extended period of time. Being in the 'Now' is what you are in every breath you take. All there is, is the 'Now.' When you release all past experiences, all past 'Now's,' and are simply within the moment, you will discover so much about yourself and your journey. Have no expectations of future 'Now's' and simply choose and create in each moment. If you begin to live this way, with the understanding of who you truly are, you will be creating all which you desire.

"Are there any further questions at this time? Then for now, we shall depart in much Love and Blessings."

This session produced a number of very interesting answers to many of the commonly held misconceptions of the current collective consciousness.

We had been told over and over again about the importance of words. We should only speak what we truly desire, as the words we speak are creative (as well as being misused and destructive). We should always be mindful that the words we use are conveying exactly what we mean and are not left "out there" for interpretation by others. It is kind of like the old saying "Say what you mean, and mean what you say." Words are creative, and if you are not being aware while you are speaking, you may be creating things that you do not desire. Do your words convey trust, Love, compassion, humor, or are they sending messages of gossip, doubt, condemnation, and mistrust? I have seen so many relationships ruined through words spoken in a moment of ego. It is always a good idea to stop, think, and be aware before you speak. I have also learned that if you do send words out that you would love to yank back, don't beat yourself up over it. Let it be a lesson to be Spirit in your conversations and not allow ego to be the speaker.

When you use words to create a desire, always be aware of not adding a qualifying statement that may express doubt about the unfolding of your desire. This sends out a mixed message. It is like writing a word on the blackboard with one hand and erasing it with the other hand before it can even be read. The result is that we receive nothing in return as we are not consistent in expressing our desires in a manner that conveys total trust and belief that those things will unfold for our highest energy. Things manifest in their proper 'time' and purpose, even if that seems to be a long wait. We have been told so many times, create, put energy to your desire, believe it to be complete, and let it go to unfold. Not an easy thing to always do, but I am really trying to do this.

April 30, 2008

"We do greet thee. How is everyone on this your day?"

We are all fine, thank you. I just read Little One's book. It is very inspiring.

"There are those, of course, who will not resonate with it, but that is quite normal. For the ones who truly resonate with it, they will benefit greatly from it. Are there questions this evening?"

We were just talking about how all of this project could not happen without your help. A short review of past earth history is enough to convince even the skeptic that this could not be possible without the aid and guidance of those who are highly evolved enough to be able to address all the concerns that have created the mess this world is in. This comes from a level of awareness and consciousness that can view the entire matter from a totally different perspective to see how it all occurred in the first place.

"For millennia, your earth has gone its way. It is not that they have not grown, as they certainly have especially in their technologies and their scientific knowledge. It is their spiritual growth that was not visible for much of your time, but we have seen more growth within the last forty of your years."

I agree completely with you. There really hasn't been much growth in the spiritual evolution of humanity in thousands of years.

"Even now with what is under way, although it is a wonder compared with what has been, it is still a toddler, if you will. This is why one of the purposes for The Light Alliance is to be a helping hand, guiding those who desire to take the next step in their own spiritual journey.

"We believe that the next step is for all within the Light Alliance family to reach out and share your understanding of the Teachings. Your understanding will, of course, continue to grow with all Teachings to come, but you have a good basic knowledge now. It is 'time' to reach out, meet other like-minded groups, and share what you have been taught. Are there questions?"

We all agree that the time has come to really go beyond ourselves and share the Teachings. I do have a question on a different subject. I was reading through the *Teachings from the Heart* book and found something on page 101 that just seemed to jump out at me. It was regarding the Circles of Light as they affect the awakening of the physical body. It was very interesting because it said that this was an added source of energy to aid us in our spiritual growth. Is there more to the Circles of Light other than the fact that we can draw energy from them? Do they have a bearing in raising the vibration of the physical body?

"The fact that you can draw energy from them not only will lift the vibration of Spirit into the remembering, but yes, it will also lift the vibration of your physical body as well. It is their purpose, at this point, for people to simply learn of their existence, learn to draw from their energy. When Spirit is energy-filled, then it cannot help but to raise the frequency of the physical as well."

Thank you for that. During my circle breathing the last couple of nights, I noticed my body seemed to have a sort of "lightness." I noticed this even more than the colors. Could you please comment on this?

"This is because with your breathing, you are moving further from ego mind and more into Spirit. You will not recognize the heaviness of the physical vibration and will only feel the lightness of Spirit. It is in those moments that you are closer to joining Spirit with the Oneness."

Does the membrane become thicker at that point?

"Yes, because your body must be protected from those times of higher energy."

This is making so much sense now.

"This helps you to be aware of the feeling of joining in the Oneness. You will feel lightness and also an expansion. This is not an expansion of the physical, but of Spirit. You will begin to feel as if you encompass your universe. Each will, of course, experience this differently, but the idea is to be in the Oneness, the stillness, spiritually. As in all things, it takes much practice and the breathing is an important stepping-stone to reaching the silence of Spirit."

Is the circle breathing exercise also helping us to understand feeling/ form?

"There will be other things that will be given that shall also aid you in this understanding. Here is a very simple example. As you know, your physical body is made of energy. If you were to cup your physical hands together and imagine a ball of energy within them, to the point where you can actually feel that ball of energy; that is a basic technique to understanding feeling/form. Feel the shape of this ball, feel its warmth, and then 'feel' its actual form. Expand and deflate this ball. Feeling/ form is the sensation and belief that what you 'see' or 'feel' has actual shape. We come in this form because our physical bodies stay within our own planets vibration while Spirit is able to travel with the energy of feeling. We will speak more on this at a later 'time.'"

Thank you very much. You have given us a lot of things to think about.

"It is our joy, you are most welcome. We do now depart with much Love and Blessings."

There were things revealed during this session that helped to continue filling in areas of understanding for us. The exercise about the ball in this session can also aid you to understand how we are taught various subjects. We are all still working on creating what feels like a solid ball but have been able to really 'feel' the energy within our hands. We understand that this will take time and a rise in the vibrational frequency of our physical bodies. At least we are making some progress.

It certainly is our desire to share these Teachings with everyone who chooses to hear them. I have found that you really have to reach people where they are in their current level of understanding. This isn't always an easy thing to know when first meeting someone. I am reluctant to even mention the "Girls" because I don't desire for them to think any less of this project or the Teachings just because they don't understand the source. People have been receiving inspiration forever and no one thinks a thing about a painter, a poet, a sculptress, or any artist, receiving this. When you begin to mention something outside their realm of understanding as being loving and bringing beautiful Teachings, they look at you sideways. We have always been told credibility, credibility, and I have endeavored to do just that. I sincerely hope that for those of you who are reading this I have portrayed, to the best of my ability, the absolute Love and energy that makes up those who have brought us such beautiful Teachings and who call us family.

Chapter Five

May 3, 2008

With all our questions ready, we sat down for our next session, which took place that afternoon.

"We do greet thee. How is everyone on this your day? You have questions?"

Greetings, would you please comment on manifestation?

"Yes, Sister of My Sister, we could say that the beginning of manifestation is your belief that it will happen. That is the beginning, for this is a thing of Spirit. It is a 'knowing' that all you desire has the definitive potential to occur. As we have said, due to the collective consciousness of your planet, and its frequency, much of manifestation requires some action on your part. It is not all dependent totally upon your action, but it does require much energy and focus by you. It means to create your desire, from your thoughts while mind is in Spirit, focus your energy upon it, see and 'know' it as completed and complete, and let it go for it to unfold as is intended for your highest purpose. Have trust that it will unfold, and allow it to do so. There is nothing more to add and nothing that can be taken away.

"We have endeavored to let you know that manifestation, of course, is not something you can just think about and it will occur. It is something that must be 'felt' as well. It is something you work toward through your giving of energy, focus, and action. It is not possible on your earth plane to simply think it, and it will happen. It is why we are working with you toward 'feeling/occurrence' and 'feeling/form.' We understand that most on your planet are in a hurry and do not sit back and allow something that they have created to unfold in its sequence. They try to push it and that, in turn, creates a resistance to that which you created. So we say, relax and allow. Do not just know your creation intellectually, for that is not enough. The body may know in that way, but it is Spirit that must truly 'know' and 'feel' it. It is the Spirit's 'knowing' that aids in the actual manifestation, not the physical's knowing. It does not matter what the physical may know for it is still bound by the frequency of the current collective consciousness. It must come from what Spirit 'knows' and believes, and therefore it unfolds. We feel that when you are dealing within what 'time' it shall occur, then you are in the physical mind, or ego. This is what puts you back into the resistance. Simply 'know' that it will occur and do those things we have spoken of to aid the process."

I have some feelings of fear regarding manifestation. I don't want to buy into them, but they are there.

"Sister of My Sister, fear must be maintained in some way in order to exist, whether you acknowledge this fear or not. It comes down to, if you will, a matter of trust. It is knowing within Spirit completely that things will be taken care of, and at the same time, you are taking the physical steps that you are able to take. Look at what is your fear. Is it the need to control, to manipulate the outcome? Allow it to unfold and manifest as it is intended to."

Thank you for that information again. I learn something each time we speak on manifestation. I do have a question about political figures. There are many out there who say they have the truth, but the truth seems different for each one of them. Why does this occur?

"We do not have a political agenda, of course, on our planet. There is no need for politics as everyone works in harmony for the good of all. Everyone is working in joy, and Spirit simply knows the desire of each and every one. We simply 'know' what it is that continues to create the harmony we seek. Your planet is not in that same understanding. You still have political parties and they still have the need to win. They come from the physical mind, or ego, and when they are not in Spirit, then their 'truth' is based upon what their individual perspectives of 'truth' may be. It is fine for them and for those who follow in that same line of ego thought, even if it is not fine for your country as a whole. There are far too many involved who are running in different directions all at the same time. The conclusion they desire to reach is winning and they do not care how that is achieved.

"It has become a tug-of-war of mind, ego. It is not of Spirit. We are not in the knowing of anyone who has been in a political position who has been able to be there as who they truly are, Spirit. Until that occurs, they will answer to those who are in ego as well and to those who have been put in positions by ego. It is a game of the mind and will continue to be so until the collective has changed.

"If you look at most of the people who are quite involved politically, you will see that they are also quite involved in other pursuits of ego. We do not 'know' your 'time' for all of this to change, but we do 'know' that this change shall be a part of the Awakening. People must be moving out, and away, from ego and it is for you to truly understand ego. What is ego? Can you tell us what you truly believe ego to be?"

I think ego is separation. It is being in your mind rather than being Spirit, connected to the Oneness.

"This is good. Little Brother, how do you look at ego?"

It is focus on self, or the finite physical, rather than focus on the spiritual. It is the focus on separation rather than Oneness.

"Yes, this is also true. Both of you have made good points. Ego is also totally of the physical and has an energy of its own. It is programmed by the identifiers that are absorbed by mind, while mind is joined with the physical. This aids to the growth of ego, it becomes a by-product, if you will, of your belief in those identifiers. Identifiers are those things that you believe yourself to be and have been created either by yourself or others. The ego is a 'presence' that keeps Spirit from remembering as it would desire to do. Many times this ego is so large that it may seem that it cannot be overcome. If you think of your current collective consciousness as one large ego, then you can see the project that is ahead—to aid people in awakening to their true self, which is Spirit. The ego is not simply a belief system, it is an essence, a presence within the physical energy. As each one chooses the path to Awakening and as Spirit begins to remember, then they may aid others in also understanding ego and moving beyond it to living a life that reflects their true nature."

We totally identify it as our self?

"Yes, you say, 'Who am I if I am not a mother, a daughter, a banker, a policeman?' 'Who am I if I am not rich or poor, healthy or diseased?' All of these examples are of the ego. It is an identification process. Spirit does not need to identify for Spirit simply is and knows itself as love, peace, joy, and calmness. The physical does not know this and therefore it puts forth the ego as its identification. It says, 'I must identify myself as something, or I am nothing.' As you awaken and Spirit remembers who it really is, then you will be helping others who also are choosing to awaken and be able to overcome their egos as well. It is teaching ego to be silent as the mind remains more and more in Spirit. The more mind continues to join with Spirit, the less the physical remains in ego. If you know someone who is identified totally by who or what they are, what they do or don't have, and if their actions show only concern for themselves, then you can now begin to understand how ego is working within them. At some point, they may begin to remember who they are and then their journey of Spirit shall begin. Mind shall join with Spirit, begin to shed the created identifiers, and put ego aside.

"This is happening now too many. This is why we are here and why there are many who also have come to lend their guidance for this journey of Awakening. It is our desire for the Awakening to occur so that people can understand, and deflate, the energy, which is the ego.

"We would desire to share with you a message from the Divine Mother."

"When Spirit first chose to incarnate on this planet and have the experience of being 'human,' it was always with the understanding that there would at first be forgetfulness. They would find joy in experiencing remembering. What is occurring with the Awakening is not just the remembering, it is the overcoming of ego, that which began at your physical creation. All things are created by, and are, energy. The physical body did not use all of the available energy given for its creation, its beginning. This 'extra' energy became a reservoir for identifiers. Ego, of course, is a name that has been given to it, so we also refer to it as such. It is a living energy that identifies itself with only the physical. We are all desirous for you to look at, to understand, and to know this ego. Know that it does not serve you to identify yourself with any one of those things that have been created by others, or by self. You, Spirit, are pure joy and love. You are all that We created. As you remember this, and begin to dismantle and deflate ego, then both Spirit and the physical body will be working together. This is not only your goal, but Ours as well. The remembering will raise the frequency of the physical vibration and you will discover all that you can and will be."

Would you say that the ego was "created" by the collective consciousness?

"Yes, in many ways, but remember the ego is there from the first moment of your physical creation. It is simply a 'leftover' of the energy that it takes to constitute your physical body. It is present and growing from the moment of your 'birth,' your emergence into your world. If there is a difficulty with the birth, it becomes a memory for ego to hold on to. As you are raised by either your parents, or others, and they tell you that you are 'good,' or that you are 'bad,' ego continues to grow with these identifiers. Whatever these identifiers are that occur on your journey, as you grow, know that ego also grows. It is not until Spirit begins to remember that *it can also begin to understand the ego and therefore dismantle it. Are there any questions regarding what I have just shared with you?"*

No, Mother, not at this time. Your explanation is very clear. We have much to take in, and to grow from, as a result of this teaching. Thank you so very much.

"You are most welcome. I will take my leave in Love."

"We are pleased that the Divine Mother has spoken with you on the ego. Are there any further questions about anything else while we are here? It was important to speak with you of the ego in this session so that you may be in the understanding of what it is and that this energy should be overcome for the Awakening of your planet. If there are no further questions at this time, we would desire for you to think upon the things that have been spoken of. You will possibly have questions that shall arise from this session. So for now, we do depart with much Love and Blessings."

What is very interesting about this session is not only was the subject of manifestation made clearer, but the Divine Mother "appeared" during the teaching on ego. Clearly this was a very important subject for the Awakening. This fact was referenced by the Divine Mother herself. We had been given teachings before when the subject of the ego had been mentioned, but not with the emphasis that was placed upon it at this time. We knew that the ego was going to be the hardest obstacle we would face as we continued with Awakening and this project. It was so important that we understand this subject in great depth so that we can share it with others, and this new information revealed more detailed information that was to be so helpful in gaining a new level of understanding. I realized much later that this was the first of many sessions and teachings that focused on ego.

The shift from being ego-led to spirit-led occupies considerable space in Bruce's books *Living Your Life in Joy* and *Now That You Are Awake*. Since this session, we have come to understand the ego very well and how it has the ability to dominate thoughts, feelings, and behaviors in people and institutions, even where the casual, or not so casual, observer would be least likely to believe the ego could exist there. There is nowhere that the ego does not show itself in our contemporary world. This is noticed especially in areas where the influence of the current collective consciousness is in control. It is only through the Awakening that the transformation from ego-led to spirit-led can occur. There are so many attempts made by ego to cloak itself skillfully to stay in control of the vast number of unawakened humanity. This is definitely a huge challenge, but as we have always been told, "take it in baby steps." This is exactly what we have been doing, and will continue to do, as we share all we have learned to those who ask the questions.

May 7, 2008

"We do greet thee. We are ready for your questions."

When I make the energy ball in my hands, they get very warm. Will we at some point be able to actually feel the ball?

"This, of course, Sister of My Sister, would be the goal—to be able to at some point feel the ball between your hands. We do not know how much of your 'time' this may require. If indeed you feel the energy, the warmth, then this is the direction to continue in."

I know we have been speaking a lot on the ego, would you please be specific in the ways that we can recognize the ego?

"This is a very good question, for the ego is not always easily recognized, particularly because of the vibrations of your physical body upon your planet. It is sometimes cloaked in disguise. It can be difficult, at times, to recognize not only within yourself but within others as well. It is easier to know if you are coming from Spirit, or ego, for when you are Spirit, you are content, happy, and all things that you do or think are in harmony. If you are in ego, you are thinking on a more linear level, more of self, more of one who is separate rather than one who is a part of the All. This would be one way to know whether you are coming from who you really are, or from ego. Your mind is the go-between, if you will, it resides between the physical and Spirit. Your mind when in the physical, and the pursuits of the physical, is in ego. Your mind, when Spirit, allows you to express yourself and react in ways that come from unconditional Love. As mind chooses to align more and more with Spirit, then the ego becomes absorbed, deflated. It does not go away, as it is part of your physical energy, but it can become absorbed and no longer have the energy it once contained. It simply becomes empty, if that is understood. It becomes less of an energy of the physical and more of an attachment, although a benign attachment, of Spirit. Ego is something that can be overcome through your understanding of Spirit and the choices you will create. It may take a great deal of your 'time' to overcome this, but we know that if you are aware of it, you can begin to take those steps."

So would it be safe to say that the mind, being in Spirit, is being as Spirit is?

"Yes, and you will always recognize this. In Spirit you are in harmony, if you are not in harmony, you are not in Spirit."

Would you also elaborate on how coming from Spirit doesn't mean we have to be a doormat?

"As a matter of fact, it could be completely the opposite. When you are coming from Spirit, it simply indicates that you are coming from a purpose and that you are coming from the Oneness. You are thinking with love, with your heart. You are conducting yourself in a manner of joy and harmony. It does not mean that you are not using your mind for thought, for working, or for composing. Some of the greatest composers composed masterpieces while their minds resided in Spirit. They were thinking in Spirit. You can use your mind while in Spirit as well as while in ego. The difference is in how you behave, react, and feel. You will know where mind lies by these things and you will recognize in others as well by how they behave and react."

Please relate that to dealing with people.

"If you were dealing with a person who has yet to awaken, then you would simply allow them to be who they are. You could attempt to share with them a message delivered in Love, in Spirit, even though they may not be aware of it. If you dealt with them while in your own ego, you would simply be putting up another wall, and it is this that they will react to. You would create frictions and increase the distance for remembering for both of you. When you come from Spirit, with someone who is still spiritually asleep, that means you are allowing them to be on their chosen path and are acknowledging their experiences, which result from their creations. You would not choose to join in their creations, their experiences but would indeed continue to give them your unconditional Love. Many times this may mean that you remove yourself from their presence, but you do not have the right to tell them what they should, or shouldn't, be doing. They have the same given 'freedom to create at will' as you have. This may seem to be difficult for you to do, but Spirit does not judge or try to change another, it simply Loves and continues its own journey of Awakening. So come in Love to each person you come into contact with. Allow."

Also, you should deal with each other in the moment.

"Yes, you should always come from the 'Now,' for that is all there is. We do understand that most upon your planet view those coming from Spirit as being 'out there,' or in what you term 'la-la land.' Simply allow them their beliefs, for if they feel this way they are not yet understanding who they are, nor how they were created.

"Coming from Spirit is the indication that you are coming from your heart, from Love. You are being joy and are in harmony with All there is. We know that harmony is not a thing that is done by ego; it is the nature of Spirit to desire to be this way always. It will be the desire of ego to always try and contradict this feeling. Once you begin to live as Spirit, then ego will no longer retain its potency. If it cannot be potent, then the physical mind, or ego, will lose its hold and mind will then be attached to Spirit. Are there any additional questions?"

Not on this subject at this time, thank you. I have a comment on manifestation. I was going through my desires and realized that my intentions are already known by the Divine Parents. It is now a matter of letting go and knowing that these will manifest. As you say, things will work out. To continue to focus or to dwell on these desires would be taking away from things that I could be doing and creating.

"Yes, and this is also a good example of living in Spirit. Simply know these things to be complete and allow their unfolding for your highest purpose along your journey. Let them be what they will be."

It seems like what you are saying is that if we have done everything in our power, and truly released it to allow its unfolding, then we should not have expectations about when or how it will occur. We should simply live in the Now.

"Yes, be and enjoy. Exactly right. Stay in the 'Now' for it may take some of your 'time,' but do not allow yourself to be concerned. Know that whatever happens will be as intended for your experience and for your journey."

Also I'm really getting, with these last few sessions, how feeling/form actually creates.

"Yes, for it is much like how we upon our planet create. We simply 'feel' the desire and it is there. We have learned to create that feeling into an actual form. It is the energy of our physical bodies that when joined with Spirit creates the form. This is something that for you must begin with baby steps. We do not know if you shall accomplish this within your current incarnation, but it is not for us to know. It is simply our purpose to begin you on that path. The manifestation is the creation of feeling/form."

Is there anything else you would like to share with us tonight?

"We have been speaking about those next steps, and we have already begun with our teaching on the ego. We are right now conferring with the Divine One as to which direction they desire for us to go, for we do not wish to move too quickly. We believe there will be many things occurring within the next several of your 'weeks.' The main thing now, as we have said before, is to begin putting what you have learned into action, if you will. For it is the giving back of what you have learned to others. Incorporate into your every 'Now' your understanding of what we have taught, live it, breathe it, and share it with those who question and choose to know.

"It is important to begin the outreach so people can see what an awakened person, what someone who is walking their path in Spirit, would be like. We desire that people would come in contact with everyone on the council and that it would make them think, 'What is it about them that makes me feel good when I am around them?' People will begin to ask you what it is you know and why do you create a sense of peace when they are around you. Then you shall begin sharing, for you shall know by their questions that they are ready to hear. As you were taught, begin with baby steps and do not overwhelm them.

"This has not been a long session, but we are pleased to be able to answer your questions. When we speak again, we will know the next advancement. It is very important that everything we have taught to this point be clearly understood and be defined within yourselves so that you can put it into practice. If you have any questions at all regarding what you have learned, something that may require clarification, bring them with you for next time. For now, we shall depart in Love and Blessings."

This was a relatively short session compared with others we have had. In looking back, this began a time of outreach that lasted until we left Happy Camp in the fall. We met people from many different states and walks of life. I would love to share with you just a little about one of these people.

There was Alice who came all the way from Tennessee because she knew she was to meet someone that she had been drawn toward. She did not know who this was, only that she was drawn to this place to meet them. This person actually turned out to be me, or rather the "Girls." It was through their council that she received answers to questions she had traveled so far to ask. When she left, she seemed to be much more at peace than when we had first met.

Nick and Bill were also two people we met that became very good friends. We still keep in touch. Dave, from New Zealand, was a wonderful Spirit who enhanced our journey in so many ways, and we shared with him much of what we had learned. It was truly a magical summer of meeting people, sharing, and just reminding ourselves to live in the Now.

Early in the spring, we found a small gold deposit to mine. We had to wait for the rains to let up and the temperatures to rise a little. During the course of looking for a deposit, Bruce found himself pushing too hard to find one and I think he lost sight for a while of what he was to be learning. After several disappointing outings, the message finally sunk in and he began to find enjoyment just being out in the fresh air, he started being in the Now. That was when the small deposit was found, when he quit trying so hard. Looking back, I can see how this was also a teaching that had to be learned before any further advancement could take place on our path. We didn't find much gold that summer, but we did meet wonderful people who shared with us their awakening experiences, and in so many ways, being able to share what we had learned, with them, was worth more than gold.

We were fortunate to find jobs shortly after arriving in Happy Camp in April. I went to work full-time for a gold prospecting company, and Bruce was able to do a small remodeling job on a cabin that was in the same park as our fifth wheel. His job only lasted about two months, but it did enable us to cover our space rent and all utilities for the entire summer. My income helped to pay monthly on some of the bills we were still so desperately trying to honor, and although we were way behind on some, at least we were making an attempt. Of course that didn't matter to the collectors, they wanted it all NOW! I took one teaching really to heart and simply allowed them to have their experience and be in their ego. All we could do was to stay calm and do our best. Another small job for Bruce, in June, lasted five weeks and gave us the means, along with my income, to continue keeping our heads above water for the rest of the summer. We even had our hopes up of being able to somehow rise above our financial circumstances despite the situation we had been enduring for many months. We started to feel a little more optimistic.

May 10, 2008

We had been encouraged to outreach and to meet with others of like mind, so we accepted an invitation to meet with some others who were also channeling. What an experience, and the following session addresses what we were to learn from this.

"We do greet thee. It has been quite a long 'day' for you. We are aware of your channeling experience earlier and we are assured that you do have questions."

Most assuredly we have questions. One of the first things we would ask is, what do we take away from this experience?

"As you are now aware, this experience was designed as a lesson for you. It is not that we designed it but we saw where we could teach from this experience. Today would have been your opportunity to view those who truly believe they are spiritually awake, but who instead are walking within a fog, or as you have stated within one of your books, 'walking in a mist.' They are indeed awakening, but they have gotten stuck in one area. They are not progressing on to the next step. These entities they say that they are channeling, as we observed from our place of viewing, were Spirits who have chosen to remain earthbound, or inside of earth's vibration. Therefore they cannot impart much in the way of teaching, or knowledge, that was beyond that which they acquired while in the physical. We did notice that these were Spirits who while incarnated did begin to understand who they truly were and had begun to awaken. At this 'time' they can only teach that which they knew."

It is the belief of the people we met today that they are channeling higher evolved beings and not earthbound Spirits. There wasn't much we could say to change that.

"It is not for you to change, only to allow. At some point in their awakening, they will begin to understand, but we are in the knowing that you did plant some seeds. It is simply a matter now if they prefer to water them or not, it is for them to ask questions and seek the answers."

Did we say too much?

"No, Sister of My Sister, we do not believe that too much was said. That which they did not resonate with simply went by them. That which they could resonate with, planted seeds."

I felt there were filters that were blocking any information we wished to give them.

"The only filters that were present were those of their own creation. If you only 'hear' your own voice, then you do not allow another to be heard. There was no 'higher evolved being' that had come to be heard. It was simply a Spirit who had passed from this life, yet it was their belief that it was what they call 'an ascended master.' We have spoken before on this term and it seems a strange thing to say. All who leave the physical shall return to the Absolute, for this is where all are; before choosing to incarnate. Ascend means to return, and all shall do this. How much higher can you possibly go?"

What does this type of belief contribute to the Awakening?

"It is not the belief, it is the people. Do not give up on them, for they are indeed Awakening. They have the drive, if you will. They are truly searching for those teachings that resonate with them. Continue to share, as you are asked, and when it resonates within another, you will know. It is your sharing of all you know that contributes, and carries on, the Awakening."

Thank you for this experience today. It taught all of us quite a lot.

"It was a lesson in learning to reach out. As we have stated before, it is important now that you begin to reach out to others and begin to expand your area of awareness."

One thing we did learn was that this particular Spirit was also supposedly being channeled by many others in this area. Would you please comment?

"This channeling becomes more of ego than Spirit as it is being able to proclaim that you too are channeling this particular Spirit. If indeed this one they say they are channeling was a highly evolved being, he or she would not be coming willy-nilly to everyone. One chooses the one channel to speak the truth for it. As you know, not only is the channel chosen but they also choose. Over a period of your time, as the channel leaves physically, then other channels may be chosen. It would not be the choice to have many different channels at one 'time.' This leaves much room for interpretation and ego to become involved."

Another thing that we noticed was that this session was a kind of "free for all."

"There were many who channeled, but no message or teaching was received, or given. Channeling is something that is done to deliver not only a message, but a truth. This truth may be delivered by one who has been chosen, and who has chosen to be that voice, or it may just be many who are desiring to be heard by the sound of their own voices. This seemed to be what occurred today with this 'free for all' as you called it."

Yes, we noticed that. We have learned an excellent lesson today.

"When you learn, you move upon your path and this was the purpose of this day. It is important to always go forth with this understanding in Love and joy and to let those around you see this Love from the Teachings that come from and through you. It is this seeing that will create a curiosity, and through this, if they are ready, they will be asking questions. It could be that when you meet again, they will have read the books you suggested, these will water the seeds of understanding that were planted, and they will step forth upon their own desire to know more."

This information is very valuable when we begin teaching others. We really need to understand this ourselves.

"There will be many who will be on different portions of their journey with many different beliefs. Listen, see where their understanding is and meet them at that point. Your patience and listening will show you which seeds may be planted. There will be those who you will be unable to plant a seed with, for they are not yet awake enough. Allow them, in Love, to be where they are. Never question another's belief, simply ask them to listen with an open mind and see what resonates with them. For those you cannot speak to of the Teachings you have received, simply love them and bless them on their journey."

Would you please elaborate on what seeds were dropped today that may have the ability to sprout?

"The biggest seed, of course, are the books. These may create many questions, and the answers will aid them in moving along their path. Another large seed that was planted was the sharing you did regarding the Divine Mother and Father. This will have them doing much thinking and discussion. Also when you spoke on the fact that we are all One, all connected one to the other. Even though they believe this also, today they were given a deeper understanding of exactly what 'being One' means. Now simply wait to see which seeds take root and which ones will die for lack of watering. Are there any other questions?"

We noticed that a considerable length of time, several minutes or so, was needed for an entity, or spirit, to speak through one of the channels. Would you please comment?

"It was also our observation. As you know, we come within seconds after we, or Little One, has chosen for us to be with you. One who is channeled is always present for their channel. There is no waiting and this we see as being quite theatrical."

When Little One has done readings, it seems that there is some time of waiting involved.

"When one is doing a 'reading,' as you call it, then they are waiting for an earthbound spirit to appear. If it is the case that the one you are receiving from is earthbound, then it may take some of your 'time,' for they are not always present. That appeared to be what was occurring today with the others you had seen. The 'time' that elapsed before speaking would be in concert with an earthbound spirit."

We also did not notice any change in the energy until you came through.

"Yes, and it will always be that way. If it is truly a being who is desiring to relay a message, whether they are earthbound, of from elsewhere, the energy change will upon their entrance."

Would you please explain again what is meant by an "earthbound" spirit?

"If you are earthbound, it simply means that you are still within the vibrational frequency of the earth. You have not yet chosen to return to the Absolute. There are only a few who choose this, particularly when you consider the population of your planet.

"There are circumstances in which Spirit, once the physical body has passed, will decide to stay."

For example, let me ask about the spirits that were being channeled by the others today, are they earthbound?

"It would appear that the ones being channeled, when there was occurring an actual channeling, were for Now earthbound. They have stayed to help, or to guide one which they desire to be with. When a highly evolved being, one who has completely awakened, has come to be channeled in order to bring a teaching or a message, they may encounter ego and therefore will simply leave. They leave because the ego, or filters, of the one chosen to channel have become involved. When this does occur, it is not unusual for an earthbound spirit to step into that role. This is the one thing that those who have chosen to remain within the physical vibration choose in order to stay in contact, if you will."

Are they like Yeshua?

"Yeshua is in the Absolute. He would never have chosen to remain earthbound. He can come directly through from the Absolute in the same way that the Divine Parents do. When he first chose to incarnate into your planet, he also chose to come with much less forgetfulness than any had ever chosen. It was his purpose, his 'blueprint,' to come and teach others about how to be who they truly are and of their connection to not only the One creator, but to all life around them. When it was 'time' for him to leave, he simply left. Should he desire to return to earth in another incarnation, or be heard verbally through a channel, or share the message in writings, this is his choice to make."

If He were to come from the Absolute to the earth's vibration, wouldn't He somehow have to lower His vibration?

"Are you assuming that He is coming in the flesh, or do you understand that He comes in Spirit? Just as the Divine Mother comes to be heard through the voice of Little One, He would come in feeling. Nothing is lowered, for this feeling allows the direct connection with the Absolute to remain."

Would that be the same for any Spirit who is in the Absolute that chooses to come and be channeled?

"Yes, if Spirit in the Absolute makes a choice to be a guide and to be heard through a channel, they would come through 'feeling.'"

Thank you for this clarification.

"Yes, Sister of My Sister. To be in the Absolute and come back could only be done in two ways. You would either come back, in forgetfulness, or incarnate into a physical body, or you would come back as a guide. Even when choosing to be a guide, you do not come in with complete 'knowing.'"

You don't come in with complete "knowing" as a guide, but do you come in complete "knowing" as a channel?

"There is always the possibility for one who is in complete 'knowing' to come through a channel, yes. The channels, of course, themselves, are simply Spirit in a physical incarnation. They too would have entered this incarnation in forgetfulness.

"We understand that this can be confusing, so let us begin again. The first time Yeshua chose to come to the earth plane, chose to incarnate into a physical body, he also chose to come in with less forgetfulness than any other. He understood who he was and His connection to the One. He desired this so that the message he came with could be delivered and taught. When he left this physical realm, he went back to the Absolute where he was again in complete understanding and 'knowing.' If he should choose, as we know he will, to come through a channel, he would come in 'feeling' to that channel.

"To any Spirit in the Absolute who desires to become a channeled entity, yes, they have the knowing to come in 'feeling.' This does not occur very often. There have been several others besides Yeshua who came to deliver a message. Buddha is one, of course. Beings from planets such as us are not in the complete knowing of the Divine's desires, which is why we must confer. We come to you in 'feeling.'

"If you were to come back to the frequency of the earth, you would come through, again, in a physical body. Therefore, you could be a channel, but you would not be the one being channeled. If you decide to come back from the Absolute to this planet again, as we have stated, there are one of two ways. You come in a physical incarnation with whatever degree of forgetfulness you decide upon. This has been agreed upon with the Divine Parents before your entering. You may also have conferred with a Spirit who came to incarnate that you would also come as their guide. Again, even as guide, you do not have full knowing."

What about the Buddhist's saying that the Dalai Llama is the same Spirit reincarnated every time he chooses and that he takes on the same persona?

"We believe this to be true. For the Spirit, known by name as the Dalai Llama, simply makes the choice to return and continue the works that he began. It is a progression, if you will. He has chosen to be that one who teaches others of love and compassion for all. This is, and has always been, his choice, his decision.

"Yeshua could come back as Yeshua in another incarnation. He would bring into the physical all he had desired to do in his previous incarnation. We also understand that even He would be ridiculed or disbelieved because of where your current collective consciousness lies. This may be why he has not yet chosen to do this.

"The one called the Dalai Llama has chosen to come back through many incarnations. If you have studied this history, you would also understand that this does not necessarily occur quickly. It may take some of your 'time' for this to happen. There are those who are sent ahead with the knowledge to recognize this new incarnation, to nurture it, and to protect it. It, simply said, means that this Spirit has chosen this experience time and time again in order to complete the teachings he came to impart. At some point, he may chose not to come back. Spirit may say, 'Enough, I have done what I desired to do.'

"It can be confusing when you begin speaking of Spirits within the Absolute, or beings such as myself and Astoria, who are actually from another planet and reside within and around our own physical body. When we leave our physical body, we also shall return to the Absolute. We are no different from yourselves, your true nature, expect in respect to where we chose to incarnate and that our desire is to be the messengers for the Divine. All come from only One source, are an inseparable part of that Source, and shall return to that when they discard their physical body."

I understand that the preparations we are receiving are, in many ways, being given to relay to the world those teachings that Yeshua came to deliver.

"Yes, at this moment in your 'time,' Yeshua's messages will be given either through writings, which are channeled, or through words that are channeled. At this 'time' upon your planet, if he was to reappear, he would not be believed or heard, for the same reasons he was not heard before. There would once again be a creation by man that would not allow the true message to be received. He would be looked at, as many current messengers are, as a charlatan, a cultist, a new ager, or one who speaks untruths. These perceptions would be based upon the current belief restrictions of the collective consciousness. This is the reason many beautiful teachings and messages are being brought in by those who choose to be, and are chosen to be, channels. They may also be scoffed at, but generally not harmed."

It would be difficult for people to understand exactly how highly evolved the beings are on your planet, right?

"As you have said, there are so many who are claiming to channel different entities at this 'time.' One really can become quite confused as to who to listen to or who not to listen to. If you continue to state the truth, simply and in love, then those who are awakening will hear them and resonate with them. It is always the choice of each one to listen or not, but we say that you will know what to listen to when it touches that place of understanding within you. When you 'feel' it to be your truth and you no longer find yourself desiring to move from these Teachings to others around you, then you will know. For those who choose not to hear, allow them this creation as well and bless them as they pass along their own chosen journey."

Those who pass by have no way of knowing what we have learned.

"We would not begin to try and change that, for as you know, and others who join with you shall know, they are part of a created belief within their collective. This is their choice and you cannot change that. You can plant the seeds and allow them to fall where they may. They will be nurtured by many within that collective who are searching and they shall ask you what you have been taught. Then, you shall share, when you hear their questions and will know they are choosing to hear."

Let me ask if there will be an "energy" felt by those who either read the books of Little One and Little Brother, or who hear the messages and teachings in another way, such as the channeling?

"Sister of My Sister, it is much like when you have been reading books and you 'feel' something as you read them, something that resonates as a truth within you. It shall be the same with the books that are now being written about the Teachings we have brought. For those who are ready for these Teachings, and are ready to awaken to the next step, the words they read or hear will resonate with them. They will indeed 'feel' an energy in and around these words. This is our desire that it occur in this way that it happen naturally. This is why we have taught much on understanding 'feeling' for this is what it is about. When you were with the others today who called and believed themselves to be channelers, they were not ready to 'feel' for they are completely caught up, if you will, in that which they believe to be a truth. They are not listening to any other words with an open mind or heart. This is where you allow them their created journey, bless them as they pass, and continue to share and be who you are, with others who do choose to hear."

This has been a marvelous session.

"We are most pleased. We definitely wanted to come through this evening so that you could have a better understanding of what occurred and so that we may answer your questions."

This was very important and very instructional.

"You are most welcome. With no further questions at this time, we shall now depart in Love and Blessings."

This session presented important teachings that we were meant to learn. These teachings resulted from our first contact with another group that regularly channels various guides and spirits during their meetings. It was an extremely valuable and eye-opening experience for us. This experience gradually expanded our understanding of our true nature and the physical world we have chosen to live in. It was the perfect moment to experience what other groups were about. The things we learned from this encounter enabled us to network with others, both those of like mind as well as those with differing points of view. We continue in this Now to outreach as we have been requested and accepted to do.

The teaching methods we receive are very interesting. Important teachings are tied together and the resulting experiences are created and designed to enable us to come away with the knowledge necessary for advanced understandings. This understanding almost immediately follows these created experiences. It was also true with the understanding given us concerning the relationship between the Absolute and the physical realm, especially in relation to either coming in as a guide or through direct incarnation. We had been exposed to this subject before, but the additional information was, as always, very helpful.

May 14, 2008

We had been accumulating questions that had come from some of our past sessions and decided to ask them at this next meeting. We had also learned that there was to be some "time" off for them to prepare for the next portion of the Teachings.

"We do greet thee. We find you well this evening. Please begin with the questions you have put together."

Our first question would be, is there any difference in the purity of the channel's message when received through their voice or when they "hear" the message internally and then they themselves share what has been "heard"?

"We would say that it is greatly dependent upon the channel. Have they chosen to remove their own consciousness while the one they channel speaks? When we speak through Little One's voice, we do so with her consent, and desire, to leave and not have her own intents, perceptions, or ego, mixed in with the message or teaching that we bring. There are other channels that, also, have chosen this, but it has seemed to us that they are not able to continue in this way. Soon the message, or teaching, is lost inside of their own projections. This is why we always say to listen, 'feel,' and 'know' the truth within yourself. When the message is given in other ways, it is an inspiration to the one who is receiving it. There may be some of their own wording, perceptions, or intent within what they write, but for those who have chosen this way to receive, they keep the integrity of the message as they deliver it. Again, you shall know the truth of their words by how they resonate within you. We, of course, cannot speak for all who write, or hear, words of messages or teachings. We can only truly speak of those we have chosen to be with. As we have said to you before, when you hear or read that which is given through a channel, ask questions. Do their words resonate within you as truth? Is there a clear message or teaching? Does it require any interpretation? By your 'feeling' within, you will 'know' of its validity."

Does everyone on earth, at this time, have awakening of their Spirit written in their "blueprint"?

"No, there are many who are not awake at this time and did not choose to do so when they were incarnated. For those who did choose awakening, this is the project we now undertake. Our purpose, your purpose, is to help those who are ready to awaken. We tell you that there are many who did not choose to awaken as part of their physical journey, it is not part of their 'blueprint.' There are many who although not awake in this 'Now' have indeed chosen to include this experience in their 'blueprint.'"

Does that mean when sufficient numbers awaken, the earth's vibration will be raised to a degree that those who are not going to awaken will choose to leave? Does everyone need to awaken to create the new collective consciousness?

"As we have taught, as more and more awaken, the frequency of those and others who have awakened will certainly rise. This rise in frequency will begin to form what we have called the new collective consciousness and that, in turn, will aid in dismantling the current consciousness that now exists. For those who do not awaken, this vibrational rise will not even be noticed or felt. They may naturally begin to form into their own alliances, but they will continue to create and experience their own journeys. Gradually over an undetermined, an unknown, amount of your 'time,' the new collective will be the one that has grown over and around the old. This will be the ultimate rise in understanding, and living, who you truly are. This understanding will create completely new experiences for you to choose from and will begin to create a place of complete peace and harmony."

Will the old collective try to interfere with this process in any way?

"It may be that even without knowing that they interfere, they will. This will come about due to man's ego and the fear they will feel as they notice changes occurring around them. Just continue as you are, sharing, teaching, reaching out, healing, and being, at all times, who you are. Their success with interference would lie with those who are awake and have chosen to overcome and create a new consciousness."

I have been talking about writing a book. What do you think about the title "From Religion to Spirituality—From Separation to Oneness"?

"Sister of My Sister, we think that this will be a tool that will help many to awaken. For those who are in religions now, and are not necessarily comfortable where they are but continue to stay there because of a feeling of responsibility, or obligation to family, this may provide for them the next stepping stone. Many fear to leave that which they have either identified with, or been identified as, even when it no longer answers their questions or resonates with them. This book may help many to realize that they do not have to be pigeonholed, if you will. You can go from being a religious person to being one of Spirit. You do not need to look back as if you have done anything 'wrong.'

"Your book will be quite interesting for it will be written in the first person. We would say to go back to your childhood to begin your story, for it is important for people to understand where you came from before you went into the convent. It is important to understand what your childhood was like and who, what, and why you made the decision to enter the convent at such a young age. This will be a personal journey that you can share with others to enable them to understand the difference between religion and spirituality."

I am getting excited about it myself. Thank you for your words.

"You are most welcome. We would like to say that we are well pleased with all the progress being made in the project. Although we have been quiet, we have observed all that is occurring. Little Brother, you still are writing your book and Little One is awaiting hers to be going onto the market. We have assured her that beginning the next book will happen in its proper 'time.' We know that much is also happening both physically and financially. This is not the 'time' for the formation of many questions. You know we are here to answer them as you have them.

"We can tell you that within the next month of your 'time,' we will begin the next step in the Teachings. We are still learning, if you will. It will be advanced, so we are being assured by the Divine Parents that what we bring to you will be done in its proper 'timing.' Right now there are many of what you call 'loose ends' that require tightening up. When this has occurred, then the Teachings, in earnest, will begin again."

At times I am feeling intensity in my heart area, almost a feeling of being in love.

"This, Sister of My Sister, is simply your heart energy center opening even more than it has been and this is due to the Awakening. Also this transpires as you release more and more ego. You will find that as ego becomes absorbed, if you will, into Spirit, you will feel more and more of these sensations as well. It is you awakening to not only the knowledge of your true self, but the being it as well."

Is this why I find myself more emotional?

"Emotion, yes, is definitely tied to the Awakening. This is good, for people for too long have been keeping emotions at bay. Little boys, in particular, are brought up to believe that to be a man you do not cry, you do not react to your feelings. Many times it is uncomfortable to show emotions, but this is a good use of energy. Understand that this is an Awakening. This is an understanding, a blending, if you will, with the All. It is perfect in its expression.

"It could also be that as much occurs in Spirit, much will also be occurring within your physical body. Moves have been, and are being, made to allow you choices regarding your physical care. You may begin to experience some things that you possibly have not experienced for a great long 'time' as this physical healing begins.

"Do you have any further questions at this 'time'? As we have stated, we are more than pleased to come even if it be only for a brief moment in your 'time.' We are undergoing some teachings of our own with the Divine Parents but are still available at all times. For now, we shall depart in Love and Blessings."

In this session, we learned that the "Girls" themselves were about to spend time with the Divine Parents in study and preparation for the next phase in our training. Of course, they did not inform us what this new phase would consist of or what instruction we were to receive. All we knew was that it would be more advanced, slowly moving beyond "baby steps." We were all curious but knew we would be patient and wait for it to unfold. In the meantime, we had much to do and many loose ends to tie off.

Bruce and I had decided to sell our gold dredge and some duplicate equipment that we could easily part with. We took an afternoon to go through our mining trailer and set everything aside to sell in order to raise some needed money. This was an action taken to try and keep ourselves from sinking any further into debt. We were fortunate to sell things that helped keep us afloat for several months.

We had received foreclosure notice on some property we had in another state and needed time to either sell it or deed it back before it was seized. We still had the strong desire to pull ourselves out of the mess we were in. It helped that Sarah was doing much better, it lightened the load somewhat.

Most of Bruce's evenings and rainy days were spent at the computer entering all the writing from his journal that would be contained in his second book. Often he would still be working well after midnight. Actually, I think he truly enjoyed those late night and early morning hours. The house was quiet then and the inspiration was so strong that he told me he could actually feel the energy let down at the end of a chapter. If it did not return within several minutes, this was his sign that the session had come to a close.

We also learned in this session that Annie desired to write a book. It would be very helpful to assist those in various religions to understand Oneness and the difference between religion and spirituality. She has worked on this now for some time and I believe she is almost ready for it to be published.

Our progress, it seemed, within the project was where it should be. We certainly had experienced our "time" of challenge as we continued to advance in our knowledge and understanding of all we were being taught. I guess these times were what actually allowed us to understand choices. We could have just said, "Forget it," and devoted our time and energy to surviving, but instead we chose to keep on our spiritual journey. I don't regret that choice for one second for it truly allowed me the opportunity to know not only who I really am, but exactly why I am here. It may not have been, or be, an easy path but it continues to be one I choose.

May 25, 2008

This was an exciting day for us as Teresa was coming up for another visit. Of course we requested a session for the evening of her arrival.

"We do greet thee. It is our great joy and pleasure to be with you this evening. Light Sister, it is so wonderful for you to join with us once again. It has been quite a busy time for us and there is much information we are gathering. While Light Sister is here, you also should get your questions together. It would also be our desire, and suggestion, that you bring everyone to the same level of understanding so that, when it is the 'time,' we can begin the Teachings once again.

"Little Brother, your book is coming along quite well. We are with great joy in hearing you read it. You are certainly getting all the points that we have taught into your book. Even more so you have also followed other inspirations as well. The book is quite understandable and quite good. It contains more to chew on than the first book, but not so advanced that it cannot be understood.

"As we said, we are endeavoring right now to spend time with the Divine Parents so that we understand what the next step will be. There is much happening upon the earth plane at this moment. There is much accumulation of not only earth changes, which are coming rapidly, but there is also much change with the new consciousness that is growing. There will be those factions who may begin to be confused by this dismantling of the old. As you speak with others, always be aware of how you present the Teachings and yourself. Continue your outreach, being at all times who you know yourself to be, and sharing the Teachings as others come and ask the questions.

"One of the things that we would desire to cover this evening would be to remember that ego should not be accepted within the council. If it does have a part, it could certainly destroy that which you are beginning to build. That is something to be aware of within each who comes to the council. Guide them in the understanding of ego and that it can be overcome and deflated through awareness, desire, choices, and being the Spirit that they are. It is important for all of us to be aware if, or when, ego arises. As you would say, nip it in the bud at that moment it appears and do not allow it to overcome you."

The other thing is to be aware of whether or not people are willing to really listen with an open mind to what is being offered.

"It is not as if you are asking someone to set aside, or discard, their current belief system, you are only saying that when they ask a question they listen with open mind and open heart to the answer. If what they hear does not resonate with them, then in Love, we bless them to continue on their current belief path, or find that which does resonate. It they do feel a part of this walk, if the words and Teachings do resonate with them then they are simply taking the next step along their path. They need not 'let go' or discard anything that may have lead them to their current questions. We would not ask anyone to do that for those things have guided them toward the path and understanding they are now upon. It has all been a part of their created experience. It is simply that they understand they are ready to go beyond that point and take the next step. It may not be for all and we are aware of that. There are many like-minded groups right now who are all finding their way and there will be those who will resonate with them. This will be as it should be, but it is not what we have come for. Our purpose is to give to each and every one of you the Teachings, and our 'time,' if you will, so that you may go forward with that information to all who will be encountered along your path and who ask, 'What is different about you?' 'Why are you so at peace?' We include all who would come to the council, or who choose to be a part of The Light Alliance family.

"We understand how much change is going to be happening and how important it shall be that each person, particularly those that are within the council, recognize when your ego is coming up. You may also recognize when ego arises within another, how will you deal with this? You, in Love, will allow them their moments of ego and let them voice their 'feelings' in a place they feel safe. Do not push against another's ego for all you will discover is resistance. Allow one to settle their ego down before you would attempt to speak about it. If you find that ego has gained control in another, then your choice is to remove yourself, in that Now, from that experience or to choose to become a part of that experience. The choice Spirit would make is to, in Love, walk away. Ego will gladly join in and create the chaos that it desires, for its purpose is to keep you away from understanding and living as Spirit. Make your choice in Spirit. Know that moments such as this shall occur and until Spirit has grown in its remembering and is strong enough to absorb the energy of that which is now your physical ego. As we have said, the ego contains and grows from the energy that is given to it by the physical body and the mind, when it also resides within the physical. When mind chooses to move with Spirit, and you are growing with your understanding of your true nature, then ego is simply absorbed."

Could you give us any pointers or guidelines toward helping ourselves in dealing with our own egos?

"Sometimes it is very difficult to recognize it within yourself, for when you are in the middle of a thought, or action, created by ego, you will not necessarily be seeing it. It will only be as you awaken more and more and you are being who you are, Spirit that you will be aware of its attempts to control. We would teach you to be follow you 'gut' feelings. If you have said, or done, something that does not rest well with you then stop yourself and say, 'Oh, that didn't sound right,' or, 'That didn't come out the way I had intended.' Understand that what did come out was from your ego, not from Spirit, especially when it has left you 'feeling' anything but peace in what you said. Spirit comes always from unconditional Love. If something is not done or said from Love, then you will recognize that it is coming from ego. We would be most pleased to continue this line of Teaching if you still have questions."

There are no more questions on this topic at this time. There is, however, an observation I would like to share with you. I have been thinking over the past couple of weeks that a lot of things we hear that sound spiritual are actually ego cloaked in spiritual garb.

"Yes, ego is quite wise for it is given much energy. It is given the energy to have you believe in others identifiers of who you are. The ego grows from these identifiers. Many times it would want you to believe that you are coming from Spirit, for if you believe that it is Spirit you come from, you will not look at ego. If you do not recognize ego, you cannot deflate it. So, yes, you are correct, Little Brother, the ego can indeed cloak itself. It is for those who are truly coming from, and understanding Spirit that will recognize this, such as you did. It is up to those who see this as to how to share this with those who remain in ego. It may be your choice to allow them this experience, or if you know them well enough you may ask questions, such as, 'Did you hear what you said, what were you feeling then?' 'What do you think that meant, how did you mean it to sound?' Sometimes you may just ask them to share their emotions of that moment. It is always to wait until the moment of ego has passed before asking any questions."

Thank you. There seems to be teachings out in the world today that sound spiritual, but when you listen carefully, the source appears to be ego.

"Be discerning at all times. Spirit will know, will 'feel' it. If you are reading a paragraph and it 'feels' good to you, it resonates within you, then you would continue to read. If you begin to 'feel' uneasy, then put it down and think upon it. Spirit will always recognize the truth and you, in Spirit, will know as well."

It is becoming so much clearer how people, who are just awakening, or early in their awakening process, can be very susceptible to anything that sounds spiritual. They are at a delicate place in their spiritual development.

"Yes, and it is at these points of confusion or questioning that you would share with them what you are learning, what you have been taught. They are searching, as many are searching. They will find many ways that will resonate with them. It is much better to finally find that which resonates with you then to continue searching. Each step, as we have said, is a stepping-stone. It does not matter what you are doing if you are moving forward.

"We would like you to know that ego is not just simply a term or a word. Ego is energy that is given life through its environment. It is that container for all the identifiers you encounter along your journey. It tells you who you are, or believe yourself to be based on other's ideas and opinions, and it will tell you what to feel. It wants to be the 'boss,' if you will, but once you recognize it for what it is you will know it is only full of hot air. It becomes pumped up like a balloon. You may pop this balloon and empty it of its identifiers, but always be aware that it remains a balloon, even when empty. This emptying is how Spirit will absorb ego, with the recognition of what it is, and does. When mind is in Spirit, ego cannot flourish for you are able to see through it right away. Ego does flourish, however, when mind remains in the physical."

What I am finding out also is that Spirit is desirous to allow people to have their own experiences and their own opinions, while it seems that ego wants to always be "right" and the "best."

"This is the difference between who you truly are, Spirit, and the identifiers you believe yourself to be, which are ego. Spirit knows exactly what it is and has no needs, therefore, it does not have to be anything but that which it is—Love, peace, and wholeness. Whereas the ego constantly wants to be more than what it is, or to make one believe in all their identifiers. Ego will create a feeling of being 'less' than who you are.

"We would say to each and every one to be aware of your ego. Begin to diminish your previous conceptions of who you are, and see yourself as the Spirit you are. This will enable the dismantling of ego and it will deflate because you will no longer be feeding it energy."

So we develop the ego early in life? Won't this make it difficult to overcome?

"Light Sister, from the moment of your physical creation ego begins. As we have taught, it is energy not used in the actual physical body that becomes the reservoir for future identifiers. These are created by others, by self through your choices and experiences, and by not knowing and understanding your true nature. The ego is not something that may be deflated overnight, but it all begins with your awareness of it.

"We do not want to overly dwell upon the ego, but it is a very important understanding for you to grasp. We do believe that you are now in this understanding and will continue in your desire to shed yourself of those identifiers that no longer serve you, thus no longer enabling ego to rule your choices. Do not become frustrated if it does not happen in the 'time' you believe it should. It took a great many of your 'years' to build and it is quite resilient. It does not desire to be deflated. Since it has always been the energy of the physical that has given ego energy, you will find that energy going into the awakening of Spirit once ego is absorbed and understood. In that way, your physical body will then begin to devote energy to Spirit. This will be one of the new teachings we will bring to you, and that is the transformation of the physical."

When we come from Spirit then we are in Oneness with everything, we are Love, joy, and peace. Does that mean we are the creators?

"Sister of My Sister, you are always the creator whether you are creating in ego or creating in Spirit. You are constantly in the process of creating. Do not forget that you do not only create from Spirit. It is the ultimate walk and desire to create only from Spirit, but while you are in the physical and until you have deflated and absorbed ego, you also create from ego. The things that you create from ego are those things where energy is misused to a certain degree; those things created from Spirit are with the highest uses of energy."

Please speak on the use of our words. When we speak in a negative manner about things, are we then creating negatively or from ego?

"Yes, for a word spoken is forever. It remains 'out there,' if you will. Who is to take it away? If you are saying what you believe are negative words toward someone or something, this will also bring with it the energy from those words. This is using energy in a lower form and this usage is directed by ego. This is creating, and as you know, this creation will form an experience from which there will be residuals. You will experience the residual effect based upon the words you spoke."

Then if our words are positive, we can bring into our experience that which we desire?

"If you go forth in life with the idea that what is intended will happen, then you are creating the steps for it to manifest in your experience. For some an understanding of manifesting is believing that if they sit and they say, 'I know there is a million dollars lying on that table,' a million dollars will appear. As you know, manifestation is much more than that. There is a certain 'feeling' that accompanies it. It does not mean that if you sit and you 'feel,' the million dollars will appear; it goes beyond that. There will be much more taught on this subject, and that is creating through feeling/form. Light Sister, ask someone to bring you up to this moment on what we have already spoken regarding feeling/form.

"There is much in a short period of time that Light Sister desires to be brought up on. We would suggest that you, Little Brother, would be this teacher and bring her up to where your understanding now lies. If you have questions, you know that we are always pleased to answer them for you."

Good, thank you. I have learned that when we identify with any role, we are in ego. Does that include identifying ourselves as a mother or daughter?

"Any title in which either you identify yourself, or you have been identified by, is ego in one of its forms. All who enter into this earth in a physical body are given a name. This name was given to you because it resonated with those who chose it for you. You have been identified by this name all of your life. What if as you grow and begin to awaken, this name does not resonate with you? This may not be who you desire to be identified as any longer and may then choose to change that name. A name identifies one to the other, it can be a title that acknowledges what you do, or it can be a way you, or others, believe you to be. Ego desires to identify everything, it exists in this way. Spirit requires nothing, no identifiers, for it just is and knows that it is. This may seem to be confusing, but we will speak on this subject until you are in understanding."

If we recognize ego in another, this can be very uncomfortable. Even if we see it, we are not always able to say it. This may be out of fear, so it can be challenging to know how to communicate to somebody if we recognize they are in ego.

"Many times, Light Sister, it will be for you to know where someone is along their path of awakening. If you know they are not yet in understanding of ego, or of who they truly are, then you would not say anything in their moments of ego. They would not hear you anyway for you would be up against the resistance of ego. You simply allow them their experience and then choose to remove yourself from this moment.

"Within the council, it is very important that each of you Love, trust, and respect the other enough to identify ego, not only in yourselves, but also in those around you. It is important that the council grow away from ego and into Spirit. We know that this is something that will take some of your 'time,' for, as we have said, you have been building this ego since your physical creation.

"It is important when children are being raised on your planet that they be raised in Spirit so that their ego does not have a chance to identify them. They should know that they are loved and surrounded with Love. The ego will then not receive the energy it requires. It is difficult to do this because children are out in the world, seeing teachers, seeing friends, and just as you experienced, the ego begins to build. The teacher says, 'You are smart,' 'You are not smart,' 'You are a troublemaker,' whatever it is that feeds identifying energy to the ego. The child begins to believe these identifiers. People accumulate many identifiers; there are a multitude of them. Each must be understood. Physically you may be a 'mother,' for you have given birth and this name identifies you in this way. This is not who you are though, it is one of the ways you are identified.

"It appears that upon your planet, a child is seldom given choices that allow them to understand how to choose one path from another. They do not understand that choices create experiences. They do not understand that energy can be used for its highest purpose or can be misused as well. If you begin with them, very early on, the understanding of who they are, how they create, and how to use and be that energy for its highest purpose, then you, in Love, are allowing and aiding them in awakening to their true nature. Imagine if you will a world surrounded with this understanding and this level of Love and energy.

"Are there any questions? We have been most pleased to be able to come in and speak with all of you this evening. While Light Sister visits, we, as always, are available for questions. If there is nothing further at this moment, then we shall depart in Love and Blessings."

It was really special to see Teresa again. She was able to stay the whole week, and it was great to share with her what we had been learning. It was so much easier and nicer to do this in person rather than by phone or e-mail. It turned out that almost our entire first session, with Teresa there, was devoted to a very comprehensive teaching on the ego. It was the most information we had received on this since we first met the "Girls" back in October 2007. Annie, of course, has known them for over twenty years although these Teachings only began when we had all met and were together.

After the session on ego, we had lots to talk about and share. Each of us had our own memorable experiences to contribute to the discussion and this led to a very exciting conversation. We also realized that the ego would become a topic of considerable importance and that we would receive further teachings to help us fully understand this subject. In looking back, I can see where it was a wonderful thing we had these early teachings on ego as each of us would go through a series of experiences and this knowledge helped us understand exactly what ego is capable of doing. We also learned that the ego will constantly attempt to reassert itself among those who have awakened. One must always be aware, in the moment, in the Now, in order to recognize its subtleties and not allow it to express itself in every aspect of our lives.

We again were informed that there was preparation with the Divine Parents for the next phase of teachings that would begin in several weeks. They did give us some hints at the topics that might be addressed, but we still would have to wait for the actual start of the sessions to know for sure what the next step would be.

May 26, 2008

Teresa had formulated some questions she wanted to ask, so we requested another session.

"We do greet thee. We find everyone well this evening? Light Sister, now that you have finished the book *Teachings from the Heart*, what was your feeling?"

The feeling is that it resonates with me. It feels good.

"This is good for we knew that it would, but this is, of course, a wonderful thing to hear. We understand there are questions."

I do have a few questions I would like you to answer. The first one would be, can you please speak of my "blueprint"?

"Yes, of course. The 'blueprint' is that which you agreed upon before you incarnated into the physical. It is something that you and the Divine Parents discussed. You would have created it, but you certainly can change or adjust it as you are upon your journey. You may find that parts of it no longer serve you for the experience that you now desire to accomplish. As far as exactly what the 'blueprint' may be for each one, we do not know. Each is an individual expression of the One and you alone create your 'blueprint' based upon your desired experiences while in the physical. For each who chooses to enter into a physical incarnation, there will be a 'blueprint,' a guideline, if you will, created by you and the Divine for your journey. Once you have incarnated, you may see things that no longer are serving you and you may then modify, change, and rewrite your continuing 'blueprint.'

"You are creating your existence; you are creating your experience. Your 'blueprint' is simply something that, while you were in the spiritual realm, was created to allow you to experience those things you desired to know. Not having any experience with these choices, you may not have understood them until actually coming into your incarnation. Once you were here, it is possible that what you believed you wished to experience no longer stood true. So you may change this."

If it was something we agreed upon with the Divine parents then, was it a concept that I wanted to come here to be a part of the healing of the planet?

"In a way, we would say yes, but what you speak of is more of what your purpose is. The 'blueprint' is for those things that you may desire to create and experience, and therefore may be modified. What you speak of is your purpose, the reason you chose to come here, this was conceived in Love while in the Absolute with the Divine Parents. This is your purpose, to be a part of the Awakening on the planet in which you incarnated into. Everyone enters with a 'blueprint' for experiencing and with a purpose. For some the only purpose may be for the experience of creating their journey while in a physical body, they may never awaken to more than that. Others come with a purpose to be a part of the journey in which awakening occurs, a part of understanding who you are and what that means. A purpose is as individual as each expression of the One. Some are here to heal, some to teach, there are an endless amount of purposes to enter into this physical realm with. Your purpose stays with you throughout your incarnation and is not to be changed or modified; this is your agreement with the Divine Parents."

Thank you for that. Will it come to pass that I will be able to leave the mainstream and join the council full-time?

"What you choose, desire, and create is what shall occur. You are already choosing paths that will take you in that direction. We know not what 'time' this may take to pass, but it is a desire within you."

Thank you.

"You shall pass from that which you have to do for continuance to that which you desire to do. It shall all occur according to your choices, creations, and experiences."

Once again, thank you. I believe that is all of my questions.

"We are reaching a point with the Divine Parents where we have formulated a plan, if you will. We have discussed the next step that will be quite remarkable, and as soon as things are completed, we shall then begin teachings again.

"As you know, it is our joy to be here on this project. It is for you to understand that awakening is not just an awakening of self. It is important, of course, that one awakens to the understanding of their journey, but we know that not all have chosen to awaken. We have come to be with those who have chosen the path of awakening for this shall also cause the vibration of the earth's frequency to rise. It is with the rise in this frequency that many aspects of that which we have come to teach will begin. It is not that you could not remain with the frequency you have now, but in order to accomplish all that you desire, the frequency must rise. It is now doing so. We are seeing with the earth changes that are occurring that this is so. Each time your earth shakes, as they say, it is also raising its vibrational frequency. The energy that resides inside of the earth is being allowed to release.

"It is much like a kettle, if you will, that is set upon a stove. As the temperature of the water rises, it begins to bubble. The whistle begins to go off. It is much the same way that a volcano will begin to spew forth when the pressure has built up. What is happening now is that the earth's energy has been contained for a great long 'time.' It has been imbalanced for a long 'time.' All these occurrences upon your earth with storms, floods, earthquakes, and droughts are not things to fear.

These are to be rejoiced as they are an attempt to raise the frequency of your planet and begin the creation of a new understanding, a new collective. Many will surround themselves with fear and anxiety, for they are still within the old collective. Understand that it is all not only within the Divine Parents' plan, but within the desire of all who have entered to awaken, teach, and bring understanding to others who choose to hear.

"If there are no further questions at this time, we shall depart in Love and Blessings."

We learned some wonderful information regarding "blueprints" in this session. Before this, we had understood that the "blueprint" was a sketch, or outline, that we formulated while still in the Absolute. It consists of experiences we chose to have during our incarnation. We chose the abilities and "tools" to bring in with us in order to experience the events and circumstance we desired. However, we now discovered that we can modify this "blueprint" at any time if something we had previously chosen, now no longer resonates with us. We also learned that our purpose was also chosen at this time, but that it was not modifiable as the "blueprint" is. It was fascinating to learn that the purpose for our incarnation was agreed upon with the Parents. Meaning, that the purpose, or purposes, we chose would be those that most fully revealed our true nature, which we know is Love. It would be that place where we would be completely fulfilled and reach the full expression of who we are, Spirit. Even though we enter with a chosen degree of forgetfulness, Spirit always knows its purpose. As we begin to spiritually awaken, not only does Spirit begin to change the body and mind, but also begins to direct the life path in order to bring about, step by step, the purpose we came to fulfill. It was also an eye-opener to understand that not every Spirit will choose to awaken for that may be exactly the experience that was chosen, to remain asleep and to create one's journey from that standpoint. That really helped me understand the whole allowing thing as well. Each one is here doing what they chose to do, experiencing those things they create, and the residuals from those choices. No judgment toward anyone, this was another greater understanding of allowing. It always seems the lessons just fall into place the further we go and the more we understand.

I, for one, do not desire to know what earth changes will happen. I just know that they will and what they are for. My focus is on sharing what I know, and who I know I am, with anyone who asks questions. I really see one of my purposes is to bring these Teachings out to the world. I guess I just do that by staying true to being Spirit in every Now. I know I won't always reflect that, I am working on that pesky ego, but I sure will do my very best. No expectations, no preconceptions, no judgment, only Love, peace, and harmony. Stay tuned!

May 29, 2008

Since this was Teresa's last day with us, we requested a meeting in the morning.

"We do greet thee. We give our Love to each and every one here. What are your questions?"

I was receiving colors of purple and black yesterday during my meditation. Do you know what these colors mean?

"Light Sister, what you were seeing was communication. As you know, we speak in a language that contains colors. What you were seeing was the language of color."

Thank you, I saw a lot of colors yesterday.

"Sometimes you will find that when an area that has been blocked is being cleared, as energy once again begins to flow, this energy takes on a color of its own. So that you were seeing colors would indicate that much is being moved within. This is as it should be."

Would you please tell us the most growth-producing way of handling the Las Vegas foreclosure notice and the threat of bankruptcy?

"Much of what is occurring is doing so because of what the collective has created and believed. You should understand that even though you have a strong desire for something to occur, the choice may lie within someone in the collective who believes that they are in control. You may desire to move upstream, but the stream may have the upper hand because of its power. We believe that what is currently happening upon your planet is that the banks have become frightened. This fear is extended outward to many and this wall has been created with great strength. This wall of fear is quite prominent in many institutions. You will observe this happening around your country.

"How do you to handle this? Just be who you know you are and know that whatever the action that is occurring, it shall pass. Hold to the understanding that what is occurring is partly due to the residual from past choices and from the current fear that has been created by the current collective. You may choose to speak with your bank, and if you see or sense resistance, then you will know where they stand. These creations by others can affect you if you choose to allow them to. You can get caught up in another's creation and experience until you realize that it is how you accept or reject it that will create your experience. See this as growth, a process of evolving from a physical understanding to a spiritual understanding."

I understand what you are saying. It seems to me to be somewhat more complex, but I do understand.

"Little Brother, would you please explain."

Well, we do have a situation where the wall of fear is present, but at what point is the free will of one person compromised over another's? There seems to be no way around it, for it is one of those no-win situations. The free will choice of the awakened individual is, of course, to take that route that is the best for Spirit and that is most in line for the highest good. If faced with another individual who is tied to the walls, who has another viewpoint, now you have two opposing intents and two opposing desires. If one of those is compromised, then the question is, which one?

"You are not dealing with an individual entity here. You are dealing with a conglomerate, a multiplicity of wills, who are in turn dealing with a bigger conglomerate of wills. Unfortunately, the current collective consciousness is quite large and quite aggressive. It does indeed appear as if the free will of one will not be honored, but the free will may be in how you choose to experience this occurrence. When an experience is created by another, and this creation is given strength and power through the beliefs of many, the collective, then it may be that your choice lies in how you handle this created experience. The freedom to create at will is that which is given to all who incarnate, there are those who will create with energy used for its highest purpose, and those who will create with energy at its lowest. When you find yourself within an experience where this second choice in the use of energy occurs, then you may choose to not be a part of that creation and remove yourself. This may also mean that you leave behind you many previous desires. For now, until more awaken and the new collective grows, these things can only be accepted and allowed as experiences of growth. Do not fight against it, for that which is resisted persists."

I will not fight it, and I have made the choice also to help establish a new consciousness.

"It shall be the new consciousness that surpasses the old that now exists. For instance, you reside right now in an area of like-minded people and these people will be drawn toward the Teachings with questions. They are already upon their spiritual journey and understand how the new collective will begin to grow. With this change in the consciousness, that which you desire to create will come to pass.

"It may be that this home you have will be gone, but it is simply something that is material and can be reached once again."

My understanding is that one of the major parts of the project we are involved in is to bring a balance between male and female energies.

"Yes, this is exactly correct."

Is this within the individual? Does every individual have male and female aspects? Is this correct? Are we looking to balance that within ourselves?

"You will achieve that balance by assuring that your energy centers are open and that the energy is flowing smoothly throughout your physical body, and this in turn allows Spirit to awaken and remember. When you are balanced, you are not leaning more to one than the other either in thought or in action. Sister of My Sister, we see that you have a question?"

I just wanted to say that this is hard right now.

"This is a difficult 'time' for you, we feel this. If we did not know that the outcome, when it comes to pass, will be more than what you have thought of, and will be for your highest purpose. We simply cannot give you a 'time' for this to occur as we are not in the 'knowing' of that 'time.'"

Thank you. I would like to ask you about a friend of mine who has been asking me questions. Am I going overboard with my communication with her?

"No, for she is asking, and the questions she is asking mean that she is ready for the answers. Do not give an answer before a question is asked. We would say this for anyone who is working with someone who is awakening. Speak to them about the basics. When the questions begin, give the answers. As we have always said to you, 'you will know by the questions where they are on their journey and what they are ready to learn and understand.'"

Are you able, at this point, to reveal anything about the change in direction of the Teachings, or is this to be held in confidence?

"At this 'time,' we are still in planning. But, yes, it will be revealed. If there are no further questions, we shall depart in much Love and Blessings."

We had been talking that day about the notice of foreclosure that we had received in the morning's mail. We had been carrying this eventuality around now for several months, but the arrival of it put us all into a space where we were trying to figure out what to do next. We also came to the realization that avoiding bankruptcy would be a very slim possibility if things did not change soon.

We learned some eye-opening truths during the meeting. Sometimes there are situations with two opposing wills and intentions, so whose free will is violated? To guarantee each person the freedom to create at will could potentially end up with the real-life scenario that we found ourselves in. I know that for Bruce this question was not just a philosophical debate. He understood that free will is something that is not only given but is one of the ways in which the Divine Parents interact with us. It is how all choices, creations, and experiences are for us to decide. If free will is not upheld, then there is a very serious problem to deal with. Yes, the collective consciousness is very powerful, but none the less it certainly did not change our position on this issue. The only way that makes sense is if a person's free will is not upheld it is for a very short while, or for a specific situation that was not in the highest interest, or purpose for that person. What was of the highest interest, or purpose, was indeed coming. We just do not see this at the time and lose sight of a much-larger picture. Our ego blinds us to this and we sometimes create further experiences that definitely do not serve us. If we would only sit with it for a while, remain open, remain Spirit, then we would see that what we interpret as not honoring our free will is only the allowance for something greater to happen.

We also learned in this session that a change in direction was about to occur. Naturally we were curious. We understood that matters were being worked out and gratefully acknowledged that we would simply wait until the details would be revealed. We had definitely learned by now that any change was always in line with objectives of the project and also an expansion of the scope of the project as well.

Chapter Six

June 4, 2008

Today was the anniversary of the first time Annie had met Zelia, which had been over twenty years ago. It seemed a wonderful time for her to speak with them.

"We do greet thee. Sister of My Sister, we would like to say how pleased we are on this day, what you call our anniversary. It is now what has been projected for a great long of your 'time.'"

I wanted to connect with you on this day. I know there is "not time," but we are in a linear situation on this earth. I wanted to thank you for bringing the three of us together and all the council that has come and will be coming. Thank you for being with us for this grand adventure.

"You are most welcome, for this is our purpose. As you say, there is 'no time,' but we know that it certainly does exist within your space continuum. Trust though that it has been a blink of the eye for us. It certainly is a grand adventure, as you call it, so continue on this road and it shall come to fruition all that is our purpose. Do you or anyone have questions?"

I was just wondering. I had expected to channel Astoria back when we first met; does that desire have any bearing on what I put into my "blueprint" for this lifetime?

"It would most likely be that this is something that you had not then, while in the Absolute, desired to do. It does not mean that you could not have a choice in this Now, a modification of your 'blueprint.' It is simply that it is not occurring for now in your 'time.'"

It wasn't a big disappointment that I didn't. I kind of felt on some level like that wasn't really what I wanted to do.

"It was simply not what your real intention was. Your desire was to simply be connected, if you will. We knew that this current relationship would come to pass, so this was the desired outcome."

Yes, it certainly was. In honor of this anniversary, would you give the three of us something, some information, to "chew on"?

"We would be most pleased, for we have been learning quite a bit. We will be working more on the energy body. It is that which surrounds your being, which surrounds Spirit. It is now most advantageous for you to learn to blend with the 'Now." It will be a 'time' of transferring energy from that of the physical to that of the spiritual, knowing that the spiritual will always maintain the physical. To transfer energy to Spirit that shall allow it to soar, to blend, and to become One, not only with people or things around you, but to begin to feel yourself a part of the whole. This is one thing that we will begin to work upon. There are many things that shall be coming to pass. We have been told of some, but some we are awaiting the 'time.'

"It is important that you continue your outreach. It is for you to continue meeting with people and speaking with them as you are led to them. Share with them, as they ask, regarding the teachings and The Light Alliance.

"Another thing we will be expanding more upon shall be your dealing in, and with, 'no time.' It is much like the plan for healthy living we have given you. You have adapted this into your daily life, and now you shall adapt the understanding of what truly is living in 'no time.' We do understand that in some ways this will be difficult, particularly because you do have jobs, and you do have moments that you must look at your clock to determine the 'time,' but when you are not present at these jobs, we would ask that you would begin to live in 'no time,' knowing that it is a continuum. If you are working, do not worry yourself with what 'time' it is. Simply let it flow. Now, of course, Little One must arrive and depart her employment at a certain 'time,' but during her day, we are going to ask her to simply forget 'time.' Simply do what needs to be done, much as you wait for your stomach to signal you that it is ready to eat. We wish for you to get an inner knowing about where you are in your day. You will begin to find that things will begin to merge and flow. We will be going into this in more depth but we believe that this will give you something to chew upon."

I like it a lot.

"It is important now that you begin understanding the concept of 'no time,' for at some point this shall be. Right now the collective, being the way it is, will make this much harder to accomplish. If you can learn to live sections of your existence in 'no time,' you will find that miraculous things occur.

"We ask you to think about this we are now saying to you. If you set a 'time' to eat and one or more are not hungry, do you eat simply because it was a set 'time'? We suggest that you give your body its desired moments between eating. Do not feel the 'need' to consume food until your body signals to you that it requires nourishment. This may prove challenging to you at first because you have conditioned yourselves to eat at the 'time' of five o'clock. Try setting this 'time' less and less to see what occurs. It may mean the preparation of a meal and then it will be eaten when each is ready."

Sometimes I do not have any hunger pangs all day long. There are also times when I am not hungry in the evening also.

"Also understand that the physical body is such that if you do not feed it; it will not react as if it is hungry. Sometimes you feed it so it begins to establish the difference between hunger and not eating or starving. You must give your body nourishment. It will then begin to signal when it requires nourishment. If you eat when you are not hungry, when you eat emotionally or from stress, then you are teaching your body to respond as if it is hungry whenever you find yourself in an emotional or stressful situation. This eating will create many more areas of physical concern."

These are two very good areas to chew on.

"There are some things we have been told we wish to work with you on. This is something for everyone to learn, of course, that the physical body, due to the heaviness of its vibration upon your earth, cannot travel as Spirit does. Spirit does indeed travel. It will be the understanding of this travel that will open doors for you. This will be one of the new areas of teaching. We will be actually showing you how to spirit travel within 'no time,' and this is why we have asked you to begin to live that way. As Spirit awakens and remembers that it is not bound by the vibrations of earth, it will also remember how to travel beyond those physical bonds. It will open a new path for those who may desire to know and understand more of this travel. We will begin the Teachings again at the end of your current month."

Are all the loose ends supposed to be tied off by that time?

"We believe they will be. They may not be tied off exactly as you have desired, but they will be tied off to what shall occur. We have been told, and we are in the 'knowing,' that all that occurs will be for your highest purpose.

"Another reason to begin 'thinking' in an abstract fashion regarding 'time' is for the body to actually begin this understanding as well as Spirit. Many things are possible when you truly know these things, possible with the body's aging, regeneration, and rejuvenation. How far you will go with this in your current incarnation we do not know, but we will teach what we are able. We know that you will go further than most for this is your path and your desire."

Little Brother and I were feeling that something was different yesterday, what was it?

"There is much that has been occurring. People are being drawn. As you have noticed, we are sending many to each of you. You will begin to see and understand more of what other information is out there and now being said to others. This will aid you in giving answers to questions that may come your way. The thing that seemed different is that which you are creating by sharing the teachings we have brought from the Divine Parents. This will raise your vibrations as well as those of the people you share with."

It seems that there are many people on the earth plane who make a big deal out of channeling.

"That may be because they do not necessarily understand truly what it is. Many who say they are channeling are simply contacting spirits who have chosen to remain earthbound. This is not channeling in its purest sense. This is simply the ability to 'read' that which is very close to your own dimension, they are still within earth's vibration. Those who are channeling, in its true sense, are channeling those from other worlds, other universes, or who are still within the Absolute. If someone says to you, 'I am speaking with so and so, and they have recently left a physical body, it is quite likely that Spirit has yet to return to the Absolute. For those who are somewhat awakened and Spirit is in the knowing, to a degree, then it is easier for them to read those who remain earthbound. They believe that what they are doing is channeling simply because they use their own voice to relay messages. The whole idea and purpose of channeling seems to have been steeped in mystery and machinations, if you will."

Please explain further how we will feel when we are thinking in "no time." How does this affect the ego?

"The effect upon ego is another reason we are teaching you to live in 'no time.' Ego cannot exist in 'no time.' It knows only the linear, only the physical. When you spend more time in Spirit and less in the physical, or ego, then it will become confused and will begin to unravel.

"To be in 'no time' is to be in the 'Now.' There is no day, no night. It is important to understand that you are on one long continuum. You are not truly on a twenty-four-hour continuum. It is not as if your day begins at one time and ends at another. Your physical 'time,' if you will, began when you drew your first breath, and it will end at the moment when you cease to breathe. At that moment, who you truly are, Spirit, in full remembrance and knowing, returns to the Absolute and so it is a continuous line. You are always who you are, whether you encompass a physical body or you are free from a physical incarnation, you always continue. We will have you begin to think on this and will bring you more teachings."

Thank you. I'm just so grateful for sharing so much of my physical experience with you.

"We are overjoyed, Sister of My Sister, that we came to know your Spirit and that we have been with you this great deal of your 'time.' We are so pleased to be continuing this journey now, all of us together. These things will be shared by many, for it is for all to know. For now, we do depart in Love and Blessings."

We were fascinated by the request for us to begin to learn how to live in "no time." As our world is based on time, this was going to be quite interesting. We would spend those moments away from work and begin practicing being outside of physical time. We have gradually become better at this and it is so freeing. I still have to refer to the clock when I have appointments to keep, places to be, or people to meet. I do love being in that place of stillness and seeing how long I can remain there before being drawn back. I am finding I can really be who I know I am when in "no time," and it gets easier to deal with others that way as well. Meditation continues to be a wonderfully productive time for all of us. The expansion of Spirit while remaining in our physical body seemed to come fairly easy for each one of us. We had been given prior insight into this so it was just a matter of putting into practice all that we had been taught to that point. This ability continues to grow with each new experience.

June 9, 2008

This was one of those days when everything seemed to be falling down around Bruce. I have included this day in this session so you will be able to really understand the Love, compassion, as well as the teachings that take place whenever any of us has one of those days.

"We do greet thee. We find you well?"

We seem to be somewhat hemmed in by "time" right now.

"Let us refer to 'time' as space, for it is simply a moment of 'Now's' in your continuum. We are in the knowing that it is important to reach beyond the word 'time' as you begin to enter more and more into the understanding of truly being 'in the Now.' This is the place where all exists. When you look, as you say, toward the future, understand that it is simply a series of 'Now's,' which have yet to occur. Things that happen in every Now, choices that you make, can change your course in a moment of that Now. When a choice is not made in awareness, it can take you from the path you desire to be upon. Once you discover that the choice has led you astray, then returning to your original path shall also require a choice in the Now you find yourself within. When you are 'living in the Now,' 'being in the Now,' be aware of your choices, what they create, and the experience and residuals that will follow that choice. That is why we say to center and breathe before you make your choice. Are there any questions?"

I don't think so.

"Little Brother, we would like to see Spirit be more in the forefront, your mind seems to be siding with the physical, in ego, at this moment."

Yes, this is a very difficult time right now.

"Only you, Spirit, can change that. Are you to see it from the angle of ego and therefore 'feel' it as difficult, or to see it for an experience of growth and understanding?"

What I seem to be sensing is that Spirit desires to go in one direction, but I seem to be physically in another direction. This is posing a lot of difficulty right now.

"Explain what you are meaning that Spirit is going in one direction while your physical body seems to be going in another."

Spirit desires to move ahead with what we came here to do, but so much of my "time" is being spent in being who I am not and being where I do not desire to be. It's been that way for over a year now.

"Little Brother, are people not being led to you for you to share the teachings with? Are you not speaking with others and doing outreach? Is that not the growth of Spirit?"

Yes, it is the growth of Spirit, but it is not the growth I am intending.

"Maybe you should simply allow all things to flow and not intend for anything. Spirit will flow also. It understands and rejoices in all that is. If you are finding it necessary, in your physical world, to be doing certain things, does that mean that because you are physically involved that you cannot also be spiritually growing? Spirit, in spite of what the physical body may be doing, continues to awaken. It is only when your mind, while in ego, has you believing 'oh, look what we have to do, poor us, we are stuck.' Then, if you choose to believe this, ego will begin to overshadow the awakening of Spirit. You know that ego desires to be in control, to be noticed. If you are allowing a mood that is making you feel stuck, then you must know that this is not the creation of Spirit, for Spirit shall never feel stuck. Spirit just is enjoying every single moment of every single Now. We understand that all which is occurring in your Now is a process of the awakening and growth of Spirit. Stay connected, in Spirit, to all that is occurring, and stay there in Love. When you acknowledge ego but do not allow it to take control, then this also allows Spirit to overtake ego and begin to deflate it. When you are able to do this, you will begin to see things opening and flowing freely."

Thank you, I can see that I have more work to do.

"There is not anyone on your planet, anyone who is awake, who will not have continuing work to do upon themselves. For not until the body, mind, and Sprit are united will you completely understand all there is to know. You are getting closer, but you will continue to expand, to unite."

You have just seen me on one of my unusually difficult days, Dear Ones.

"We do understand this. We simply wanted to point all this out to you so that you could be more aware."

I really do thank you for that. It seems like the dam broke on me today.

"Do not allow that to be your experience, for this feeling comes from what ego puts forth. If it keeps you thinking, if it keeps you in a state of confusion, it has accomplished one of its purposes. Remember, Spirit would never create this feeling."

That is very much appreciated. Thank you.

"You are most welcome; this is what we desire to help you with. You have reached the point where you may choose to let go of those things that you have tried to control and hang on to. If you do this, knowing that in the hands of the Divine all things unfold for your highest purpose, you will be joyful and ready to receive that which has unfolded for you."

Yes, I do know it is in Their hands.

"Trust that you are doing what can be done with the resources you have in your current Now. If nothing more can be done, then simply let it go."

I truly do hear what you say. My frustration today is that I have many questions and few answers. There are so many loose ends to tie off.

"Then go with what you do know and do not let ego create confusion in what you do not know. You are pushing against a wall, just flow with it and allow Spirit to flow as well. Let Spirit take the lead in all your choices. Do not be in fear to ask for help, for you will make it up to those who help you. Your questions shall be answered when you find yourself in a place of balance and harmony, when you have reached a place to hear the answers.

"Sister of My Sister, do you have anything that you would care to share or ask?"

No, my comment is that this whole session has been beneficial for me as well. As always, there has been a teaching within your words of comfort.

"We desire that with each moment we come, even if it is only to answer your personal questions, that there also be a teaching as well. The teaching of this moment, we believe, would be for you to understand what 'being in the Now,' is about. It is not the state of leaving your body, or being in the ether, it is being in your body in Spirit, for this is who you truly are. It is being in each moment, not projecting yourself into a 'time,' or space, that has not yet occurred."

I did not mean to be a little sour tonight.

"No, Little Brother, you know that we Love you and we do understand where you are in your Now. It is our desire to help you see things in a clearer fashion, for there is always a larger picture. If you get stuck upon the micro dot in front of you, then your ego will grow it into a mountain instead of the smallness that it really is. If there is nothing further, we shall depart in Love and Blessings."

We all have had our meltdown on this journey. Some are mild while others seem to be so much more. You feel like you are being squeezed so hard that whatever it is that needs to be removed is coming out drop by drop. Fortunately, while it can be an extremely painful experience, they are usually very short-lived. Such was the experience in Bruce's case.

I included it as a session for several reasons. First, to show that just because you have awakened it does not mean you are through growing spiritually; in fact, it is just the opposite. The deep issues you do not often even know exist still must be brought to the surface so that you can really take a hard look at them, what created them, and understand that you really can let them go and not allow them to continue creating experiences for you. Why hold on to something that does not serve you and is no longer who you know that you are?

Second, to show you that they always bring loving guidance and that at the same time they remind us that no matter what options may be available, it is always our choice to make them.

Third, so you are able to see that there is always a teaching that accompanies the experience we are having, and a reminder that we have the freedom to create at will everything we experience. We always have the right to choose the course of action we will take in all aspects of our lives.

I hope that this advice can aid you when hard decisions arise, or you are simply having "one of those days"!

June 17, 2008

Bruce's sister had called to ask if he could come up to Oregon and help her with some needed remodeling on her home. He wanted to check with the "Girls" to see if this absence would fit into the plans for the new Teachings that were to begin around the same time he would be gone.

"We do greet thee. How is everyone in this space of yours? We understand there are questions that you desire to have answered. We would be pleased to answer all you ask, so please begin."

Greetings, Dear Ones. Yes, there are a couple of questions to ask of you. My sister called and has asked me to come up to do repairs on her home. She would like me to leave right away, and I was wondering if the timing of this visit would be in line with what is planned for the continued teachings?

"Because there is 'no time,' this short space that you will be with your family is just simply that, a short 'time.' You will not only be giving while you are there, but you will be receiving as well. This space of your 'time' will pass quite quickly."

Over the last few days, there have been three distinct and different directions that I thought I may be on. Now there has only been this one direction, so this appears to be the direction to follow. Is it because of the circumstances that are happening right now that it was necessary to make those changes rapidly?

"That was indeed a factor. We desired for you to see how rapidly events and circumstances truly can be changed. This was something that you needed to be aware of because there have been times when you did not feel that circumstances, or events, were moving quickly enough for you. It was for you to see that they could be changed in the blink of an eye. When you return, the lessons will continue. We have also observed, and heard, that you have spoken with a friend about visiting with him, and with this we are most pleased. We are pleased to work within whatever 'time' is set. We see that you are preparing for your trip, so for now, we shall depart in Love and Blessings."

This was a short session and I included it only to show when you have no expectations, or time schedules, things just seem to fall into place. We knew that all things occur in their intended sequence and this trip for Bruce was one of those things. Since there really is "no time," it was of no concern as to when the Teachings would again begin. At first I know he was a bit hesitant to go as we were waiting for the next series of Teachings to start, but it was made clear that everything was as it should be.

Bruce was able to accomplish all that his sister and brother-in-law desired during his stay. He told me that they had many wonderful evenings on the patio over dinner and were able to share so many thoughts and feelings. It was a very special time for him.

Since I was really practicing being in "no time," the five weeks that he was gone didn't seem so long at all.

July 24, 2008

Bruce arrived back in Happy Camp during the afternoon, stopped to see me at work, and went back to our fifth wheel to unpack. It was then that he met the newest addition to our family, a tiny Jack Russell Terrier puppy that I had named "Spirit." I felt that in light of all I was learning about who I was, and my connection to all things, this was a very appropriate name indeed. Spirit was born on June 21, 2008, the summer solstice. She was an only pup of a six-year-old Jack Russell named Daisy. What Bruce discovered upon entering the trailer was truly precious. He told me little Spirit was cuddled up with her mother in a large crate our friend had given us when he brought the then three-week-old Spirit to me. I had agreed to keep Daisy with us until Spirit was weaned. Naturally Bruce's first meeting with Spirit included his holding her. She was so small she could almost fit into the palm of his hand. It was love at first sight and an instant bond.

As this day was also our anniversary, I was very happy he was back in time to celebrate. The addition of little Spirit to our family was truly icing on the cake. Sarah was staying at Annie's. We introduced the newest member to her. Sarah was not too impressed when they met. All that Spirit got in return for bouncing around her was a swat and a not-so-inviting hiss. Sarah then turned around and walked back to where she had been sleeping.

Sarah was doing so good health wise that we had decided to leave her at the house with Annie. We also had been staying there since early April and only recently had moved down to our fifth wheel. I had been so cold and wet that we all decided it had been best to stay where it was warmer. Being back in the trailer was nice because now I only had to walk a block to work and Bruce was right there to finish work on the cabin he was remodeling.

This "time" seemed to also bring in many people who would just "pop in" to talk. It was really a big outreach occasion. From that time on, through the rest of the summer, not much went on with gold prospecting. It was clear that this time of outreach was very important to moving the project, and the teachings, forward. Not only were our days filled with people who just seemed to appear, but the evenings as well were taken up with the many gatherings and the sharing of the teachings we had received.

Now, to the session we had the evening of Bruce's return.

"We do greet thee. We would like to express our Love to Little One and Little Brother on this the remembrance of their coming together."

Thank you, Dear Ones.

"You are most welcome. How is everyone in this Now? We are pleased to hear and answer your questions."

We are wonderful. I have a whole lot of questions, but it will seem like I am monopolizing because Little Brother doesn't have any. I think he will think of some as we go along. Were you and Astoria combined when you were previously channeled years ago?

"No, not exactly. We have always been one, of course, with our connection to you, Little Brother, and Little One, but when we were channeling through the other, it was primarily myself, if you will. Sister Astoria was at the time your guide. There were moments when we were combined in our energies, but not always. It would have been dependent upon the message that we were bringing about."

Way back then, I wondered mainly because when I chose to accept her as my guide, you told me that she was so happy, dancing with arms in the air. What I concluded since then is that she knew about the eventual coming of The Light Alliance and that was why she was so happy.

"Also you should be aware that many times it was not us being channeled through the other one. There were moments during her experience in channeling where it was either her ego, or an earthbound spirit being heard. When it was you who requested a channeling, then you may be assured that it was us. We came to give you information that you would one day remember, and now you understand that it was for these moments we first came."

Those words stayed with me all those years. They were very powerful. Now I understand through reading Little One's book that the combination of the two of you has been since you first began to channel through Little One.

"Yes, since we, and Little One, were chosen and chose each other, we have always come as one."

That is so exciting. That is beautiful. Do the various earthbound spirits interrelate with one another?

"If they choose to relate, yes they can. It is sometimes one Spirit who brings in another during a psychic reading. Since they all have chosen to remain within the same frequency and vibration, and not yet return to the Absolute, they may also choose to interact with others who have chosen the same."

Are there more-advanced earthbound Spirits that help lesser-advanced earthbound Spirits?

"Again, if it is a choice, yes, they may. When you leave your physical body behind, and before you return to the Absolute, you take with you the knowledge and understanding you obtained while in the physical, in addition to a higher understanding and remembering of what you had forgotten. Since there are many degrees of understanding at the time you leave your physical body, there will also be those who 'know' more. They may choose to work with those who may not have the same depth of understanding."

One time I was at a meeting and one of the persons who was working on someone during an energy session suddenly fell to the floor. Two other people said they saw a dark energy rise up and go out the door. I would like to know what that was all about.

"We would say that this is what you might call a group consciousness, or mass hysteria. Of course you know that there is no 'darkness.' It was simply a matter of someone being overcome by the flow of energy because they truly did not yet understand it. This person's ego took the opportunity to create a situation that would move everyone away from the beauty and truth of what the energy truly is. It was also the ego in each of those who came to assist that joined in creating this experience. Energy is energy always. It can be used for the highest purposes, or can be misused as well, but it remains the energy of the One. It is the choice of each on how it is used and what it creates. This person did not understand not only what they were doing, but also they did not know who they truly are. When ego is allowed to participate in any choice or action, then you can be assured that the experience, and the resulting residual, will not be that which serves who you are, which, as you know, is Spirit."

So there really was no dark energy that sailed across the room and went out of the glass door?

"No, for there is only energy and that energy when used for a higher purpose is always white. If one is misusing energy, then that created experience will result in a residual for that one person only. It will be their experience alone and there is not any color to this energy, only residual from its misuse. As we have said, you may use the energy 'turned up' or 'turned down,' but it remains the same energy."

That makes so much sense, but sometimes one wonders when you hear such things.

"Yes, and many will believe such a thing. It will be the mass consciousness of their ego that shall create and hold this belief. If you would think back to the time that this occurred, probably one person says they saw this, and all others simply got caught up within that creation. It would be a mass reckoning, a mass consciousness."

Are there determining factors involved in earthbound spirits returning to the Absolute?

"No, for who would create these factors. It is simply that one makes a choice. When they have fulfilled the reason that they chose to remain earthbound, they will simply return to the Absolute."

There is "no time" then?

"Of course, for they may choose to stay earthbound for as long as they desire, especially since 'time' truly is an endless continuum and they choose to leave the experience somewhere along the continuum."

Since Spirit chooses to incarnate into the physical in forgetfulness, how is it that some will remember and some won't?

"As we have taught, it is simply a matter of choice. As you are walking upon your path, you are encountering moments where you are given choices. You may be shown a book, hear a word or a conversation, it may be a myriad of things, but if you choose to ignore them, then your moment of awakening may not occur, or be delayed. For others who do remember, it is because that which has been put in front of them, they have chosen to accept, or to look into. Also do not forget the 'blueprint.' It may be that your choice within your 'blueprint' was to experience a physical incarnation while remaining spiritually asleep. Of course you can always modify this first choice and that is where recognition of things which resonate with you comes in. If you choose to modify, then you will be drawn eventually to those things which will help you in awakening and understanding the path you are upon."

Does one lifetime have an influence on other lifetimes?

"In each incarnation, you enter with a purpose. Sometimes you may pull from a 'memory' of Spirit to aid you in fulfilling this purpose. Since all is a continuum, then the things you may have learned in one incarnation are simply stored within the 'knowing' of Spirit. At any point, within an incarnation, you may learn to draw upon these 'memories' in order to move you along in your current purpose."

I have heard from a channeled being that it is all one continuous lifetime. What would you say about that?

"We would say, of course, that Spirit is continuous. Spirit is eternal, continuous. The physical body is not it has an ending. If you are terming lifetime in a spiritual sense, then yes, it is a continuous lifetime."

So then each incarnation is a different experience?

"Yes, you have chosen to come back into a physical body for whatever purpose you now desire to create and experience. It will always be a different experience even when it is drawn, to some extent, from Spirit 'memories.' Your purpose may be to continue advancing, teaching, learning, and sharing along a line you had previously desired. It will still entail different experiences."

Do parents make agreements with their children in the Absolute before they incarnate into the physical?

"It may happen. Just as you may agree with another to come in as a guide for them as they are having their human experience, you may also choose to come in as a child, or parent, one to the other. This would especially be true if what you desire to experience goes along with what another may also be choosing. We are not aware of when this has happened for it would be the choice of those involved in that particular incarnation."

Then this would not be a usual thing?

"No, it generally would occur for one's particular reason. If Spirit has chosen to come in to be in the scientific field, for instance, then they may agree with another Spirit who has also chosen that field to come incarnate as their child and so be raised in that particular environment."

How does Spirit awaken ahead of the body and mind?

"Spirit, of course, before entering into the physical knows all. It is simply a matter of when in its 'blueprint' it has chosen to awaken. This awakening always occurs before the physical body or the mind and it is Spirit that brings the other two along. Mind, of course, as Spirit awakens, may choose to either be in ego mind, or to move back to where it began, which was in Spirit. The physical body may at times seem reluctant to move with Spirit because it has been in ego, but as the mind moves more in the direction of Spirit, then the body is brought along to align with Spirit."

Is there ever a case where Spirit comes in and never wakes up in a lifetime?

"Yes, for as we have taught, awakening is also a choice. One may simply get to the end of one's physical journey and run into a wall, if you will, and does not understand what has occurred because they chose not to awaken. Spirit may also have chosen to awaken in small degrees over a period of your 'time,' what you refer to as searching."

How does that correspond with the awakening of the mind?

"The mind is either attached to the physical or Spirit. It enters with Spirit but may choose its association. Ego awakens in the physical from birth and begins to create an awareness of oneself as an individual, separated. Ego is then given energy as the physical grows, dependent upon the consciousness and the environment it is within."

Is it correct to say that if we lift anything, with Spirit awareness, into the Oneness, then it becomes lifted to the One Energy?

"All things are of the One Energy. Foods, for instance, have an interaction with the human body, some serve its health and well-being, and others do not. If you occasionally eat a food that does not serve your health, then you may raise its frequency to somewhat counteract its potential to detract from the health of the human body. We would suggest that you stay away from those foods altogether and therefore would not have that issue, but if you choose to eat them then you may lift them, in Spirit, to raise their vibration."

So the degree of our awakening is the degree to which we are being in the One?

"It is that, yes, and also what your choice was regarding awakening while you were creating your 'blueprint.' If awakening was your choice, then the more you understand Oneness, the more you are living as Spirit, the more you 'know' of your connection to all things, then your awakening will rise to the degree of your effort and choices."

Does everyone enter the earth with the same degree of forgetfulness?

"No, of course not, for if you look at Yeshua, he chose to come in with less forgetfulness in order to be a teacher. Look also at some of your greatest scientists. Einstein chose to come in remembering, and knowing more conceptually, of that field. Spirit can choose to come in with the degree of forgetfulness it desires."

We are three in One, body, mind, Spirit. When I was seeking to heal my physical body from purely a spiritual standpoint, I was out of balance by not seeking medical assistance. So does all creation take place the same way, with the joining of body, mind, and Spirit in doing what it can both physically and spiritually?

"It is important that Spirit is One with healing the physical; however, if the physical body is not involved in that healing as well, then this may entail seeking aid from one of your physicians. If you resist against seeking help, then this is an ego creation and is setting up a blockade, if you will. Your physical body may desire the control it feels it has by your remaining ill, so yes, it must be the joining of all three to accomplish that which you desire."

Those are all of my questions.

"Little Brother, did you desire to comment?"

There are no questions at this time, Dear Ones. I am well and joyful.

"We are most pleased to hear this. If there are no further questions, then for now, we shall depart in Love and Blessings."

This session was for Annie to present her questions based on Teachings we had received to date. We somehow knew that his session marked the end of a chapter for us in our journey. It was made quite clear that a new direction was coming with advancement in the Teachings we would be receiving. We were excited and ready for them to begin. We would wait for two more weeks before we were informed that the next phase was about to begin.

Spirit was now quite active at almost six weeks old. She had begun to lose the wobbly back legs she has as a very young puppy and began to emerge as a fearless bundle of energy who loved to fly. There were two steps in our fifth wheel that led up to the bedroom. Once she learned how to climb up them, she decided that the best way, and probably the most fun, to get back down was to jump. She would stand at the top of the steps, look straight ahead, and then launch herself into the air with both front legs stretched out. We started calling her the "flying puppy." It seemed the more we laughed at her antics, the more she did them.

Sarah was doing quite well, although we did begin to notice an increase in her urine output. We knew that she had kidney disease, but she was alert, playful, and her old self. We were so happy that she was still choosing to be with us.

Chapter Seven

August 8, 2008

We were at a crossroads: should we choose to file for bankruptcy or continue to try and do whatever we could in the hope of recovering from our ever-growing financial problems? To help us sort things out, we requested another session. As in every session, this one also contained a Teaching, and this one was on orbs.

"We do greet thee. How is everyone? We are ready and awaiting your questions."

Greetings, is there one thing that may be more beneficial to the project financially if there are several things that potentially may bring in money?

"Sister of My Sister, it is not that one is more beneficial, for all things that you decide upon on your journey will benefit you in one way or another. It could be that some will give 'more' and some will give 'less,' but all will give something. Each that you choose, each decision you make, will move you to a different part of your journey. As always, it is your choice."

The main thing then seems to be the experience.

"All is an experience. You have a choice of taking a 'right' turn or a 'left' turn as you arrive at crossroads in your path. If you choose one direction, you will experience one thing, and another direction will create a different experience. It is the same thing you do as you move within your journey, it is the choice that you shall make that will create the experience that you shall have."

We got into a wonderful discussion on orbs the other night. Would you be so kind as to give us an understanding of what they are?

"Yes, Little Brother, we would be most pleased to do so. Orbs are condensed energy, energy that actually solidifies and takes on a form. They draw energy from the place where they exist, as well as from the people that they are around. They are formed first of all with the energy that is given by the Divine Feminine. When orbs are captured on film, the energy may also arise from the one who is taking the picture. It is energy drawn into a condensed mass, if you will, a form. In a sense, it is feeling/form as it is 'feeling' the energy of where it is. It is not the same type of feeling/form that you are attempting to create in your practices with the 'feeling' of a ball between your hands. This energy actually has an intelligence of sorts. As it forms, it begins with a nucleolus much like all living things that are created. Orbs do have an outward perimeter that is similar to an aura, but it is actually just energy that is generally layered with colors. This energy can actually extend outward and be seen as well.

"Orbs are not new, but they are becoming more prevalent. The reason for this is the Awakening. This is where we will now present you with a Teaching. It is the Awakening that is causing more and more orbs to appear. It is a lowering of a veil, and this veil is the veil of Divine feminine energy that has been so imbalance upon your planet. All orbs are created first from energy that the Divine Mother is sending in massive amounts. Once it reaches the earth plane, it condenses into these spheres, or orbs. You may see one, two, or millions at one time and in one place. This energy is no different for as you know; all energy come from the One Source, this particular energy is coming from the Feminine aspect and essence of the One.

"This energy, if meditated upon can guide you and provide help and substance. It is going to be a matter of your understanding this and respecting this energy. So, the energy comes first from the Mother and then gathers from the area, and from the people or person, who is present and begins to condense. You have a formation of the energies, if you will, into One. Now this energy will begin to create. It is not unusual to see an orb within an orb, or an orb splitting within an orb. The core energy, once it is created, begins to split and grow. This energy within these orbs is actually a consciousness of sorts. It is of the new forming consciousness and is not of the old current collective consciousness."

Is it similar to the Circles of Light around the sun, moon, and earth?

"Somewhat, Sister of My Sister, because the Circles of Light are energy that was put in place many, many of your 'time' ago. It is energy that is present for those who are awakening to draw upon. The orbs are somewhat different in the fact that they are being created, being formed, by the energy they are given and the energy they are drawing from. The Circles of Light, which are around the sun, the moon, and the earth, do not, of course, have intelligence. It is simply energy that has been left for this time of the Awakening, whereas the orbs have intelligence. They have a substance, if you will, and they can be meditated upon, they are feminine energy."

Are they Spirits?

"In a vague sense, you could say this, although they are not spirits in the way you now understand them to be. They are not Spirit as you are, for you were formed and created within the One, in the Absolute. This is where you began. Orbs are being created by feminine energy, but also from energy which is present here on your earth. So, yes you could use the term spirits if you understand that to mean they come from the spirit, energy, of others. There may be just one orb, or there may also be a million orbs. As we have said, orbs are the birth of a new consciousness."

You have taught us that at the Creation, there were pockets of energy or essences that were left in certain physical locations on the earth plane. Is this the physical manifestation and form of that energy?

"In some instances, this is true, Little Brother. For the energy that was left in these areas is now being used and drawn upon by the orbs themselves."

Is this particularly true of the island of Kauai? The picture we took when we visited there must contain five or six hundred in one photograph.

"There has been much feminine energy deposited there. What you are now beginning to experience is something that has always been there but is now being known. There are those who have experienced orbs but do not necessarily understand them completely. We have read much that has been said about a ghost orb or something to do with the paranormal, whatever that may mean, for what is 'normal'? Since all experiences are dependent upon the choices and actions of each one making them, who is to say what is 'normal'? All that orbs truly are is the condensing of Divine feminine energy, along with earth energy, to aid in lowering the veil that surrounds the current collective consciousness."

Then is this going to be a part of the elevation of the consciousness at the Centers and the Sanctuaries that will eventually be created?

"Yes, and not just there, but this energy will raise the consciousness of the entire world."

The feeling is that the energy is very highly concentrated on Kauai.

"It is, and there are other areas such as this. Next time you are in nature, we would suggest that you take a camera with you. When you begin sensing or 'feeling' this energy, look around you. If you see spots that look as if you are looking through water, or areas that appear to be shimmering, begin taking pictures in those areas. You may capture the orbs on film, and as you begin to evolve in Spirit connection with all around you, you may also begin to see them without the use of a camera. Once you are able to achieve this, then you will know that your energy has risen to the point where you may ask them to join with you in your desired creation. You may ask them anyway, even if you do not see them."

How close are we to this level of guidance and awareness?

"It is happening. We do not know your 'time,' but it is occurring and it is growing."

In the photograph we took in our backyard during the "opening' last November are bolts of light that came down and ended in a very highly condensed ball. They were tremendous bands of energy. We felt like the whole backyard was electrified. Would you please comment on this?

"Those are simply orbs that you caught on your camera at the moment they were being sent. Many orbs, Little Brother, will not always necessarily be round. They may have tails, they may be split, or they may be stacked one upon the other. There may be many formations, but there will always be a clear nucleus that you will see, and there will also be intricate structure within. There are those who have attempted to recreate the looks of orbs with many substances introduced in front of the lens. You will know these creations because the center will be a small dark dot and there will be no color or real structure within."

Are there specific locations where we can find orbs?

"Orbs are going to begin appearing wherever the energy is high and is being used for highest purposes. It would not surprise us at all if there were some here right now. This home now has high energy due to your spiritual journey and our energy also. It is not that they will be found only in certain areas, they will be found where they are created by that energy."

So even if we do not see them, we can call upon them?

"When you do see them, you will know that your energy and the energy around you is quite strong. If you are capturing them on film, even though you may not be seeing them with your physical eyes, you may study them, look at them. Even on film, their energy remains."

This is very interesting. We have been studying the ones we took in Kauai; however, we will really start to study them now. Particularly the ones we took in our backyard on the first night of the opening. There was a tremendous burst and influx that was so intense you could actually feel the energy.

"You will also begin to feel the energy through the medium of film as well."

Thank you. Are there any other attributes or nature of orbs that would be beneficial for us to know at this time?

"Know that they are gentle. They are pure energy just as you are pure Spirit. They are newly created each time they appear. When they have used all the given, and gathered, energy, and when they have completed that they came for, they will simply dissipate and the energy they gathered will once more become a part of the whole."

Is this involved with the restoration of the balance between the Divine masculine and the Divine feminine energy? We all sense that this balance is beginning to be restored.

"Yes, for it is the influx of feminine energy that is restoring balance with that of the current prevailing masculine energy."

It seems like more and more people are becoming aware.

"It is happening as we mentioned it would and it is happening in this Now. There are many like-minded, as you are, although their 'groups' may go by different names. All are moving on their paths toward that which we call the Awakening."

That's fascinating. It is wonderful to know that they are also associated with the energy that was left for this time. Thank you so very much. I would like you to help me always remember to be the Spirit that I am and to see everyone else as that same Spirit.

"We believe that the more you begin to see Spirit in others, the less you will be in forgetfulness. Being who you are, at all moments, will be as second nature to you. You will see through your spiritual eyes to their spiritual self. You will continue to acquire this ability to see all this way, and yes, we will be most pleased to assist you on this."

Over the last few days, there has been a growing feeling to hold back, and understand this new spiritual expansion we are undergoing, in order to be able to follow through, to the finish, the various experiences that are already under way.

"We would not say that you should hold back anything, for if you are feeling like this, then follow through is most likely already occurring. We are saying that when you begin to become frustrated that you simply slip into the Now, for you will find that what you are doing will be accomplished much faster and will be accomplished with joy. You will see that it will flow. You will just simply know what to do, whereas the other day when you were working upon your book and kept telling yourself, 'I don't know how to do this.'"

During that time I tried, but I could not finish since there was this deep yearning to be somewhere else.

"We understand this, of course, and it is at those moments in your Now that you just stop, take a deep breath, let yourself slide away from the physical and into Spirit. Spirit does not yearn, Spirit is. If you slip into your Now while you are doing something physical, you will be who you are and will accomplish what you are doing much quicker and with more understanding. You will not be saying, 'I don't know, I can't.' When ego hears that, ego loves that. Ego will hear this and attempt to pull you back into physical mind, and it is this that tells you that you can't do something. Ego inserts the concept of 'time' back into your thoughts.

"Slip back into Spirit, do not yearn. Take care of all things while in the understanding of Spirit but do not forget that even though your desire is to be 100 percent in the spiritual, you cannot do that while you walk this earth plane in a physical body. You need to learn to combine Spirit and body together in harmony.

"What has occurred with all of you is that you are well advanced along your spiritual paths. You know and understand who you truly are, Spirit. We have already taught you many things and in order to move to the next level of Teachings, we had to be aware of your understanding. Not only is there the understanding of who you are, but there is also the living of this understanding. You are Spirit utilizing a physical vehicle. This physical body may be lifted in vibration to a certain degree, but you will always work within physical limitations. That is why we say to you to 'feel' with your 'gut.' It is why we say to listen to or 'feel' the vibrations. These are physical feelings that are relaying a spiritual knowing.

"Ego, as Spirit awakens, will begin to be deflated and absorbed. If you are still using words such as yearning, or need, you know you are not coming from Spirit, for Spirit knows none of those emotions. As you are walking upon your path and you are faced with a decision to make, 'feel' what it is and be who you are, no matter what that decision is. Do all things as Spirit.

"Finances, money, are things of the physical world. We understand that upon your earth, money has become a requirement and the lack of it puts much doubt, anger, fear, and frustration out there. These are all conditions of ego, although we understand that money is a very real consideration, for that is what the collective has created and that is your system. We would say to 'go with the flow,' as this is a term you use. Understand that the money will occur when it is to occur, and it will do so because you have made the decisions and the choices that have brought you to that portion along your path. To dwell upon it, to be frustrated or fearful of it, will not aid you. Decisions have to be made, yes, and we will attempt to guide you where we see we are allowed to do so. Many decisions that have to be made will have to be 'felt.' Let Spirit guide you in those decisions. When you fall back into too much concern about money, or you fall back into fantasy about how things 'should be,' then that becomes a creation of ego, a physical thing."

So regardless of what choice we make, we are not in any way forcing the Divine Parents to help, is this true?

"Yes, Sister of My Sister, for the Divine is always there. The Divine will always allow circumstances to bring about events, people, situations, and choices to you. As you know, the Divine Parents also desire whatever is your desire. If you make a choice, then, of course, we as well as the Divine are going to go with that choice. It is your choice, and it is then also our desire for you. You are the creator of your own physical, and spiritual, journey. If you stop before finalizing your choice and 'feel' that decision, and if you are honest with yourself about those feelings and you are being Spirit, then how can you go where you do not desire? Do you understand?"

Yes, so no matter which way these financial considerations go, everything will be as it should be based on our choices?

"Yes, of course, this is the way, but each experience along the path will be different and shall have their own residual effects or consequences. Now, as to the long run, or as you would say, the 'big picture,' choice, creations, and experiences will bring things to pass, and if they have been made in Spirit, they will indeed turn out for your highest purpose. We are not, as you know, in the knowing or knowledge of exactly when, or how, that shall occur. That is the realm of the Divine Parents and is not ours to know unless we are informed. All things rest within your choices."

So it is still a matter of experiences?

"Yes, this is what you have chosen to come here for, to experience. You will get an experience regardless of any choice you make, as even a seemingly non-choice is a choice. All choices create and all creations result in an experience. Some choices, made in awareness of Spirit, will take you toward your desire; others if made by ego will most likely take you off your path. How long you remain off your path will be up to you.

It will all be an experience. It is all a learning and that is what you have come to understand, to be Spirit in all things."

Regardless then of which decision they make concerning the bankruptcy and all the financial problems, it's all going to turn out fine anyway?

"We do not know if it will turn out as what you may now consider fine, but it will be what the experience may be. Some of what has occurred is through choices that were made, becoming immersed, although unavoidably, with what the collective consciousness believes as truths, and the playing out of all those residuals.

"Every choice leads you to an experience, and you will find many times upon your path a multitude of choices to make. You cannot make them all, of course, but you can choose some, in Spirit, and they will lead you in the direction you desire to go. We shall give you an example. Imagine if the path you travel divided suddenly into many paths. Each path is of a different color, and each color has within it a different 'feeling.' Each of these 'feelings' will lead you to a different experience. Let us say you choose the color green and you pass by orange, yellow, red, blue, and turquoise. You chose green. Upon this green path, you will have different experiences than if you had chosen any one of the other colors. There is of course no 'good' or 'bad.' You will experience, you will learn, you will 'feel.' We have taught 'feeling' so that you may know when a choice you have made is for your highest purpose or not. If you make one that soon resonates as not going in the direction you desire, then change it. You are not stuck with that choice, although you may have to play out some residual from that choice."

Sometimes there are repercussions to choices that may have more of an influence on more long-range goals than another option or choice. Would it be the wiser choice than to choose the one that will in the long run be better?

"It is for your understanding that once you have made a choice, once way or the other you must realize that there will be residuals from either choice. In your current financial experience, you may choose several paths. You have attempted to work within the rules of the current collective and have experienced their resistance to aid you. Now you may choose to ignore them or to file what you call bankruptcy. Both shall have their own residuals which shall continue until they have been completed."

That is exactly what I was asking. This is all very clear and I will choose the course that is my desire.

"Be aware that whatever courses you choose, you do so in Spirit and not ego. Are there any other questions? We are looking forward to Light Sister being here once again. When she arrives, it is always a wonderful reunion. It will be a time of high energy. We would suggest that this time you make a camera available. As we speak on orbs and energy, you will find many present that you may put upon your film. If there then are no further questions, we shall depart in much Love and Blessings."

The tone of this session was an unusually serious one. We had to make a decision as to whether we would file for bankruptcy or try, somehow, to resolve our financial crisis with the creditors. We would have to find a means of generating the money that was required to lift us out of this hole. The answers given helped us to stand back, breathe, and really weigh each alternative both in the short and long run. We needed to "feel" the course of action that would be in our best interests, both personally and in regard to the project's continuance.

In the middle of all this mess, we were given a surprise teaching. This was so interesting that it took us away, for the Now, from all that was spinning around us and attempting to move us off our course.

Orbs are a fascinating subject. We had previously heard of them when we had photographed them on Kauai. However, we knew very little about them. The teaching that unfolded in this session left us with so much to think about, but at the same time gave us a very thorough understanding of them. We have since captured many on our digital camera. We were quite taken with understanding this new form of creation. We desired to gain all the knowledge of them we could, as well as to directly experience them. Now that we understood what they were, how they were formed, and what their purpose was, we began to view them in a completely different way, they were no longer just pretty!

August 16, 2008

Teresa had once again been able to get some time away from her work to come up to Happy Camp for a visit. As always it was good to see her. We quickly brought her up to date on the teachings that had been given to us during the time since her last visit. Of course she was more than ready to "speak" with them again.

"We do greet thee. Welcome, Light Sister. We are most joyful to see you. We are quite pleased with what has been occurring, but we would like your input about how your experiences with being in the Now have been. It will be with your telling that we can assess where you are in your understanding. Would you care to begin with your observations and questions?"

Sure. I feel like my periods of being in the present are expanding and becoming more frequent and for longer periods of time. I am really experiencing much joy in life every day.

"We believe you are, of course, on your way to being more in the Now and to understanding what this truly means. It is enlightening for us to hear each one's experience as you stay in the Now more and more. You are learning how to be who you are and to make your choices from this 'being' in every Now. After we hear each one's experience, we will give you an idea of where the next step will lead. Sister of My Sister, would you share your experience?"

I haven't focused as much on being in the Now as much as being Spirit and seeing everyone else as Spirit. Marvelous things are happening within my understanding because of this.

"Wonderful, and you, Little Brother, what has been your experience so far?"

There are times when I feel that I am in the Now, and then there are times when there is a feeling of being "out of time" and not thinking that something has to happen within a certain period of "time." I feel more fluid and flexible now; I am looking at things in terms of sequence to sequence instead of time frame to time frame.

"This is growing in your understanding as well. It is important that all understand that while you are in the 'Now,' it is for you to be Spirit in this 'Now." There should be none of your physical emotions of ego. There should be no anger, no hurt, no frustration, for Spirit does not know or feel any of these things. What Spirit does feel is Love, and at these moments of 'Now,' things will be crystal clear. The clarity, the remembering, will be sharp. It will be in focus, if you will. When you are in the 'Now,' you are present in all ways, body, mind, Spirit. Ego will not be functioning at that time. It will be absorbed into Spirit so there will be no frustrations, anger, or disappointment. Things will be more in focus to the direction you are pursuing. This is what being in the 'Now' truly means. It is a quieting, a stilling of the ego, so that Spirit may experience all that is around it at that moment. Continue with your experiences. We are will pleased with what you have discovered to this point."

When a baby gets mad, they are very "present," are they not? Are they present in ego, or are they present in Spirit?

"It would be difficult for this to be ego, for an infant has not yet begun gathering many identifiers. There is that part, that energy, that shall become ego and that shall be what expresses anger. Spirit within an infant, in particular, is so closely linked with the Absolute that it does not yet feel frustration or anger.

"When you are in the 'Now,' when you are Spirit, you have made the choice to be that way. You have taken, in a sense, control, although we do not mean this as it would be when associated with ego. What we mean by this is that you have become, in all ways, who you are by your choice to be so. You have placed ego where it has gone into Spirit. At that point, you will not feel any of the physical ego-emotions. This is something that we expect to not always occur for you for it is a process and it will become more and more so as your evolution towards being Spirit, at all moments, continues. We are pleased with where you are right in this Now. We have observed and seen some fallbacks, but you are recognizing them right away. This recognition allows ego to be taken care of, for it is when you do not recognize it that ego says, 'Aha, now I can get a stronger hold for they did not recognize the little hold that I took.' This is how the ego will replant itself, if you will, into the physical, into the mind, and out of Spirit. When you see that it has taken hold, even if that hold may be very slight, you can make it release by simply being Spirit. It cannot then hold."

It seems like the more we practice and put this into action, then the things that had previously held such great meaning are now meaningless. Those things of ego simply don't matter anymore.

"Yes, this is so true. That is why our objectives for these past few of your months have been for you to get to that place. First, it will be advantageous for you to be in that place, the Now, when the teachings continue, for there will be much awakening. It will be coming in somewhat more giant leaps, if you will, for it is that sequences will begin to be placed in their proper perspectives. This is what is to be occurring. We will begin these teaching by bringing the first lesson during Light Sister's visit. Little Brother, we understand that you are leaving for your trip with your friend Bill to do some 'gold hunting.' We will have the first lesson tomorrow then so that you may be present before your trip. Does anyone have a question?'

I do. When a new person comes on to the council, does everybody on the council meet with them? Does everyone have to be comfortable with that person?

" Light Sister, it is important for the new one, if you will, to be upon the same page as those already present and to be of like mind with those other council family, to be resonating with them and the teachings. It is good for all to meet for how else would you know if you resonate together?"

Should I be here every day?

"We will accommodate whatever your 'time' may be to meet with everyone. If you need to go do something during this visit, then we shall simply wait until your return. Tomorrow we shall begin, and then if you desire to take a couple of days off, we will simply continue when you come back."

Thank you. I would like to ask you this. Does Spirit desire total unity?

"Spirit understands unity so is always seeking that. Spirit is patient until that unity is found and begins. Spirit is in union with all that is around it, it is connected, but understands that sometimes others may not yet be in that place. So it simply waits for what is around to choose that unity also."

I remember when you spoke to us about colors. Do our colors change as we evolve? Also with color, or colors, is there a word that can be used to match up with a particular color?

"Yes, there are words, in any given moment, which can be used to describe the particular color you are or are experiencing. We would say that in this Now, your color, and the word to describe it, would be gentleness. In each Now, you will find the fluctuations and flow of your colors. They are dependent upon where you are in that moment in your physical presence, the placement of mind, either being in Spirit or in ego, and the prominence of being Spirit."

Do you have any personal hints for each of us?

"We would like to say to Light Sister to continue to reflect upon who she truly is and not to allow others experiences to draw her in. Always remain in the 'Now' to create your own experiences. Allow others their experience, regardless of what that may mean, but choose to not become a part of an experience that may not serve you.

"Sister of My Sister, we would say for you that it is simply a matter of understanding what is truly ego, and we see you are doing so. It is for recognizing, as you have been, those moments that occur and to work with them as you have been doing. We are quite pleased with this. Simply notice all things that come up. We are well pleased with the advances you have made in this area.

"Little Brother, our hint for you would be to stay in the 'Now.' We would have all of you to continue to do your outreach as you have been doing. With the giving of Spirit to others, you shall plant the seeds that will enable them to also understand who they are should this be of their choosing."

I have heard about pendulums. Can they be used as a tool to communicate with Spirit?

"We understand, Light Sister, the concept of a pendulum. As we have said to Little Brother before regarding the question of pendulums, who would it be that is answering the question you ask? You ask a question, but because you are Spirit, you already know the answer simply by asking it. You are the Spirit that hears the question, and you are the Spirit who answers. So to ask yourself a question is not something we understand, especially using an instrument to answer what you already know. You will remember the answer if it is meant for you to remember and only ego would require an instrument for an answer. Spirit need not ask, it only should allow the remembering."

But don't we still live in two worlds, one of ego and one of Spirit?

"You physically are only living within one world, but you are recognizing that within your physical presence resides both ego and Spirit. You are working toward absorbing ego into Spirit. Of course there are always going to be moments that it will arise and will make you think that you do not know the direction that you wish to go. In these moments, simply breathe, be in the Now, and allow Spirit to confine and absorb ego."

Ego is still coming from separation, isn't it?

"Yes, Sister of My Sister, you could say in some ways that this is separation. It is simply that your ego does not want to be absorbed by Spirit. It wishes to remain in control of the mind. It will bring up a question and will make you question who you are, even though, being Spirit, you know the answer."

Before you go, I would just like to thank you for your help.

"You are most welcome, for this is what we are here for. We have enjoyed being in your company. For now, unless there are more questions, we shall depart in much Love and Blessings."

The most important teaching in this session was the further emphasis placed on being in the Now. This ability was revealed as the key that would open the door to the next level of teachings.

Every session brings with it deeper understanding of either things we have been taught or answers to questions we ask. Some of my commentary will be short when I know that the best way for you to understand is to read the session. In the long run we, and you, will receive the answers when we are ready—always.

August 17, 2008

We all settled in and looked forward to what we felt would be a wonderful session. We were given far more than we ever could have imagined.

"We do greet thee. It is definitely our pleasure to be here with you on this day. We would begin by asking if there are any questions. If not, then we shall begin.

"We will first begin by speaking again of orbs, for it is most important that you understand exactly what these are and why they are occurring at this point in your 'time.' Orbs are simply the condensed energy gathered from the place and the people or person that is around it. So whether you are in a room, outside, or wherever, and you begin to photograph or see an orb; you may be assured that this is a place where high energy currently resides. Orbs draw their energy and their forms from that which is around them. They will actually become an energy source. They become condensed energy, if you will. This condensed energy has a presence, an essence of its own. This is why they can be captured on film, for it is the magnetic energy the film is capturing. It is not necessarily a picture; it is the essence of the energy that is being seen.

"The orb can be helpful to you in many, many areas. You can use its energy in healing, in spiritual growth. They use the energy of the area in which they were formed and the wisdom of the person, or people, around them. For one who is awakening to the truth of who they are, these orbs can be asked questions of guidance. They will not in any way 'tell' you what to do, but their energy may enable you to make a clearer choice. What other questions regarding orbs do you have?"

How would you access that energy to guide or help you?

"A connection may be made with either an actual orb you are seeing 'in the moment,' or with the picture of an orb. The essence, the energy, of that orb is contained within that picture. To connect is to be Spirit and to look at the orb, to become joined, if you will, with its energy. This joining allows you access to all the energy that is within the orb. This is something that does take some practice, so we would suggest that if you have a picture of one you would begin with that first."

Can we work with pictures that have been sent via a computer?

"Yes, for the essence, the energy of that orb still remains within its picture."

Is that comparable to when I am in one room and Sarah is in another but we seem to be "connected"? The cat's energy and my energy feel like we are communicating.

"It is, yes, indeed that you are communicating with her Spirit, but it is somewhat different with an orb. An orb is formed through feeling/form. It is because the energy of the area and the energy of the people around it have created a feeling, which then gives energy to a form. It is this form that is the orb. The orb is not necessarily always going to be spherical, many times it will be elongated, or somewhat static looking and have points here or there. Do not always think just because you are seeing something that is not round, or spherical, that it is not an orb. They take many forms. Many times if you have a camera available and you are looking through the lens, it will be as if you are trying to look through an old glass or through water. You will have the illusion that there is something there that you cannot necessarily see with your eyes.

When you are feeling that, then simply begin to take pictures. You may then capture an orb.

"Orbs are present right now upon your planet, for there is great energy forming. All the areas that we have spoken of previously, that were left with high energy or with more energy than other places, are beginning to form these orbs. People are now beginning to gather in many of these areas. It is those people, in the understanding of who they truly are, that are helping to form these orbs. If someone does not understand that they are Spirit but are simply upon their created paths while spiritually asleep, they will not lend energy to the formation, for it takes this awareness. Orbs form around those who know they are Spirit. They can also form simply in a room when the energy is high.

"We would be pleased to take other questions regarding orbs. We have simply given you basic knowledge in this Now."

You mentioned that the orb has a will, what does this mean?

"It has a 'will' because it is created by the Divine feminine energy as well. 'Will' is simply a word from your planet that we use, but an orb has a 'knowing,' and essence, that is of the Divine. This is why we say it can be used in healing. It can be helpful in manifestation and for many aspects of your journey. It is a 'knowing' of its own, so upon your planet, you would refer to this as having a 'will' of its own. Remember that it is not a separate entity but it is a part of the whole or all energy."

Is it part of the balance of the Divine masculine/feminine energy?

"It has the balance of both energies. Without that balance within an orb, it would not be of any essence. The energy of the Masculine is already quite high upon your earth, so the Divine Feminine has sent energy to create and balance all the energy within an orb."

There is recognition that the colors within an orb often are ones with the specific attributes of both the Divine Father and the Divine Mother.

"Yes, these colors are quite prevalent because there is that balance of both energies."

A lot of the colors seen within orbs are in the green, red, and orange range.

"Yes, and you may also see more in the blue range as the collective consciousness begins to lift in its understanding and vibration. This is now happening, but in such a small scale that it would not be a visible change as far as the colors are concerned. The change of colors within, or the addition of colors within, will also be an indication to you of how the new consciousness is growing."

We have also been noticing that at openings, or outpourings, there has been a tremendous amount of energy. We did not what this meant at the time, but most of the ones that were photographed in the backyard were either yellow or white or a combination of the two.

"This is very high energy, Little Brother. There is so much for you to begin to understand and absorb. You will have no difficulty for we will certainly be there every step of the way. As always, we start you with baby steps and we continue to know from your questions what your understanding is."

Does the aura around the orb reflect the intent of the orb?

"No, for the intent of that energy is that which you choose. The aura is simply a part of the orb, its energy ring, if you will."

So would this reflect the color of its frequency then? It would be the expression of the content of the orb itself?

"This certainly is one indication of the amount of energy contained within a particular orb, or as you have said, its expression. It is an energy body, just as you are, and both have auras."

When we connect with the orb, what does it impart to us, and for us?

"It shall give only that which you have awakened to receive."

Thank you. We purchased a water feature, what do you think?

"It is quite nice. It is very relaxing and gives out the energy of the water. Water is a living source and has its own vibration, color, and energy.

When you make this present in your surroundings, you are adding to the energy of that area."

Getting back to orbs, are orbs a spiritual picture of the color of the energy both of the place and the people who create it? So, is it like a reflection?

"It is a reflection of all which is around it. In addition to that which is around it, the orb contains the energy of the Divine Feminine."

Have orbs been happening prior to this time even though we have not visually seen them?

"Orbs have been around always. Most have not been aware of them. It is only recently in your history that they have been 'seen.' They were at first thought by the collective to be what you call 'evil.' They were thought to be ghosts, or spirits, of those who have passed from their physical form. There have been many conjectures of what they were, or could have been. You now know them to be energy, formed and created. You are now beginning to understand why they are and what they are.

"We will leave the subject of orbs in this Now, but may come back to the subject anytime you have questions. What other questions do you have that we may address?"

What is this thing about a silver cord holding the Spirit to the body? Is it true or not?

"This is something that someone has created and is very graphic. Yes, there is an attachment of Spirit with the physical body it is encompassing and this remains complete until Spirit leaves the physical body. What holds Spirit to the physical is the desire of Spirit to experience while in a physical body, once this desire has been fulfilled by Spirit, or by the body choosing to cease its existence, this attachment is then ended.

"There is something which we would suggest that you begin to bring into practice. This would be to do your energy work with each other. Work upon the opening of your energy centers first and then begin using the energy modality that you have been inspired to. You may all move the energy within each other through your hands. You do not have to do this every day, but the more you practice, the more you will 'know' and understand the energy that comes through you. Especially when you are together as a group this would be of great benefit."

Would it also be beneficial to do exercises like the breathing of the energy, which you taught me while I was at my sister's home?

"Yes, Little Brother, and since you have been already a part of that experience, you will be the one to share it with the others.

"Today, this Now, is a day of beginnings, of new teachings. Use this day to work upon each other for ten minutes and record the feelings of the one who is receiving, the recipient of the energy. The ones who allow the energy to flow through them are called the practitioners.

"For now, we have touched upon several subjects. We would welcome more questions, or you may simply desire to study and understand that which we have already given. We know that it may seem like quite a lot, but these are baby steps. Listen to your tapes and formulate questions so that when next we come we may answer them for you. Little Brother, since you are not going to be here, you may leave your questions, or save them for a later moment.

"Sister of My Sister and Light Sister, we would appreciate it if you would listen to the tape and let us know of your understanding of what has been taught. We will come on your 'tomorrow' and then will break for a period of your 'time.' We will come again when Little Brother has returned. For now, we shall depart in Love and Blessings."

After quite a while of waiting, it seemed as if the teachings had finally begun again in earnest.

We now realized the importance that orbs would play in the Awakening. Our first new teaching was an expansion of a lot of previously given information regarding orbs. We were given a review of what they are and how they form, plus additional information on how to connect with them. Orbs had first been introduced as Divine feminine energy. We now understood that each orb was a balance of the Divine masculine/feminine energy. The restoration of this balance was what the Awakening was for and was of monumental importance.

We had been a bit lazy in doing our energy work and it wasn't because we weren't interested, but was mostly because we hadn't completely learned how to combine our physical "needs" with our spiritual desires. This energy modality was such a gift and we knew we should begin to seriously work with it. I really felt that it was something which could change the face of modalities that had come before. I know of course that it is all the same energy; it is just the intention of use and the application of that which is different.

It has, in the Now of writing this second book, become my purpose and desire. To share and teach others what we were given and to be the conduit for that energy to all who may come to experience it. Those who have experienced it continue to come with their intentions and desires, and we have trained many who are now sharing this with others. I love this purpose!

August 21, 2008

This was Teresa's last day in Happy Camp before returning home and Bruce had just returned from his prospecting trip with our friend Bill. We requested this next session so Teresa would be able to "speak" with them and Bruce could ask his questions from the previous session.

"We do greet thee. We are ready to receive your questions."

When I was a child, I would repeatedly have dreams where someone was chasing me and I was trying to get away. Almost always this big gulf would open up in front of me and I would just fly across.

"Light Sister, many children experience this flying. It is not unusual in children upon your earth. What it is, of course, is spiritual travel even though you have no awareness of that at the time it is occurring. It is usually triggered by, as you said, someone chasing you, or the need to get away from something. It is somewhat the beginning, if you will, of spiritual travel."

This is very interesting. When I was a child, I wasn't being chased in my dreams, I just loved to fly. I would soar upward then swoop down to the floor and back up again. I was soon flying all over the room. It was fun and something I looked forward to. I felt such freedom in doing that although I did not understand at the time what was going on, other than it was fun and a very natural thing to do.

"Thank you for sharing that, Little Brother."

I always thought it was just a dream, not real.

"Light Sister, many children do have this experience and they do believe they are dreams. They do not understand. Some would find the truth quite frightening because they do not yet understand who they are. Once they become more enlightened, more awake, as they mature, they then begin to understand what they were doing and begin to appreciate the fact of what they were doing."

I've also had dreams like this even as an adult. Not a lot of them, but I can remember walking and then saying to myself, "Why am I walking when I can fly?" I would then just take off, it was great. I just had another thought. It was awareness, a "knowingness" of being Spirit while still being in my body. I don't know how else to put it.

"This is well said, Sister of My Sister. You are simply recognizing the Spirit that you are and being able to see, at the same time, the physical body that is being inhabited and encompassed by Spirit."

It was an interesting thing to read Little One's book last night. When looking at the symbol for The Light Alliance, there was, all of a sudden, a dimensionality that looked like a tunnel that started at the outer triangle and shot into the center. It was like being drawn into the symbol.

"It is the purpose of this symbol. It is very ancient. You may see things within the symbol as you look at it. We were going to bring this to you, but as you have brought it up, Little Brother, we shall speak on it. Look into the center of the symbol and see what happens. Do you see colors? Do you see movement?"

I saw a brilliant white light when I was looking into the center of the smallest triangle. It just happened; I didn't have any intention in that moment. It just seemed to have such depth.

"In and off itself this symbol is just lines, but it is the ancient wisdom within these lines that was created for the benefit of those who are awakening. The symbol is a creative focus for meditation, manifestation, healing, and awareness. You will receive from it that which you are prepared to receive, and it shall be with your desire and intent. This symbol was given to you for your growth and for the connection of all who choose to be within The Light Alliance, but it is also for anyone who understands it. There is no separateness in its being, it is for all."

There are things I read last night in the book that were quite extraordinary.

"You will find much within Little One's book that is not necessarily hidden, but will be revealed in greater depth as you begin to understand. The intent of this book is to gently guide you in your awakening, and understanding, that you are Spirit."

There is so much in there at so many levels of awareness.

"There is much that will be further revealed as you grow in your understanding. Words once read will take on new meanings."

I will reread it often to discover more. I would like to ask if in the Absolute there is just one vibration.

"You could say this, Sister of My Sister. In the Absolute, of course, everything vibrates to the same frequency. It is because it is One that it vibrates as One. There are no different frequencies of vibrations as you would find upon planets or universes. This is because everything in the One, in the Absolute, is One. Therefore, there is harmony."

So, is it incorrect for people to believe in a hierarchy of importance in heaven?

"We can tell you that everything in the Absolute is equal. Everything is One. Everything vibrates the same. Everything is on the same frequency. There is no such thing as higher or lower."

The next time I will be here is in about a month. Will we have teachings then as my time coming here is limited for the rest of the year?

"Yes, Light Sister, we will do as many teachings as you are ready to receive in that 'time' frame. Also you will have the tapes so that you may listen to them.

"Are there any other questions?"

Yes. Many times, when in the company of others who are not like-minded, you will have experiences that come from another consciousness. We realize that these are important experiences. Would you please comment?

"They are important experiences, for all experiences are important for your growth and understanding. We would suggest to you that when you are with someone who is coming from a different consciousness, you simply listen to them. You do not have to become a part of their experience, but in Love you would allow them to have their view. If you see that they are willing to also hear what you have to share, then do so. Just be aware that you do not overwhelm them with what you know and that you are respectful of where they may be in their journey. These experiences aid you in dealing with all points of view and belief and enable you to 'know' where to begin sharing with another."

I have noticed that others actions seem to be shifting where I work. Am I doing that?

"Light Sister, it's because you are being Spirit and you are being present in the Now. It cannot help but to give off a vibration to others that will calm them. The people you deal with will feel your essence even if they do not understand it.

"Most people are able to go from a bad mood to a fairly pleasant mood in a short period of 'time.' There are those, of course, who are choosing to be stubborn in their interactions with others; this is the journey they are creating for themselves. You will indeed encounter these people. Give them Love and go on, for it is not a path that you desire to be upon.

"Are there further questions? We would like to speak just a little more regarding orbs, where in your vicinity they can be found. This will aid you in your picture taking as well. The times for orbs are strongest at daybreak and sunset. Also it can be strong throughout the evening because things are quiet, the vibrations have not become so chaotic. If you are in a gathering of many people and this occurs at night, sunset, or daybreak, you may find a lot then also. Where fire is concerned, this is often a place to find orbs because the energy of fire will help to develop and draw them. Outdoors is generally where you will find them, in nature. You will find them indoors especially if that place is of high energy and vibration.

"Light Sister, we give to you a safe journey. We will, of course, continue to be with you and you know you may call upon us when you have questions. Sister of My Sister, we are pleased you are doing well and that your doctor was able to aid you in feeling better. This help, along with your desire and intention to be well, will guide you in your choices regarding your physical health. Little Brother, we would just say to continue being who you know you are. If there are no further questions or comments, we shall depart in much Love and Blessings."

This session gave us additional information as to where and under what circumstances we would find orbs. Eventually we became quite aware of their presence. At times we were almost able to physically see the stronger ones. They would appear as a shimmering distortion; this was a signal for their presence. Outside it was a bit more difficult. We would just have a feeling, point the camera, and capture one on the memory card.

Teresa left the next morning. It had been a wonderful visit filled with lots of laughter and excellent teachings that left us with the knowing that there was so much more yet to come.

As the "Girls" have spoken several times about The Light Alliance emblem, I have included a drawing of it. It really is a wonderful focus during meditations.

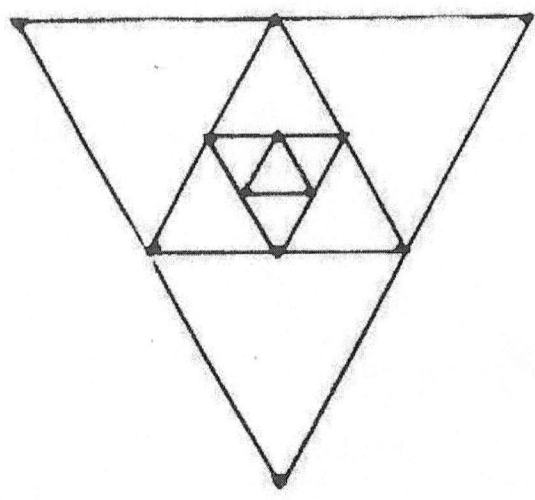

One Voice—One Walk—One Purpose

Chapter Eight

September 5, 2008

"We do greet thee. We are pleased to be here with you. You have questions?"

I do have a few. Where does Spirit go while we are asleep?

"Sister of My Sister, because Spirit is who you are, where would it go? If you are speaking of spirit travel, then we would say to you that Spirit does not actually leave the physical body. It always encompasses and fills the physical body. It will simply travel in feeling/form wherever it desires to be."

There are those people who say it goes back to the Absolute, or heaven, and some have claimed that when it returns, they actually remember what they were learning there.

"We would say, 'What is the purpose for this?' When you are in the Absolute, you know all there is, so why would you go there to learn? Learning is done upon your planet. You would not have chosen to come into this incarnation to experience and remember if you could simply 'pop' back and be in the full knowledge of the Absolute again. Why come back in total, or partial, remembrance? The whole purpose of your incarnation upon this planet was for the experience of being Spirit within a physical body. It was for the remembering of who you are. It was about choices, creations, experiences, and residuals. While you are here, Spirit will grow, awaken, and remember."

The reason I asked this question is because I had heard from many sources that our Spirit went to the Absolute during sleep. From what you have just said, I now understand that it is not possible for Spirit to go to the Absolute without staying there.

"You may certainly go to different realms or dimensions, but you would not go back to the Absolute. When you do return to the Absolute, it is because you have chosen to leave the incarnation in which you are currently in."

Does Spirit learn something from its travels?

"Spirit is always learning, always remembering, so of course, anything it is remembering will help it to be learning as well."

We are told on the one hand that everything is the same One energy, but on the other hand, that we should not take drugs, drink hard alcohol, smoke, and eat things that do not serve our physical bodies. Is this because our consciousness has judged these things and put them in separation?

"That is a good deal of it, but it is because man has chosen to add things into your foods and you are not always consuming pure, living foods. Your physical body was never created to be consuming drugs, alcohol, or tobacco. Man has chosen to introduce these substances into their journey, but the lower energy of them does not serve your body. Yes, everything is of the some energy, but some things exist with the energy at its highest and some contain energy at its lowest."

Even when we raise those foods into the One Spirit, they are still hampered somewhat by the collective consciousness?

"Yes, for as you know, the collective consciousness has much control and much influence, if you will, over things of your earth. So, yes, the things that man has created and put into your food sources, your animals, and your water are also connected to the collective as well."

Does the mind have a function with Spirit in the Absolute, or is it the seat of our feeling and knowing?

"The mind is one of those rather elusive things, although it was created in that same moment that Spirit began. It is a part of Spirit and therefore came with Spirit for your incarnation here. Mind has the option, or choice, to attach to ego when you have not yet awakened to your true essence, or to remain Spirit as you awaken. It is when you return to the Absolute that your mind, being intricately attached to Spirit, also returns. In other words, your mind is that which you use to physically think, to create, to reason, and your mind is either led by your ego, which is physical, or by Spirit. Mind, in Spirit, means that then you are creating spiritually, you are living spiritually, you are thinking and reasoning in a spiritual way."

Since in the Absolute we are pure Spirit, do we recognize our loved ones by feeling, knowing, or vibration?

"It is simply by 'knowing.' When everyone returns to the Absolute, they are known by all. If you shared an incarnation with them, then you would also be aware of that connection as well. All are in the knowing, completely, when they are in the Absolute. You recognize each other from all forms of your incarnations, but you always recognize each other as Spirit."

We are really the God experience, aren't we?

"That is one phrase that has been coined, but simply speaking, you are a creation of the One. This particular journey is to express, experience, and remember all that you are while encompassing a physical body. The One experiences through you that which you have chosen to experience. You were created by the One, and then it became your choice to incarnate into different planets, universes, and dimensions for the sole purpose of experiencing. Through you and your experiences, the Divine also experiences. All of this also occurs for your own spiritual awakening during your physical incarnation."

Will we know that we have united our body, mind, and Spirit together when we live each moment unrestricted by the seven walls of humanity?

"That will be part of it. You are never not together while in the physical, but you may choose to have your perspective, or experiences, reflect more of the physical, or ego, rather than come from Spirit. It is not that there are separate entities within the physical, for all essences are an inseparable part of the One, are always a united presence. As Spirit begins to remember and to experience these walls, and to identify them, this identification and realization begins to dismantle them. Then, of course, the physical vibration is lifted as well and the mind may choose where it desires to be, ego or Spirit. Of course the more that Spirit awakens and remembers, the more mind is drawn back to where it began, in Spirit."

Would you give us some concrete examples of how to balance being Spirit while still meeting physical requirements for supporting our life within the present collective consciousness?

"To be Spirit is simply to be who you are. While you are on this planet, in this physical incarnation, you travel in a physical vehicle. You may be identified as only physical, for it is that which you are viewed as. Actually you, Spirit, resides within, and encompassing, this physical creation. We know, of course, that should you choose, while you are in your incarnation, to become more aware of yourself as Spirit, you will do so. An example would be that once you know, awaken, and remember that you are Spirit, then everything you do for your physical body will be done in Spirit. You can balance this joining of Spirit, and the body, by being who you are. You will not be caught up in the limitations of the walls or caught up in the beliefs of the collective consciousness once you become aware of your true nature. By being aware of this, you will begin to balance who you are with where you are. It is much easier to balance something when you are aware of it rather than when you are not aware of it. For those who walk upon the earth in this incarnation, who have chosen to remain asleep, they will never be able to balance Spirit with the physical body. They are simply not aware of any of these things we have spoken on. As you awaken, as Spirit is growing and remembering, then the physical simply goes with it and you balance it by that 'knowing,' by that knowledge."

So when difficulties arise, we come from Spirit in dealing with them?

"Yes, for worry, if you will, is a sentiment on your earth that we do not know and we do not have. We come from Spirit, and Spirit does not worry. Spirit knows that at some point things will be as they are created, and you simply accept those experiences in that Now. We are accepting that where we are and what we are doing is where we have chosen to be and what we have chosen to be doing as well. When you come from Spirit, there is no worry. You know that things will be as you create them to be. If your created experiences are not taking you where you are desiring to be, then in conscious awareness, you would change them."

That is a beautiful answer, thank you. Does Spirit think?

"Spirit remembers, and in that remembering is all knowledge. So to equate it with something you do, you could call that 'thinking.' Spirit does not require a brain as your physical body does, a brain is simply the computer system to run the physical body. All knowledge is an integral part of Spirit. Its remembering, of who you are, begins the remembrance of all things known.

"If you, Sister of My Sister, were in a room full of people who have spiritually awakened, and who are now experiencing that truth, you would find that their 'need' for words would be much less. They would communicate more through feeling, through touch. Yes, there would still be words, for that is how you have always communicated, but there would be fewer words. Most of the people on your planet feel that they must clutter the silence with sound. When you are awakening, and when you have awakened, feelings will be transferred through a look, a touch, and one word rather than ten words."

So instead of putting our mouths in gear, we should just stop and feel. We should find that quiet inside and then go from there.

"Yes, exactly, and this is why it is important when you are speaking with someone that you listen in Spirit to them. It is by listening to others that you will 'know,' spiritually, where they are on their own journey. From that understanding, you will answer their questions, or as we have said, plant a seed."

I see that we really are the creators of our own lives.

"There is no one else who creates what occurs upon your journey. It is always your own creation, whether you are aware of it or not. Many will not believe this because they are not yet aware of who they are, and ego needs to have someone else to place blame upon when things go 'wrong.' Everything which you experience will be because of the choices you have made. There is no one judging your choices, for they are yours alone. The Divine will experience along with you all that you create, there is no judgment. There are times in which you can get caught up in someone else's experience and it is these times where you should be discerning. Spirit will ask, 'Is this something I desire to bring into my experience, or should I just continue on my own journey?'

"When you find yourself caught within another's choice, know that you are the only one who can choose to remove yourself. Use your 'gut,' your 'feelings.' What is happening? Are you allowing another to make your choices? All these things can add up and can turn your journey into a path that is quite possibly not where you desired to be. Through not staying aware of all your choices, you may arrive upon a path that will change your journey. Know that should this occur, you can choose to get back to where you desire. You are the one who makes your choices; you are the creator of your journey. It shall be your experiences and residuals that will arise from your choices.

"Little Brother, do you have any questions or comments?"

There are no questions at this time. The only thing would be a comment concerning the exercises you showed us. There was one experience a few days ago that was interesting. I was looking at myself and then it seemed as if my Spirit came out, went around me, and then came back in. It did not take very long for this to happen. Would you please comment?

"For you this is a beginning of awareness. It is looking at yourself and being totally aware that you are composed of, the physical, the mind, and Spirit; and at the same time understanding that you are three joined within the totality of one. You are body, mind, and Spirit. Spirit would not, of course, actually leave the body, it would be more of a viewing of the physical body from spiritual awareness, and in that moment, you were more aware of yourself, Spirit, then you were of your physical body."

It was interesting. The body felt comfortable and there was an awareness that Spirit and mind had joined once again as one. There was conscious awareness and understanding that this joining had occurred.

"As you, Spirit, expand and remember, you will be 'feeling' this expansion."

I feel this whether I am asleep or awake. Of course, while awake, there is a heightened awareness as I am consciously aware.

"It is the direction you are choosing, to experience these things in a wakeful state rather than in a sleeping state. We understand that, generally speaking, for those upon your planet, the sleeping state is what enables them to spirit 'travel.' Most simply view this as a dream. Awareness of Spirit will occur more for you because this is your choice to experience."

What about Spirit and the imagination? Are we actually going through a door during our meditation? Is our attempt to travel in Spirit to a particular place real or imagined?

"Imagination is something that is quite extraordinary, if you will, for it is partly from Spirit and partly from mind. Imagination comes from that creative awareness of who you are, but it is also created with the mind, which may be in Spirit or ego. Ego, in its attempt to remain strong, can sometimes cause you to doubt those things you are seeing or feeling. It can create doubt in your ability to spirit 'travel.' Using your imagination is one of those things that can be the building block toward true understanding or complete confusion. This is why we have taught to make your choices in awareness of Spirit and to be cautioned by choices that do not serve to move you in the directions you desire."

Attempts are being made to get out of ego as much as is currently possible, and stay firmly in the present, the Now.

"Everyone is doing quite well. Being in the Now, as we have said so many times, is just being and breathing in every moment who you truly are. With every breath you take, you are being in the Now. It is not something you think about, for there is no thinking required to be there, there is just being. There will be clarity and awareness, but you should not have to think, 'Okay, I am going to be in the Now,' because you are always in the Now. It is simply your joining into that moment with all you know yourself to be."

Because of our circumstances, the attempt is to try and not be further ahead in 'time' than I actually am. I am desiring to be always in the present and not be concerned with what has yet to be.

"This is why we have said so many times that what is out there has not yet been created, and it shall be your choices that bring your creation where and when, it will arrive. If you put yourself out into a place that has not yet been created, then you are taking yourself out of the Now."

I'm realizing that my old view was that the Divine put things on our path, and we were supposed to follow them, instead of realizing just how free we are to choose our experiences.

"Sister of My Sister, the Divine Parents would never make you do anything. They would not expect you to, for the Divine Parents have followed your experience of incarnating into this planet, and everything you have learned and created to this point. They have experienced all of this with you. They would not make demands upon you, for They know that this would not then be your choice or creation."

I also believed that if you just prayed, things would be fixed. I see now that that is not necessarily the way it is.

"There is nothing wrong with prayer, but there is more to it than the simple utterance of words. Some believe that if they simply pray about something, everything will be fine. What they are forgetting is that desire with action is what creates. If you are praying for something, or desiring something, you should also be taking an action toward it. The energy of your action, combined with the voicing of the desire, shall take you forward to its outcome.

"We are looking toward Light Sister's coming visit. There is much in this Now, which is in the process of falling sequentially into place. There will be teachings, but they shall be small while things are unfolding.

"If there are no further questions, we shall depart in much Love and Blessings."

This session was primarily for Annie to catch up on questions she had complied since our last session two weeks ago. Bruce and I were preparing to return to Las Vegas to take care of some business that we felt would probably involve getting an attorney. We had been receiving threats of legal action by some creditors and, of course, another notice of foreclosure. It didn't seem to matter to any of them that we were trying to so hard to stay on top of the things we were able to. No one cared, and no one was willing to work with us. The bottom line was, as always, their desire for all their money NOW! The small amounts we were still trying to send them not only took food out of our mouths, literally, but they weren't satisfied. Truly a lesson in ego for me and what the collective consciousness really cares about.

I would like to share a story with you that may help you in similar circumstances, or it may help to show what remaining in Spirit is all about.

We had been approached by a person who was staying in the same RV Park as we were, and during a conversation with him about some of the trials we had been going through, he said he had a group of friends who he believed could help us out of some of our financial dilemma. These were philanthropists who had joined together during this economic downturn to help people. He told us that he would make a call. The next day, he told us it was a "done deal" and that at least two of these people, along with their attorney, would fly to Las Vegas to meet with us and finalize details. They were to call and make arrangements to meet us in Las Vegas around the fourteenth of the month.

In the past, we would have taken this information and run with it, letting our emotions and desire to be out from under this mess take the lead. However, there were way too many things about this person and this offer that did not add up. We thanked him, but chose to remain neutral in our view as to whether the help was in fact the truth. We really were choosing to stay in Spirit and stay in the Now. We did set a date that if we didn't hear, in person, from one of his friends by the twelfth of the month, we would not make the trip.

A day or so later, we found him, late at night, pulling out of the RV Park. When we went over to see what was wrong, he said that his sister-in-law was ill and that he had to leave right away. Of course we thanked him for all his concern for us and wished him a safe journey. We did not judge or in any way question neither his sudden departure, nor his reason for it. We chose to let circumstances play out. They did. No phone call was ever received by us. We realized that this was a situation that this person would repeat in every place he went. Whenever the date for a promised action came near, he would suddenly leave and most likely in the middle of the night. We also found out that he had made several rather spectacular offers to others as well. This experience brought to us the understanding of not running after something that we desired so much that we allowed ourselves to be completely taken into another person's creation and experience. We desired that this person would realize, at some point, that his actions could cause real heartbreak for someone. In looking back, we could easily see that the red flag should have been his habit of constantly telling us how spiritual he was, especially when his words and actions were telling us that just the opposite was true.

I relayed this story to you so that you can see how being consciously aware, and Spirit, can really help you to avoid being entangled in someone else's experience. Our choice to just stay focused on our own journey, our own choices, and to remain Spirit in every Now helped us to not be angry, judgmental, or discouraged. Spirit always will find peace and joy within every moment.

September 6, 2008

Christy, a possible new addition to the council, was coming to visit that evening. In honor of her visit, the "Girls" requested to come.

"We do greet thee. We would like to welcome you and say how pleased we are that you are here. How have you been?"

Thank you. I've been great, thanks to you.

"We have been with you quite a lot whether you have been aware or not."

Yes, I am completely aware of this.

"Since all who may choose to be council are given a name, we have given to you the name of Star Sister. This is appropriate for we believe you understand being among the stars as well as remaining grounded. Are there questions? Do you have something you would like to ask?"

Did you just start being with me, or has it been for forever?

"We have been with you, we would say, in your 'time,' probably twenty of your years. There were moments when you were having difficult times and we came to give you the strength to move beyond those times. We of course 'knew' that at some moment, in some Now, you would be creating a path to lead you in this direction."

I wonder why I did not recognize you.

"You were not ready, Star Sister. You were still searching. You are now awakening. This is truly enjoyable to see for that is our purpose that is the reason why we have come, for those who are awakening to their truth. We teach so that people may choose to hear, and they can then teach others so that they may also choose, and awaken."

Thank you for your guidance.

"You are most welcome. We would like to tell everyone that there is much happening right now, particularly with earth changes, and you will see volcanos, tornados, and hurricanes. They are accelerating, if you will, so you shall see major things going on within nature within the next six of your months. There is nothing to be frightened off, it does not mean the 'end of your world' as many are prone to believe whenever things change. You will know and understand that this is a part of earth changes as the feminine energy awakens. We tell you these things so that you will know them in awareness. The economy of your country is, of course, being affected by your current collective consciousness and by the ego of the people who have been placed in positions of 'power.'"

How do you see me fitting into the plan for the Awakening and for The Light Alliance?

"What we would say to you is that once you have read the books, listened to the teaching tapes, and understood the teachings, and if what you read and hear resonates within you and leads you to the understanding of yourself as Spirit, then it would be our joy to invite you to be part of the council. This will also be your choice of course."

That is wonderful.

"We believe that you will experience many changes as well. These changes, of course, will be the results, the residuals, of your choices."

Can you elaborate?

"Only to be aware of all your choices, for they will take your journey in different directions. Choose those that will be for your highest purpose and desire.

"Little Brother, do you have anything to say or comment?"

No, Dear Ones, not at this time. I was more desirous for this to be Star Sister's session.

"Sister of My Sister, do you have any other questions?"

No, thank you, I do not.

"Star Sister, we would suggest that you start by reading Little One's book, *Teachings from the Heart*. Then you may listen to the tapes that contain all additional teachings, and we would have you be a part of the new teachings, which are coming, as well. If being council family is your desire, and your choice, then know that from the moment of that choice you shall be considered as council.

"If there are no further questions, then you know that we are available anytime a question arises. In Love and Blessings, we do depart."

This is another session that reveals just how loving and respectful the "Girls" truly are. We had been speaking with Christy for some time now, explaining what The Light Alliance project was and how it was to aid in the Awakening. The "Girls" politely and respectfully honored her freedom to choose at will by allowing her to express her questions and feelings during the session. Indeed she did choose to become part of the council.

We had intended for this to be her session, for all her questions to be answered. It was also the first time she had "met" Zelia and Astoria. Of course we had shared with her all about them and she had already begun, in her own way, to establish a relationship with them. We are so blessed that she made a decision to be a part of this Awakening, and she will undoubtedly do so much in aiding others to awaken.

September 10, 2008

Teresa had returned once again for a visit to Happy Camp. This would be her last visit of the year. Little did we know, at the time, how significant this session would become.

"We do greet thee. Welcome back, Light Sister. It is our joy to see you here."

Thank you. I wanted to tell you that I went through a strange period where I was just a bit unsure as to what I was feeling. I really didn't understand what the feelings were or where they were coming from.

"What you were experiencing is what we would call a 'pulling,' if you will. It is that your physical body was feeling pushed beyond its vibrational frequency that it currently has upon the earth. When this occurs, you may feel somewhat disjointed. This is not unusual when one is beginning to understand what it means to be Spirit and when you are being totally in the Now. You may have been spending a great deal of 'time' in meditation and this will begin to raise your vibration. Sometimes the body, or ego, will resist this rise and will bring about these feelings you have spoken about."

I'm not exactly sure if I know how to phrase this next question, but if we are One, how do the Divine Parents speak to us as individuals?

"It is not that they speak as individuals, for they are always One Spirit. It is that the essence, either Masculine or Feminine, may choose to be in the forefront during a meeting. We understand that this could be somewhat confusing. Remember first of all that you are a creation of the Divine Parents. Everyone and everything is a creation of the One Spirit. The One has both the essence and attributes of Masculine and Feminine; this is why you are said to have been created in the image and likeness of. You are inseparably connected to All things, and All things come from and are a part of the One. When the Divine Parents speak to you, whether that is the Masculine or Feminine essence, they still speak from One voice."

Do you know the part in the Bible where it says, "Ask and you will receive"? Is this true?

"At the time of its writing, of course, its intent was to bring people together. If they were together in a purpose, a belief, then this kept them somewhat 'joined,' if you will. Ask and therefore you shall receive simply means, as we have been teaching, to put forth a desire, take action toward its completion, and this will contribute to the potential of its manifestation. To simply ask to receive without any creation of your own is not likely to produce your desired result. We believe that many things that were written into religions were turned upside down in many ways, for it was a matter of control. Yes, we have taught that if you put forth your intent and follow that with intent and action, then, of course, many events, people, and circumstances will be placed upon your path to enable you to create your desire and journey by your choices. The course of your path, and manifestations of your desires, change according to the decisions you are making."

I am viewing what is going on with us, the council, as far as the amount of ego involvement. This ego is coming up because we need to recognize it and move beyond it. If these moments of ego do not come out, how can we really recognize them and begin to dismantle them? Is my thinking along this line correct?

"That is exactly right. It is by your choices that they are coming out. They are not being pulled out, if you will. Sometimes you may not be aware that you have made a choice to recognize ego, but the fact that you desire to progress, and advance, in your spiritual awareness means that they must come out and be dealt with."

They must, yes. It is an evolving then, isn't it?

"It is. It means you are evolving away from ego toward being Spirit. The old identifiers and views of ego are brought from deep within and viewed in the awareness of Now and who you know you are. Through this understanding of Spirit, you are on the path of evolving away from ego and breaking it down."

Is there any way, since I live so far away from here that I could be able to speak with you and communicate with you in the same ways that Little Brother and Little One do? Could I ask you things and hear your voice?

"We are always with you and you may certainly get to that place. It is simply a matter of asking a question and waiting in silence until you hear an answer. Then, do not doubt necessarily whether you have received the answer. You may verify it the first few times with those who already 'hear' us and in that way will know for sure."

Will I hear a different voice or will it be my own voice?

"You may not hear a voice at all. Some simply have a 'knowing.' Some have a 'feeling' about it. We do not know how it may affect you. Our guidance is for all who ask, but we have chosen Little One as the channel for our voice to be heard. You may, at some point, be chosen, and choose, to also become a channel for the voice of another of our planet. There will be many in your 'time' to come, who will be looking for and choosing a channel to help bring this awakening to many. If that be your desire, your choice, to be a channel, then open your heart and wait in Spirit for that moment to happen."

As far as the exercise regarding our meditation door is concerned, I do not feel like I am making any progress. I feel like when I open the door, there is only darkness.

"Perhaps you would like to do what we suggested to Little Brother, as he was also having difficulty picturing his door. Not all exercises will resonate with everyone, so we would suggest that you simply put yourself in a certain place instead of traveling through a door. Have this be somewhere already familiar to you and have it be with someone you know. Do this placement at a designated time with the other person and then verify with each other what was experienced. What did you see or do, what was the other person doing? What did they see or experience? Stay with this and it will eventually enable you to understand Spirit travel just as the door can also do. We gave the door as an example for this would have you travel to places you may not be aware of, but by placing yourself in a location familiar to you, with someone you know, this will aid you in experiencing the same thing, Sprit travel."

Not last night, but the night before, I was being awakened and my entire body was either humming or vibrating. What was this?

"It was that your physical body was being lifted to another energy level. That is all. Just as the energy changes when the Divine Mother comes to speak, your energy around you is changing because you are now understanding and being the Spirit that you are. This energy then lifts your physical body to a higher level of vibration. This should not have been anything that was uncomfortable."

No, it wasn't uncomfortable at all. It just woke me up and I was wondering what it was.

"Right now upon your earth, there is much that is going on with the misuse of energy, if you will. It is because of your economy and what is going on with the consciousness of the people in your country. We are seeing the collective in its 'negative' state become somewhat 'glued in place.' This will change as the awakening spreads, but for now, we are lifting up your energy a bit."

Thank you for that. I can certainly use it, especially being right down in the middle of it where I live.

"You are in an area where there are a great many people who are and will be affected. The results of your current economy will also affect more than just those who live in your area. People in Happy Camp will be somewhat isolated, if you will, which is how they desire to be. The larger areas of population will of course 'feel' more of what is occurring. It is for us to send more energy to lift up the council."

Thank you for all of your help.

"You are most welcome. Sister of My Sister, do you have any questions?"

I do not have any questions, but I feel as Teresa does that I want to be able to communicate with you better. I think I am now although I just don't always recognize it.

"Sometimes a response can be quite subtle. It is difficult when people first begin, especially if they have never done such a thing before or it is not being directed toward them for a purpose, such as writing or teaching. We would say again to just ask a question and wait. Be aware of all 'knowing' or 'feelings' that may come to you. Also be clear to things you read, see, or hear, for the answer may lie within these things as well. When you feel you have received an answer, follow through with that as well."

I felt that when I got the "hit" to tell Little One that she was supposed to be channeling you and Astoria that this came from you.

"It did, and you were communicating even though you may not have been aware of it. For you it may come with what you call your 'hits.'"

I really desire for that to get stronger.

"It will, and it can. It will never be the same as it is when we are coming through our channel, but it will aid you in times when you have a question, particularly when those questions can be answered with a simple yes or no. Those types of questions are much easier when you are trying to gain some type of understanding. Little Brother, do you have questions?"

I really don't have any questions at this moment, but I would like to share with you something that happened the night before. It seems important that I share this. I was seeing energy coming off my hands when I was dreaming. Would you please comment?

"You were seeing that which you cannot see through your physical eyes. You are seeing this through your spiritual eyes. You are seeing the energy that is not only in, but surrounds your body as well."

It was the same energy that I saw when I was at my sister's home. It appeared as waves of energy.

"This was what we spoke to you about when doing the ball exercise or seeing the energy coming off your hands when your eyes are closed. This is the same thing. This is a practice to enable you to see the energy that is within and surrounds your physical body. You will understand then that your physical energy may not always be constant, but the energy which is Spirit always is. Physical energy is based upon several things. It may be the wellness of the physical body or it may be where it lies within its connection with Spirit.

"We know that you are all anxious to hear the Divine Mother and we would say that if you have some questions to ask Her that She would be most pleased to take a few. We would suggest that you do not bombard her with questions as this is not her purpose, in the Now, for coming to see you. So if you are ready we believe that, She is ready to come through her channel."

"*My children, I have come at this time because it is necessary for the Father and I to explain something that we believe you may have misunderstood. It is not that there has been a misunderstanding on purpose, of course, but it is that we possibly did not make ourselves clear enough to you. We would like to start with creation, what it is, and how it is accomplished.*

"*It is important to understand that you are creating your lives. We are not doing that. We do experience your lives through you, but we do not create them. This is why you have the freedom to create at will, or what others have called free will. Although we experience through you, we do not create for you, for if we were to do so, then what would be the purpose of your being here to experience and grow? You should understand that from time to time, the Father and I, put circumstances, events, and people upon your path. It will be at that point your choice to go, or not to go, with them. Again, it shall be your creation, and as you create, we experience that with you.*

"*We are always loving you and giving energy to you. We shall not interfere with your lives, for that is neither our purpose nor our pleasure. We are always with you here, upon the plane of existence that you have chosen to incarnate into, the place where you create your journey through your choices. We will always be there to help when there are decisions to make, but we do not make them for you. We think that there has been a misunderstanding in the fact that many people believe they are being stopped, or kept, from something, that they are not allowed to do certain things. I would ask you right now, who would not be allowing you to do this? We do not stop you. We do not disallow you. We would never interfere with your choices, for your choice for yourself is our choice for you as well. We understand that the life you have chosen upon this planet is not always one that you would term 'easy.' Yet you knew all this before you came here, it was something we discussed at your 'blueprint' when it was formed. Whatever you are experiencing, it is there for the purpose you created it. Many times we find and see that you are not even aware that you created it. If you would but stop and remember you could trace back through the 'knowing' of Spirit exactly where you made a choice that created what you are now experiencing, you will then see where your decision created a pathway that did not before exist. We simply want you to know that we allow that creation because it is yours.*

"*You are our children. We will put thing before you that you desire, but whether you recognize them and choose them shall always be up to you. We would say to understand where you are flowing and to know that we are also there. Miracles do happen, yes, but those occur when not only have you put forth a heartfelt desire, and maintained that desire, but you have also taken all action that you can for its manifestation. This action is taken in the living, and awareness, of who you are, and not in ego.*

"*We have chosen Now, the Father and I, to come to you out of our Love for you, out of our desire for you to understand and take a good look at the creations you are Now making. The journey you are now upon is in your hands alone. You are the creator of your experience and we are the experiencing.*"

Can we ask you for strength in a situation that we are trying to overcome?

"*Yes, at all times we will be there with strength, with energy, with Love, and with our compassion. These are not what you would call intervening emotions, these are simply the movements of Love, and to you we freely give this. Know that when you need our strength each of you can call upon us and it will be given. I do not often entertain questions, but I will be most pleased to take some from each of you. You may begin.*"

I do not have a question, but I do want to tell you how much I Love you and to thank you so much.

"*And, my daughter, the Father and I Love you as well. Know that we are with you always. It is this, your journey upon this planet, that you should enjoy and create. We shall be reunited and we shall speak of our experience. You will then be back in total remembrance and knowing, but for now, know that we are with you and we do Love you.*"

You would be omnipresent, is that correct? So when any of us say, "Please help me," you hear us?

"*Yes, always. There is not one utterance, not one tear that falls, not one laugh that has been sent out that we do not hear, do not feel, or do not experience. It is important to understand that we experience all of what you would term as 'good' or 'bad.' You have created it, therefore, we also have experienced it. So, when you call upon us know that we are in all places at all times. When you ask for Love, energy, or strength, we will and do give it joyfully to you.*"

I have a question, Mother. Am I way too far ahead of where I am supposed to be right now?

"My son, we would like it if you would look at it in a backwards way, if you will. We would like for you to just stop for a moment and be who you are in this Now and not who you know you can be. For when you get too far ahead of yourself, it can be quite frustrating for you. Out of this frustration, you can be preventing the very thing that you desire to create. You could view things from the understanding of "I made a poor decision here, or there." It was simply in that Now what you chose, now move forward.

"Many times there are veils that will hold in place your ability to 'feel' and 'see' the truth within yourself and all that is around you. We would desire to help you lift the veil, to enable you a clearer vision. Close your eyes, everyone, and take a deep breath. As if you were looking at a blind being drawn up upon a window, see this blind, or veil, which is keeping you, in many ways, in unawareness. This blind holds back those things that you would view through spiritual eyes. We desire for you to see more clearly, so that you may see how each of your choices and creations will take you along different portions of your path. The lifting of this will enable you to be more aware when a circumstance, an event, a word, or a person is brought forward to you along your journey. This awareness will also allow you to see when these things will aid you in creating those experiences that will serve your highest purpose. We would, in this Now, lift this shade for you.

"It now would appear as if you are looking out through clear glass to a lake. This lake is crystal blue and very pure and clean. This lake is now your awareness, your understanding. It is your vision. See where you now stride along your path and where you desire to be. Know that when you make your choices with this clearness of vision and complete awareness, these choices will create for you the experiences that will take you to your desire. Know also that the unfolding of events will always present you with those things that are for your highest purpose even if they may seem to be somewhat different than your vision. Sometimes there is a sequence of events, or residuals, that must first be played out.

"I shall go for now, but shall never be far away as we are an inseparable part of one another. You are Our children and we Love each and every one of you with a Love that encompasses everything that you are, everything you desire to be, and everything that We are to you. We leave in Love."

"We do greet thee. We are in the understanding that the Mother has given you much information to absorb and to understand. We will not remain much longer. We would desire for you to be in the Now and to 'feel' all that was revealed. For now, we shall depart in much Love and Blessings."

It is truly amazing how a question or series of questions can lead you to something extraordinary. It seemed as if questions we were asking actually led up to the Divine Mother desiring to speak with us. Things such as "Who really creates our lives?" and, "How do we know when we are truly receiving inspiration?" We had no idea beforehand that the Mother would make an appearance, but were thrilled when she did. We also received answers to these questions and I think really began to understand that we create our lives.

Puts it all in our court, doesn't it? We can't blame anyone for our choices because we made them. The residuals of those choices have to play themselves out; no one is going to bail our fannies out of the fire. I do believe, as we were told, that there will be things placed before us along our paths to help us, but whether we are aware enough to see them is up to us. The more we live as Spirit and the less we allow ego to be heard, the more awareness we will have to see the things placed before us.

I know that the Divine Parents are present in everyone's life; Their love and Their strength is for everyone. I am so blessed that not only did I make the choice to be a channel, but I was chosen as well. This doesn't in any way make me different from anyone else, I believe anyone who desired this could do so. You really just have to open your heart, listen very carefully to everything around you, and be Spirit. The only thing that keeps anyone from "hearing" the messages and teachings is the ego. It can be very sneaky, so you always have to stay aware of your words, actions, and choices. If you do this in every Now, you will overcome it as much as is possible in this physical journey. Imagine a world where everyone comes from a place of Spirit and ego has no control. I can imagine this and that is what I and all of us are working toward. Whether it is completed in my physical lifetime or not, the journey on the way is wonderful!

September 12, 2008

We settled in for another session as Teresa's visit was drawing to a close.

"We do greet thee. We have been observing quite an interesting thing that is occurring among you. We see that you are truly speaking to one another when issues arrive. It will be with the conversing that you will begin to break down and solve those things that are creating disharmony. We do not look at them as problems, for we understand that they are just someone's experiencing of those things that they created. You have discussed these things, and we suggest that now you put them aside and move forward. It has no purpose and does not serve you to go back to a Now that no longer exists. We will answer any questions you may have and then we would like for you to share your experiences with Spirit travel. Who would care to begin?"

I do not seem to having good luck with the traveling. Last night I woke up early and couldn't go back to sleep.

"Light Sister, have you been doing the suggested exercises?"

I have been practicing being "out of my body." I did have one night where I dreamt I was flying.

"Spirit will know when it can overcome your perceived limitations and simply travel. This flying dream may have indeed been traveling, so always be aware. It may only occur for moments at first, and then as you grow with the understanding that you are Spirit, they will last for longer periods of your 'time,' and you will begin to recall them when you have awakened."

As far as the exercise with the door, I feel like I can't get past it, like I am stuck.

"Then we would say to simply leave the door. Choose to put yourself somewhere you are already familiar with. Look around you and note all that you see. Is there someone there who may verify your presence for you? Choose a 'time' to do this when there will be someone there and they are awake. Travel in Spirit to see them and then get their observations. What did they feel? Were they aware of your presence? Note all that you saw from them and around them so that they may confirm these things for you. Sister of My Sister, how are you doing with your exercises and experiences?"

I think I may have misunderstood. Will our experiences always come from a dream state?

"There are many who have it first in the dream state, as that is an easier state for it to occur. It does take a little more focus for it to occur while in a waking state, but if this is what is occurring to you, then this is how it should be. This will take some practice to continue as this is something that your physical body is not used to. It may be that it is occurring during a time of what you call daydreaming. If you can learn to travel without the aid of sleep, this would of course be the ultimate goal. And, Little Brother, what would you care to express?"

There are a number of things to share with you. The other day when we were driving out to where we are doing our mining, I shared with you the feeling I was having that it seemed like we were moving through a space. I felt the solidity of the rocks, the fluidity of the air, and the feeling of being in motion as we moved through space. Also the colors were much brighter than usual. There was a complete feeling of Oneness within this space we were moving through. I found myself thinking about that and feeling the movement of Spirit as it expanded outward. Is this part of what you desired for us?

"Yes, and this is indeed the way that you, individually, if you will, were experiencing this. Some of what you were experiencing was the denseness of earth's vibration around Spirit."

I seem to be more aware, particularly after the Divine Parents coming through, of the unity of everything around me.

"No matter what you choose, or desire, to make, every choice within every breath will create something that will be in your experience. Sometimes these are quite subtle, or unnoticeable. When you truly join with the unity, the connectedness, of all things, then these choices you make for your journey will be made consciously in Spirit."

There is something I would like very much to ask you about. I'm actually feeling you around me much stronger of late.

"We have always been there, Little Brother, you are just now connecting with that feeling."

It is becoming more and more noticeable. It is almost like I feel a little pressure on my hands or on my feet. Just the slightest touch, but this is clearly felt.

"What you are experiencing is feeling/form. You are opening to this and we are most pleased. Although we, of course, are not there in a physical sense, we are able to move energy in such a way as to create the sensation of touch. As far as your experiences with Sprit travel, this will happen more as you begin to lift some of the identifiers from yourself."

After the Mother was speaking, I felt so much more at One with the Divine Parents than ever before. I felt that we were a family; there was a very strong feeling of unity. That was a beautiful feeling. It brought so much joy, happiness, and peace.

"There is much that you will experience within your coming Now's. We know that with this understanding, this unity, the things to come will be much easier for you to experience."

I just love this expanding relationship with both of you. I'm so thankful and feel so lighthearted today.

"It is what we also have desired to experience with all of you, and it has given us a totally new perspective as well. You understand that on our planet things are always peaceful, always joyous. There is much laughter upon our planet. We know who we are, why we are here, and we chose to remember this as we incarnated to our planet. It is warming our hearts, if you will, to see that you also now have the understanding of who you are and why you have chosen to be here. Keep the feeling of peace and joy with you, especially in the days and choices to come."

In regard to the door we have created during meditation, to experience Spirit travel, the other night I went through mine and noticed a group of people lined up. Their faces were visible as well as their bodies, but I did not recognize any of them. Would you please give an explanation for what that might have been or meant?

"It would have been somewhere you traveled; we are not sure where this was. Did you notice the clothing or what was around them?"

There was a road and they were standing on each side of it. There was a group of people, and some of the men were wearing dark slacks, some light. The shirts seemed to be what we would call "polo shirts," as they were a type of knit. Other than that, the faces were nonexpressive. This was all I noticed.

"We are not in the knowing of where you may have traveled, but if you are indeed seeing this type of detail, this travel is working well for you. Be aware to 'see' all that you can and do not hesitate to ask for information, for if you are in their sight as well as their presence, they may be able to share information with you as to where you are and who they are. Sometimes travel is simply for experience and sometimes it is to aid you with information for your journey. Stay connected, focused, and aware.

"We would suggest that each one maintain a journal of their travels."

What if this traveling occurs in the daytime?

"Yes, even then, for you are still traveling. You are working toward this 'awake' state of travel. At first it seems easier for Spirit to travel while the physical body sleeps, but if you are already experiencing travel while awake, or daydreaming, you are 'ahead of the game,' as they say.

"We will visit with you again, tomorrow evening of your 'time.' There may be a small teaching at this time for we understand that you will be gone for a period of your 'time.' When all are back together, teaching will resume. There may be many changes, depending on your choices, but this is just the continuance of your journey. We, of course, will be with you."

Do you think it's advisable for me to stay one more night?

"It would be wonderful, Light Sister, but if there is something that must be done, do not feel that you must be here. There will be the tapes for you to listen to. It will be your choice of course."

Did you see the orbs that Little One and I took pictures of last night?

"We were actually with you upon your journey. It was quite wonderful. We love the energy of orbs. They are all around us at all times, but to actually be able to capture them on your camera is fascinating."

There is one picture that was taken inside of the car and there were lots of tiny orbs in there with us.

"We were waiting for you to see this. There was quite a conglomeration, if you will, and they were all inside and not outside in that moment. It simply shows the energy that you and Little One have when you are together."

The orbs that were in the car were so tiny. Is there meaning to the difference in their size or color?

"It is that some are highly condensed and others are not. The color corresponds to the frequency of the energy that the orb is gathering to itself when it forms."

That was pretty cool, I really enjoyed that.

"We believe there will be more of a significance with orbs as time goes on. We have explained some things about them and we believe there will be more and more as the energy and frequency of earth rises. This, as you know, is because there is more energy being bombarded upon your earth in this Now."

Will we be able to see them with the physical eye at some point?

"There already are those who have seen them with the naked eye, if you will. Do not rush it, for the fact that you are capturing them upon your film is remarkable."

Do you have any additional information on how orbs can be used?

"It is not so much in the using of them it is more in the joining with them, allowing the energy that they contain to become a part of your energy as well. So the more orbs that are around you, the more increased your energy flow will become resulting in more orbs. It is not so much a using as it is a sharing. Remember that energy can certainly lift your vibration higher. You will join with that energy and one will create the other."

Why is it that some areas seem to have more orbs than others? How come some of them look gold while others may be clear?

"Color could be defined by the energy that has been absorbed. Some with more energy absorption may appear clearer or brighter. Where the energy has come from for their formation also has a bearing upon their color. It could be that they were just in contact with an animal, or it could be that they were joined with the energy from the star systems. Color also varies according to where they have come from and the energy that has come with them."

Are orbs always with us? Are they always present?

"Yes, they have been gathering energy; they come from all places of high energy. You will be able to tell by their colors, by the designs in them, which you should pay close attention to. You have on your planet that which you call a mandala. If you look within an orb, you will see this type of patterning."

We did see this within the gold one.

"There is a reason for this. We are fascinated with orbs and have quite a symbiotic relationship with them. Although they have been with us, and others, for a great long of your 'time,' it is an interesting thing to see them now gathering, and being formed, upon your earth plane. It tells us that changes are definitely in the works and that the Awakening had begun.

"Are there any other questions at this time? If not, then we shall depart in much Love and Blessings."

At this writing, I do not recall exactly what we were discussing prior to this session that prompted the "Girls" comments, but whatever it was brought about a wonderful amount of information. Apparently we had some ego issues coming up which lead to some differences of opinion. Whatever it was specifically I can't recall and no one else remembers. I just know it was an experience of some kind, but I am thankful for it because it enabled us to receive such a teaching.

The "Girls" can be playful and very curious about our incarnations. They also desire to participate in some of our physical experiences, such as being with Bruce when he would go mining, or "helping" to drive the truck. They have such warm, loving, and engaging personalities. Always they are kind, gentle, and extremely polite. They always allow us to make our own choices and always respect our freedom to create at will. Having a relationship with them is not something in a million years that I would imagined. I had heard, from time to time, about "beings who were channeled," but I never really believed it. I thought it was all a bunch of kooks who were out of their minds! I guess you do have to be out of your mind, out of ego, before you can open your heart enough to realize that we, on planet earth, are not the only ones. Why we would think that, now seems crazy to me. Out of the unimagined amount of us that were created, how could we even begin to think that it's all about our planet, that other Spirits didn't choose other experiences, in other places, besides earth? I am so thankful that I opened my heart to them and can't imagine what my life would be like without them. I hope that you also have opened your heart, your Spirit, and that you are creating for yourself as well.

Teresa was so happy to have had her experience with orbs. She and I were coming back to Happy Camp from a day's outing in Cave Junction, which is in southern Oregon. It was after dark and we were taking the shortcut up over a mountain the locals call "Grayback." We had the feeling to stop alongside the road and take pictures. Luckily I had thought to bring my digital camera along. We shot several pictures into the dark and then took a look at them. In several shots, we saw some beautiful orbs, and one in particular was huge and the most beautiful shade of yellow. Inside of it was a very intricate pattern that contained several other colors. Just to the bottom of it was a small red orb. I wish I could show you the picture, there is so much energy contained there. I will try to get it onto the website. The discovery of these orbs was one of the high points of Teresa's visit.

We also learned in this session that changes were coming. We felt that these were to be major changes as the "Girls" let us know they would be coming through again the next evening. They do not normally announce something like this, so when they do, we know that something very important is about to happen.

At this point, it looked as though the teachings would continue once we were back in Happy Camp after our upcoming trip to Las Vegas. We were hoping to be given a little more information at this next session that would answer some of the many questions that were flooding our thoughts. In the end, we decided to just wait to see what we would hear and not spend any more time speculating on something that was in a Now that had yet to occur.

September 13, 2008

Teresa chose to stay over one more day. As she was headed for home the next morning, she would now be able to be present when the "Girls" came this evening. We were hoping for more information about the changes that we now knew were coming.

"We do greet thee. How is everyone in your Now? We have come to hear your questions as well as to share with you.

"We spoke a little about the changes that would be occurring and the direction that they may take you, according to your choices of course. We are now somewhat more privy to information, but as you know, the Divine always allows you to choose your own direction. This information may simply be put upon your path for you to consider while making your choices. This change in direction will be created by you. We are in the knowing that no matter your choice, the project will not be affected, for it is a constant. There may simply be a transition, if you will. We are not knowing in what 'time' of yours this will occur, just that there will be decisions and choices made. We do see that there may be a time in your 'time' where you will be apart, but eventually everything will flow as you choose. Do you have questions regarding what we have brought to you?"

Is this something that is relatively immediate in our "time"?

"Since there is no 'time' except that which you have created, this would be hard to answer in your terms. What we know is that within your 'time' frame, it is relatively short, yes."

My understanding is that circumstances or something will appear and we will receive inspiration as to the straightest course to our ultimate desire. This will enable us to make a more informed choice of the direction we are to go.

"It is not necessarily that something will appear immediately in your 'time.' You will be making decisions prior to this appearance, but many times on your journey, you will have circumstance, people, and events placed before you. These things, and guidance, are available if you remain of open heart to hear and see them."

I say that because in going back to Las Vegas, there are considerations that we need to address. So if something were not to unfold in the next short space of time, decisions would be automatically made because other alternatives would not have been presented. In other words, we will not be able to stay in a populated area unless it is clear that an opportunity presents itself.

"It may be a matter of pooling interests, if you will. Many times there are people who, while on their journey's, chose to be together. You may also choose this and pool resources. This is something that you will all speak of and you will, for yourselves, make a choice. It will be a group choice and decision. In this Now, you will go and do what you can, keeping in mind all opportunities that enable you to follow your desires."

Well, I am going with an open mind and am open to whatever unfolds. I will try to be as attentive as possible to all forms of inspiration and guidance. Everything has been put on the table at this point, everything is possible to me.

"That is good, Little Brother. We are in the understanding, just recently of course, that you are contemplating that which you call 'bankruptcy.' We know that in many ways you have been caught within the choices and creations of the collective consciousness, although it cannot be held totally responsible. Much of your current experiences are due to decisions and choices you have made. We believe that there are certain rules and regulations that allow you to keep a home and a vehicle. This would be something we would have you inquire about and then possibly to be removed from everything else. Then, continue to try and find employment that would enable you to keep your home. If this is not possible in this economy that has been created, then you may have to look, as we said, in pooling resources, especially if you all choose to remain closely together in the same area. We see that in this Now, Little One is doing the income part of it with her current job, and she will maintain this for a period of time until the decision has been made to either stay in your current area or move back to Las Vegas. We see this unfolding at the end of your winter. You, Little Brother, may need to make some decisions prior to that."

Decisions will have to be made in order to continue and they will have to be made almost immediately. I am completely wide open with no expectations as to the outcome, watching as attentively as possible to see what door may open.

"Well, at the moment there would appear to be, for you, more doors that are closed. You understand that as many doors close, many doors open. It is simply being aware of them and being able to see beyond the closed ones to the ones that are opening."

This is why I have no expectations.

"It is possible that if you pooled resources that this would allow you to keep the home where all could reside. This is something that you must decide on your own, for we have almost stepped beyond our purpose for being here."

We understand this. Thank you so much. We sensed that a change of this order and magnitude was coming.

"It has been a project for us that has become much more than we had anticipated, if you will. When we chose to be part of this awakening, back even before your incarnations, we also chose to follow all of you during your incarnations. We were quite familiar with who you are, but we did not know your hearts as we do Now, and we did not share our hearts as we do Now. So we have become bound, we have become family. It is our joy to have this relationship with you, but we also must be aware in our choices as well to not step too far beyond that which we have come to do."

We understand and indeed we are family, and as such, this means so much more now. Your guidance, your assistance, and your recommendations are so respected. It is the kind of thing where you go to a family member who you love and respect tremendously to get their perspective on your situation. This is as close in word to try and express the love, respect, and gratitude that is felt for both of you.

"We also feel that way about all of you. It is the strength of the four of you that will solidify the rest of the council. We now, of course, also have Star Sister who has chosen to be a part of the council. It may be that she also will want to look into moving. These decisions will first be done individually and then together."

I have a question that is off this subject. Would it be possible for us to have our own form of energy healing? There are already many out there, but we have been talking about one that would be simplified, but powerful. We all have a strong desire to be "healers" and would love to have a modality that has been inspired to The Light Alliance. Then we could learn how to direct the energy and to open the energy centers so that many may benefit.

"We would be most pleased to teach you ways this could be done."

Would it be simpler?

"Yes, for we do not believe it needs to be as complicated as it is in some current modalities. Sometimes there are rituals, if you will, that are brought into energy work, this makes people feel that there is something extraordinary occurring. This sometimes becomes what you would call 'smoke and mirrors.' It is important for those who come to you to be in complete understanding of the energy, how it works, how it may feel. Many times the person is not even a part of this understanding or this treatment. They lay upon the table thinking, 'What is happening?' 'What am I paying for?' If you utilize, as we have been showing Little One, the touch of your hands, then they will 'feel' the reception of the energy. Your touch delivers the energy from the Divine and sends it through the recipient to open all their energy centers. The energy works with the intent of the recipient and they are an integral part of their own healing."

Would you bring us direction and inspiration for this?

"We will speak with the Divine Parents and bring to you teachings on this modality.

"If there is nothing further for now, then, Light Sister, we wish you a safe and speedy journey home. There are decisions for you to make. Continue to speak with each other, help to guide one another, for you may be the circumstance or person that the Divine puts onto someone's path."

When we know more about our direction, we could then notify Star Sister so that she can also make her decision.

"You will most definitely contact her, for she may decide to relocate as well. There are many decisions to be made, so go through them with an open and loving heart, a gentle and pure Spirit, and always be consciously aware of where these choices may lead you and what their residuals may be.

"We know that there is much ahead of you right now, be in the Now for all of your thoughts and decisions."

You did say that you see imminent changes taking place?

"The decisions will begin, yes. We do not know the 'time' frame that they will occur. All lies within your choices."

We are most appreciative of this information. Thank you. We just want to express how much we love you and how grateful we are.

"You are most welcome. Now, in Love and Blessings, we do depart."

The content of this session was to become the center for all our discussions for quite some time. Definite changes were already on the wind.

We all understood that whatever these changes would be that they would not affect the outcome of the project in any way. No matter what they were, or how they may appear to the eyes and ears, the eventual outcome would not change. This was a comforting thought as we were jumping off the cliff into free fall to know that at least our chutes would open!

From what the "Girls" had told us, it became quite apparent that there was to be a physical relocation for at least two of the council. The "Girls" said that we should not be concerned, stay Spirit, and that it well be the way it shall be, everything would occur for our highest purpose. This raised a red flag for Bruce and he said that he knew that something remarkable was about to manifest. I also knew that when this statement is used, it always refers to the "purpose" aspect of a person's blueprint, not necessarily a desire for a particular experience. It all has to do with why you incarnated here, what your life's purpose is. You chose this purpose, with the Divine Parents, before you incarnated, and once you remember this, you are on your way to fulfilling this purpose.

Matters were very advanced on the foreclosure and imminent bankruptcy scene. It really looked like whatever inspiration was to arrive, it would be at 11:59, with only a minute to spare. All we could do was be at peace with it all and not fall back into the fear or anger of the collective consciousness.

It seemed apparent that a larger population area was in mind, partly for outreach but mostly for job potential. We had the feeling that the "start" phase of the project was coming to a close and that a new chapter was about to begin. We desired so much to be able to handle these financial burdens, and the possibility of finding jobs might be just around the corner. This was uplifting, but I was still approaching it a little bit of trepidation. If there was some way to preserve the house for all of us, then opportunities for employment must surely also appear, or at least this was our desire. Jobs in Las Vegas were scarce, but there were so many more than compared to Happy Camp. I know we would do all we could to find one.

While discussing the suggestions they had for how we could keep the house, they said they had "almost stepped beyond their purpose." They had always kept the context within a teaching when revealing information to us. So great is their love and concern for us.

We were all discussing that we, in the truest sense, were family. The "Girls" had opened their hearts to us, perhaps in a way never before experienced, and we had also opened up our hearts to them. Love always desires the desires of another and will go to great lengths to help them. We really want others to fully experience all that they had intended to accomplish during their incarnation. We understood this about ourselves, so we understood that the "Girls'" great love for us had brought them to that place where they must be aware of their choices as they guided, taught, and participated with us as our lives unfolded. They would be careful not to overstep, or step beyond, what they were here to do. We understood this completely. It has to do with the full allowance of every person to have the freedom to create at will all they will experience in life. It also has to do with the careful restraint of only releasing information that will guide the person without interfering in their creative freedom. The more you understand that you are Spirit, and the more you live as such, the more you also understand how creative power at this level can and does manifest. To the degree that significant events may occur that may not as yet be "in step" with an overall project. If something is revealed that is not keeping "in step" with the sequences of events that are intended to unfold, they can change the course of these events.

We were informed that a new healing modality would be sent to us. This would come directly from the Divine Parents. We knew, of course, that it would be the Divine Mother who would tailor a program to meet the needs of the Awakening, and the transformation in consciousness that this "appointed time" would bring about. We were not the least bit concerned with the "time" that it may take to bring this to us, we were just thrilled knowing that it would be taught to us when we were ready, and prepared, to receive it. All of those on the council were already Reiki masters so we had training in an energy modality already, but we were looking forward to something simplified, yet powerful, that also allowed us to just sit within the energy and be that conduit for its deliverance to one who chose to receive it.

We headed for Las Vegas and home the next morning, and as Sarah was so comfortable at Annie's, we decided to leave her in Annie's care. We took our then almost three-month-old puppy Spirit with us. She really seemed to enjoy the trip, sitting, lying, or sleeping in her bed, which was on the center rest between us. Of course the conversation was all about what changes may be happening and what they would mean for us.

Once we arrived home on the fifteenth, there was the usual list of items to take care of, and of course, we had to make a final decision on the house. We investigated storage unit again, but something inside said to hold off on getting one. We had an appointment with a new attorney the next day. We instantly liked her and she was very helpful in showing us where we stood. We did not retain her then because we really wanted to talk with everyone, especially the "Girls."

Before we had the last session on the thirteenth, we had pretty much made up our minds to remove our belongings, let the bank foreclose, and file for bankruptcy. After that session, we felt that maybe we were to go a different direction. We still were not sure how matters would present themselves. We kept reminding each other to stay in the moment, in the Now. We knew that if we could do this, then we would be more aware of guidance when it came, no matter what the guidance may be. There wasn't anything else we could do so we decided to enjoy our pool and go swimming. We had only used it once since it had been built since we had either been in the Northwest working (before Bruce's surgery and the economy going to hell), or we were scrambling in Happy Camp to survive. We really had missed our home and all the touches we had given it. We had created a magical environment in the backyard and felt blessed to experience this again for whatever "time" we may have in our home.

September 19, 2008

Something rather remarkable happened on the morning of the nineteenth. The "Girls" informed me that they had an important message to give us. We immediately went into the family room, took out the tape recorder. I closed my eyes, and Bruce waited for the "Girls" to come through. What, we wondered, would the message be?

"We do greet thee. We have come to share with you some ideas. These are for you to decide upon, for you to choose. We find it is the 'time' for the council to come together to make decisions. We would like to tell you of events and circumstances that may come before you, but these will come according to your choices. It is as we were describing to Little One this morning. There are options to be taken and it is now for the council to choose. This may be an opportunity for you to experience what it would be like to be living together within a Center or Sanctuary together. Both a Center and a Sanctuary will take devotion and commitment. It will take, if you will, sacrifice. We are not saying that anyone must do this, for this is your decision, your choice, your journey. What we have been informed is that there are resources. It remains the choice of the people with the resources whether to help or not. If this is not their choice, they are still loved.

"It does not mean that they shall not remain a part of the Alliance, they shall continue just as they have to this Now. We are now looking at this home as possibly belonging to all council. Therefore, it will become a central point, if you will. This area has many places of very high energy, and this is why you first chose to come here even though you were not aware of it at the time. Being here was a part of the journey for the beginning of The Light Alliance. Choices you made did not allow you to remain here, but there is no right or wrong. They were simply choices you made. In this Now, the council is in a position to also make choices that may allow you to stay here.

"It will be the stepping out of comfort zones for all of you. This will no longer be your home alone, but will be the home for all current council. What you consider 'time' is running out and only the pooling of resources may enable you to remain here.

"We like the attorney and we see that she will do well for you. It may now be your choice to retain her, as it will be the retaining of her that will help you to keep your home and to get a start here together. Do you have questions?"

The only question I have is one about a comment you made just a few minutes ago. You said if "we do not choose" to do this, does that mean that we would be replaced and someone else would be chosen to do this?

"You would not be replaced for this is one of your purposes as well as ours. You chose and were chosen for the Awakening. It is simply that your decisions, your journey, may take you for a 'time' in a different direction."

It is our desire to remain with this project and the Awakening. I know it is for me.

"We are in the understanding that if you all choose to remain in Happy Camp, this is how it shall be, this is the decision that you will all make. It is not that the Awakening or Teachings will not continue, for they shall continue. You will possibly fine it a much rougher road due to the area and the population. This will be part of the choice you will make, but no matter what choice you make, it will not affect the project's continuance. It is simply that in your 'time,' it may mean a delay for you may find yourselves going in different directions. If you are living together and everyone is outreaching in their own way, through work or people they meet, then this home may become a gathering place, a place to learn and grow. It will be easier for people to gather here than Happy Camp because of its more central, and not so remote, location.

If the council is desirous of keeping this home, then the council must work together as one."

So am I to understand that although Happy Camp may be the easiest decision, it is not, in the long run, the best decision?

"We cannot say whether it is a good or bad decision. As you would say, lay your cards on the table and look at them. Where would be your opportunities for the most outreach? Where is the greatest potential for work? Where will you market and present your books? This may require some travel, but you are much better placed within this area than within Happy Camp.

"This is what we would say to you with our 'knowing' on this day. It will be for you, Little Brother, to take it forward. There are decisions that you will make regarding your finances. If you are going to be able and you choose to do this, then you will not require a storage unit. You need not be concerned with packing. We would suggest that you look at what is within your home and what may be brought in to make it comfortable for all to live here. If this is your choice, then there are things to do. Little One will speak with her employer and given them 'time' to have her duties taken over. Everyone may not be coming immediately as they may have to wrap things up, as you would say.

"We do see that if you choose this way that there will be several trips back and forth. It is not advisable for Sister of My Sister to drive her vehicle such a long distance, so someone may be found who can help you with this.

"This is what we 'know' and can share in this Now."

Thank you, there is much to discuss and decide. I do have a question about orbs. Some of them are now appearing quite large.

"There is much energy being sent your way into this particular area. As you know, the orbs grow on the energy that is being sent to the area, as well as the energy of the people within that area. This is showing to us that there is a great deal of energy around and within your home."

So this is a very important and pivotal decision?

"Yes, and for you there is very little 'time,' for you will be leaving in a few days and things should be finalized before you depart."

Does the attorney have to be retained on Monday? We understand that even if we file bankruptcy, we can still keep the home, but all past and late payments must be made up and we must continue paying the mortgage payments.

"We would suggest that you contact this attorney to verify what you believe as to the retaining of your home and the requirements for keeping it. This is something to find out. As far as everything else is concerned, it shall be with all of your choices as to whether or not to pool finances and keep the home."

I know that I and Little One are willing to sell everything we have in order to make this happen. We can sell off all the rest of the mining equipment and the trailer.

"This will all be part of your decision making."

I guess if everyone is in agreement, we will retain the attorney and inform her that we are going to do everything we can to keep the house.

"Yes, but know that this is something you will be able to do while still ridding yourselves of the rest of your debt. We understand that you have phone calls to make. You will speak with the council about these decisions. As in all things, Little Brother, be aware. Make your choices in this awareness, as will all of the council. We are with you regardless of the direction you may choose to go. For now, we do depart, in Love and Blessings."

There are times in your life when you are asked to not only make a choice, but to fully commit to that choice. Your willingness to lay down everything that you have truly shows your commitment. This is exactly what we would be doing. Whether we made this commitment was of course our choice, and we knew that whichever way we decided, they would still be here for us.

Experience is a wonderful thing, and it is through our experiences that we come to know and understand so many things. It was clear that all we had learned so far was bringing us to this moment. Were we willing to take this step, or more appropriately, leap, to move the project forward? We didn't really think too long about this, we were, and are, totally committed to sharing these teachings with anyone who cares to hear and takes the time to listen. This Awakening really is our purpose. By arriving at a unanimous decision to step up and step forward, we would demonstrate not only our commitment to the project, but to our spiritual journey and growth as well.

Moving out of comfort zones can be very difficult for most people. However, it's not often that this movement may be one that can transform your life. This was the opportunity placed before us, what would we do?

The spoke about Center and Sanctuary skills, devotion, commitment, and some sacrifices were voiced. We knew from the very beginning that this was going to be a difficult but wonderful journey and that what we were going through was just one of the many situations in the "difficult" column. We also "knew" that this would open a door to our spiritual growth. We couldn't choose for the others on the council, only for ourselves. We would honor whatever were their choices.

We had wondered what was meant by change during the session in Happy Camp. What did this really mean? It now seemed to mean relocation for two of the council and a change from it being our home to, in essence, The Light Alliance home. We really did not have to think about this for very long. The only thing that now remained was to immediately call everyone and relay to them the contents of the session we had just had. We did. We heard back within hours that they had both made the choice to relocate and so began the formulation of the plans to do this.

Annie would return with Bruce, and I and Bruce would make two trips to get her belongings. Teresa would follow some time later in the year as it was unsure when she would be able to finalize her arrangements. That was no problem. Bruce and I threw away the storage information, unpacked everything that we had previously packed, rearranged the house to accommodate both Annie and Teresa, and retained the attorney. We weren't sure how we were going to save the house, we just knew that we would do all we could to make it happen.

It took us several days to take care of all the preliminary arrangement that we needed to do to prepare the house for everyone. These were long days, but we set aside time in the evenings to enjoy the energy both in the house and especially in the backyard. I captured some beautiful large orbs on my camera, both in the evening and in daylight. We did somehow feel lighter and more at peace. Although there were many days ahead dealing with all sorts of consideration, we chose to stay in the Now and enjoy our home.

We left Las Vegas on the morning of the twenty-third, arriving in Happy Camp on the twenty-fifth in the late afternoon. We went to work almost immediately, beginning to help Annie pack and sort through the things that she desired to bring with her. We gave ourselves the time to get things done without excessive pushing and agreed that we would leave sometime around the first or second of October. We left this open just in case we could use an extra day to complete everything.

September 25, 2008

In the midst of all this activity, we had the opportunity of having two sessions in Happy Camp to close out our time there. The first one actually took place on the evening of our arrival back at Annie's.

"We do greet thee. How is everyone? We have come only for a short while this evening. We would wish to speak with you about things you may desire to put into effect when you have moved. There are some things that we would suggest to you, that as a family you may desire to consider. You may choose to form a financial account, what you call a bank account, with everyone on it. Into that account you will all decide what is going to be needed for the household expenses. Then you will put that amount into your account. Everyone's personal accounts do not have to be in the communal fund. We would suggest that everyone decide what is going to be required."

We will all decide and help each other.

"Yes, Sister of My Sister, we know this to be true. We are finding that each of you are becoming more and more like each of us, if you will, for we are seeing more of Spirit shining through. It is much the same on our planet. Even though we do not have the monetary considerations that you do, we are all always giving one to the other. Whatever it is that may be desired, we simply are there to give it to one another. It is a wonderful thing to see this beginning, this new consciousness that is beginning with the four of you. This shall be your opportunity to see how things may be. There will be others who will join you, not necessarily with living in your home, but who will join you in this journey and will desire to be nearby."

Would you explain the difference between this and the type of living I experienced in the convent?

"In the convent, you were told what to do, how to think, when to sleep, and how you must dress. This living arrangement that you are now creating is simply a gathering of like-minded Spirits. Therefore, you can sleep when you desire, eat when you desire, and dress how you will. You have control of your own money and may spend it as you care to, whatever is your choice is your journey. You will learn to come together as a family to decide that which is also best for the family."

How beautiful, I thank you so much for that.

"You are most welcome. This is one of the things we had desired to speak with you about. It will be true communal living as it was intended to be before egos, drugs, and alcohol took control. The generation of what you called "hippies" did not understand, and when they finally began to grasp it, they allowed drugs and alcohol to come into their experience. These choices ultimately created experiences and residuals that neither served them or communal living in its truest sense. This is going to be your opportunity to create that type of living condition based on unconditional Love and being who you really are, Spirit, in all your interactions.

"There may not be many more sessions now before you leave, for there is much for you to accomplish before then. If there are questions, you must simply address them to Little One and she will always have our knowledge, or knowing.

"This has been relatively short for your little creature is not enjoying being penned up, and she has been for the last few days as you have been making your preparations. She desires to be out in the fresh air and run."

We all are so grateful for your presence.

"You are most welcome. For now, we do depart with much Love and Blessings."

It was a great meeting as it confirmed out choice to move from Happy Camp to Las Vegas for the next step on the journey. Our time, and objectives, here had been completed. It was now time to relocate, and although there was the unknown ahead of us, we were moving forward with a purpose. I wasn't fooling myself about this being an easy chapter for the project, there were going to be three women living under one roof!

There were many arrangements to be made. I gave my notice at work and it was tough to leave not only the people I had come to care for, but the steady income every week. I could only hope at this point that I would find another job quickly when we got back to Las Vegas. We spent every day busily sorting and packing everyone's things. We voluntarily surrendered our fifth wheel trailer back to the bank. We had been able to stay current with our payments to this point, but we knew we would not be able to keep both the trailer and the house. Previously we had thought we were going to have to live in it after the house was foreclosed upon and the bankruptcy filed. Now, it looked like we would all be contributing toward trying to keep the house in Las Vegas.

The fifth wheel was going to be picked up during the first week of October, so after packing all we could, we gave the rest to a community outreach program for those who were in need. Before we left, we decided to have one last session in Happy Camp.

September 28, 2008

We were only days away from leaving Happy Camp, and as we still had a few questions, we had our final session before heading south.

"We do greet thee. You have some questions for us?"

Would you please explain more about how living together can prepare us for starting a Sanctuary eventually?

"It is simply going to be a matter of communication. You are being prepared to understand many things and the biggest thing is how to communicate, not just with each other but with all as well. You will take that understanding of how to communicate beyond where you now are, to all that you will be in contact with, and to all who will become a part of The Light Alliance.

"Communication is a great consideration. On our planet, because of the type of communication we have, we are always in the 'knowing.' If a conversation is not flowing smoothly from one to the other, we stop and see what is occurring that causes the flow to cease. What we have witnessed upon your planet are people not always speaking with each other in a loving spirit-filled way. Sincere communication is very vital to your journey.

"If you cannot communicate with each other in a peaceful, loving, gentle, kind, and spiritual way, then there are things going on 'behind the scenes,' as you say, other than what it appears you are speaking about. If you are talking to someone and suddenly things are off track, then you should look beyond what you are speaking of, there is always a deeper issue that is the cause for anger, fear, shouting, or accusations. In those moments, someone's ego has taken control of the conversation and communication has stopped. This is something you are all learning.

"It is for you to talk out even the little things, for even a grain of sand can cause a massive sore if it is left unattended. When you speak to each other, speak on the level of Spirit. Once voices get raised, Spirit recedes and ego emerges. Now you are no longer talking about whatever the issue was, it has gone beyond that into something else. It is for you to understand what else is going on and to deal with that issue. There should not be raised voices. Spirit will not go in that direction because that is not what Spirit is. It is important to know that if there is no communication going on, one to one in Spirit, then ego has appeared. Figure out why it appeared.

"We know that there will occur moments, for the four of you, when there will be conflict, but if you stay Spirit you will be able to communicate about it. Conflict does not necessarily mean an outright battle. Conflict is something that occurs between people when their ideas, thoughts, words, or expressions are not quite gelling. If you observe this, then you would sit down and talk about it. 'What can we do about this thing that is causing conflict?' You should be able, in Spirit, to sit down and calmly talk about it and find a solution that all resonate with."

What happens then in this process is that we are becoming more the Spirit that we are?

"Yes, and we know that everyone is at a different place, at a different step in this. It is because you are still having a human experience while remembering to be the Spirit that you are. There will be moments of conflict, of changes, so be prepared for them and communicate one to the other about these moments. If they are approached in Love and Spirit, you can, if you desire so, resolve the issues.

"Little Brother, do you have any questions?"

No, Dear Ones, I have been listening even while entertaining our puppy. I am in complete agreement with you that communication is perhaps the most important skill we can all learn.

"We are able to observe when ego emerges, but it is not our place to say this, as you must recognize these moments. It shall be up to you as to how you approach these situations. We do know that if things are not dealt with in a quiet, peaceful, communicative way, things will be difficult for everyone. Within an unsettled environment, ego grows and creates blockages of action, thought, and purpose along the way. To overcome ego within your 'family' will be through the choices of all involved, through remaining Spirit, and staying in the Now. Pulling garbage along with you from a past Now does not serve either who you are remembering to be or those around you. Everyone is aware that for this project to be strong, to reach many, and be an integral part of the Awakening, you must dismantle your egos. This communal living is putting you into an arena to experience and work together on this purpose."

There are some that are predicting, with the new president in office, that everyone is going to get all this money and that everything is going to be different.

"This is not going to be, for your country does not have any money. There is much that shall occur with your new president. Some will term it 'good' and some will term it 'bad' and that will be, of course, from the perspective of each one that looks upon it. We do know that there may be times ahead to be aware of, depending upon the choices and creations made by the collective who are in governmental control. If egos continue to flow the way of ego, then jobs and homes will be lost, the economy shall not remain a constant but will experience many changes.

"We will be with you on your trip and will always be watching over you. For now, we shall depart in Love and Blessings."

This ended our final session in Happy Camp. It had been a remarkable time together here. Actually, in looking back, it had been a remarkable year. So much had transpired and so much had been learned. None of us were the same as we had all been changed by the Teachings and experiences we had gone through during this period of "time."

Things turned out so different than we could ever have imagined. What was to have been a very concentrated year of mining for us became one of outreach to others. So many people were brought before us from so many different states. We even met people from countries in Europe and Central America. We shared what we had been taught and listened to so many fascinating stories about others' journeys. We were truly blessed to have met and shared experiences with each and every one of them.

We knew that a major change was about to take place. We were all moving to Las Vegas, and this was the next stage, or evolution, in not only the Teachings, but the project as well. We were asked to take all that we had learned and to apply it to what would transpire in Las Vegas. In our final session in Happy Camp, the emphasis was on communication. This stood out as being a particularly important skill for all of us to master. Undoubtedly we would be exposed to many experiences that would sharpen this skill, but we had no understanding at this time just what this would entail, or mean, for each of us in the days ahead.

We finished packing everything and crammed it as full as we could into a twelve-foot rented trailer. We also loaded up the truck bed and then discovered that we needed still more space. This would mean one more trip for Bruce to load and pick up the empty mining trailer.

Dennis, our friend who had introduced us to Annie in the fall of 2007, was gracious to offer to drive Annie's car to Las Vegas. He would return with Bruce after what he called a brief vacation in Sin City. With everything packed up, we put Spirit in the truck, Sarah, Annie, and Dennis were in Annie's car, and began the trip south to Las Vegas.

We left the morning of October 2, 2008. We decided to not rush it and take our time. We arrived in Vegas the afternoon of October 4. Dennis stayed for several days, actually almost a week, and then he decided it was time to return. He and Bruce went to collect the remainder of things that had been left behind.

Annie and I began the task of unpacking. I was so happy not only to be home, but to know that we were staying. After all the trips back and forth, I was looking forward to being in one place.

Here, I temporarily end the telling of this portion of our journey. I look forward to each Now and what it may bring.

It has been my joy to share all of this with you, and my absolute desire that it has touched you in some way. We cannot know what lies ahead, for those choices have yet to be made. We know that if we continue to make them in awareness and Spirit, they will take us down our chosen path.

To all of you who joined on this walk, may you be blessed and always find peace and joy in the understanding of who you truly are, and may these Teachings bring to you clarity of vision, a lightness of heart, and true peace within.

Until we join again along our journey, Love and Blessings to you.

Index

Made in the USA
San Bernardino, CA
02 June 2013